RECOLLECTIONS OF
92 YEARS

Elizabeth Avery Meriwether

Recollections Of

1824   92 Years   1916

EPM Publications, Inc.
McLean, Virginia

Library of Congress Cataloging-in-Publication Data

Meriwether, Elizabeth Avery, 1824-1917.
    Recollections of 92 Years, 1824-1916 / Elizabeth Avery Meriwether.
       p. cm.
    Originally published: Nashville : Tennessee Historical Commission,
1958.
    Includes index.
    ISBN 0-939009-84-6
    1. Meriwether, Elizabeth Avery. 1824-1917. 2. Tennessee—History.
3. Tennessee—Biography. 4. United States—History—Civil War,
1861-1865–Personal narratives. 5. Women—Suffrage—United States.
I. Title. II. Title: Recollections of ninety-two years, 1824-1916.
F436. M48   1994
976.8'05'092--dc20   94-23586
                                   CIP

EPM Publications, Inc., 1003 Turkey Run Road
    McLean, Va 22101
Printed in the United States of America

Cover design by Tom Huestis

FOREWORD

It is an adventure for a reader in the late 20th-century to step back in time and share the experiences of a woman who was born in 1824, and who lived for almost a century. A woman whose physician father left Lebanon, New York in the early 19th-century for the frontier of Tennessee, and in 1816, married the daughter of a former Virginia planter who had also relocated to Tennessee.

While *Recollections of 92 years,* covers many details of Elizabeth Avery Meriwether's family, her life growing up in the wilds of Tennessee, her marriage to Minor Meriwether, and her late 19th-century activities as an author and advocate for the equality of women, it is her trials during the Civil War years of 1861-1865 that are most compelling.

When reading Elizabeth's story, one soon realizes that the severe traumas of the Civil War were not limited to the battlefield. People left on the home front were often just as affected by the issue of a military order as soldiers serving in the field. Women whose husbands were in the Confederate army and happened to be living in areas occupied by the Union Army, found themselves subjected to the harshness of military rule.

In 1862, General William T. Sherman, the Union military commander in Memphis, Tennessee, issued an order that he would "ban ten wives of rebel soldiers" if the Confederate artillery fired upon Union gun boats moving along the Mississipppi River. Such was to be the fate of Elizabeth Meriwether when, in October, she was given 24 hours to leave Memphis with her two sons, ages 3 and 5 years, and only the few personal possessions that could be fitted into her carriage.

The story of this exceptional woman who, with two small sons and expecting her third child within two months, was banished to wander from place to place through the war-torn South demonstrates the incredible courage exhibited by many women. The War not only removed their husbands, fathers, sons and brothers from their midst, but subjected them to personal hardships that were beyond their comprehension prior to 1861.

Given her courage and stamina, it is not surprising that Elizabeth Meriwether was years ahead of her time in fighting for the right of women to vote. She was one of the first women in the South to publicly advocate women's suffrage. In 1867, when Susan B. Anthony was imprisoned for voting in New York, Elizabeth rented a theater in Memphis to announce to a large invited audience that she would cast her vote in the upcoming presidential election -- which she did. Her success as an author, as well as her experiences as the editor of her own newspaper, are also detailed for the reader to share. Elizabeth's crusade for the rights of women continued until her death at the age of 92 in 1916 -- the same year that Congress agreed to consider the right of women to vote.

Recollections of 92 Years, by Elizabeth Avery Meriwether was first published in 1958 by the Tennessee Historical Commission. Having discovered the long-out-of-print book in 1993, through the generosity of Elden E. ("Josh") Billings, I found Elizabeth's story so interesting that I wanted to share it with those who would not have had the opportunity to obtain a copy of the original printing. The text is presented as it was originally published, unedited and unchanged.

I am indebted to the Tennessee Historical Commission for granting permission to Fort Ward Museum to reprint the book. I am also indebted to Elden E. ("Josh") Billings for making me aware of the many out-of-print books about exceptional women of the period by sharing this and numerous other volumes from his personal library. I would also like to thank the staff of the Management Information Services, City of

Alexandria, Virginia for scanning the text that facilitated the reprinting. Appreciation is also extended to Mrs. Evelyn Metzger of EPM Publications, who shared my enthusiasm for Elizabeth Meriwether's recollections.

1994   Wanda S. Dowell
                                                   Director

Alexandria, Virginia

Lee Meriwether

This photograph was taken in 1957 on the front porch of *Beauvoir*,
the home of Jefferson Davis, near Biloxi, Mississippi.

MY MOTHER

In 1865, after fighting four years in the Confederate army, my father returned to Memphis and bought a large lot at 95 Union Street. The Peabody Hotel now stands on that lot, but in 1865 there were on it a frame cottage and a grove of forest trees.

One night in 1867 several of father's friends came to that cottage to discuss the Ku Klux Klan and how it might save Memphis and the South from bankruptcy. Among those friends were Gen. Nathan Bedford Forrest and Matt Galloway, editor of the old *Memphis Appeal,* now the *Commercial Appeal.*

General Forrest, Editor Galloway and my father agreed the only hope of averting bankruptcy was in the Ku Klux Klan. Ex-slaves were the only men in the South entitled to vote. White men who had fought in the Confederate army, which meant nearly every white male of military age, were disfranchised.

The ignorant ex-slaves, elected to City Councils and State Legislatures, and dominated by the carpetbaggers who had come from the north to plunder the South, voted millions of dollars of bonds for which little or no value was received. But federal courts ordered mayors of cities to levy taxes big enough to pay 100 cents on the dollar. To do this it would have been necessary to sell the city's parks, fire engines, and everything it possessed. At that party at my father's home in 1867 it was agreed that the Ku Klux Klan by midnight parades as "Ghosts," and by whipping and even by killing Negro voters, Negroes would become afraid to vote and so would not be elected to public office which would issue hundreds of millions of bonds.

This was illegal, fantastic, but self-preservation is the first law of Nature. When at the close of the meeting my mother served sandwiches and coffee, Editor Galloway said,

"Well, Betty Meriwether, what do you think of our plan?"

Mother replied: "It may work. Negroes are very superstitious. They may become too scared to vote; then when you are allowed to vote you can elect intelligent men to tax you and make the laws that govern you. But when will women have the right to vote? I have been taught to believe that taxation without representation is tyranny."

"There you go, Betty," said Editor Galloway. "You know very well your husband will take care of your interests."

"Who will take care of the interests of women who have no husbands?" There was no answer to this question. My mother said: "Taxation without representation is tyranny. I shall protest against that tyranny as long as I live."

And my mother did just that. She was one of the first women in the South publicly to advocate Woman Suffrage. When, in 1876, Susan B. Anthony was jailed for the "crime" of voting in New York, my mother announced she would vote in November, 1876, for Samuel J. Tilden, the Democratic nominee for President of the United States. "If I am arrested for that crime," mother said, "I shall be glad to share Miss Anthony's cell."

Mother rented the Memphis Theater for the evening of May 5, 1876, and told a large audience she intended to vote for Tilden in November. She did cast a ballot on the first Tuesday in November 1876, but it probably was not counted. The Judge and clerk of election in her precinct were father's friends; they dropped mother's ballot in the box and probably destroyed it later.

Mother said: "Counting my ballot is not important; what is important is to focus public attention on the monstrous injustice, as well as stupidity, of including educated women with felons and lunatics as persons denied the right of suffrage."

Southern as well as Northern newspapers pictured mother as a bigboned virago with jutting jaw and a steely glint in her eyes. In reality she was rather small, not over five feet two inches tall and a slender figure. Without being actually beautiful she was comely and attractive because of the light that shone in her brown eyes and the sweet smile that parted her lips even while she condemned men for denying vote for women.

Mother's voice also endeared her to all who heard her. In those days there were no microphones, but mother's voice was a "carrying" one that made her heard even by persons in the back row of halls and theaters. Thus in the final years of the battle, mother as a speaker was in demand in all parts of the country.

In 1916 both the Republican and the Democratic party promised to Support an amendment to the Constitution forbidding withholding the ballot from women because of their sex. When my mother read this "plank" in the platforms of the two major political parties she said: "Lee, my work is done. I am content now to face the setting sun and fall asleep as the night comes on."

A few months later, as a clock stops ticking, so stopped the beating of my mother's heart--no pain, no illness, no attempt to cling to life. One moment she was discussing the topic of the day; the next moment she closed her eyes and silently slipped into the vast ocean of yesteryears.

In her death I lost not only a mother; I lost the intellectual companionship of a woman who was the peer of any woman I have known in all my 95 years.

St. Louis, January 20, 1958.

TABLE OF CONTENTS

CHAPTER I

Ninety two years old to day. Why I write these recollections. My family and my childhood. Quaint letters written by my mother in 1819. Life in Tennessee ninety years ago.

To day, January 19th 1916, I am ninety two years old. This is certainly old age and in the course of Nature not many more years can be left to me. But thus far I have been blessed with health and to day as I enter my ninety third year I have no aches or pains. My eye sight is good and I still have my teeth, thirty of them, all sound and strong. When Victor Hugo's *Les Miserables* was first published more than half a century ago one of the characters in that romance, old M. Gillenormand, interested me--he was always boasting that he had his "two and thirty teeth."

It was from M. Gillenormand that I learned the number of teeth human beings have, or should have; and as I have lost only two of my teeth I know that I have thirty remaining--not as good a record as M. Gillenormand, but then he was only ninety. Many people younger than I have no teeth at all--I mean natural teeth. I suppose many people have false teeth, but fortunately I have the ones Nature gave me and to this day I like the crust of bread rather than the soft inside.

But in spite of all this--good teeth, good eyes and good health--undeniably I am getting old and find myself living more and more in the past my thoughts constantly wander back to the long ago and I am surprised to find that I can remember even petty trifles of my childhood, while important events of hardly more than yesterday seem to have become vague to me. When my son and my grand children and my great grandson come to see me I tell them stories of the past and they say my recollections are interesting and should be written down so that they may be read by their children in future years. It may be they tell me this only to please me, but in truth my recollections ought to be entertaining--how can there fail to be entertainment in the recollections of one whose memory is good and whose life covers nearly an entire century. When I was a girl men's means of travel were the same as in the time of Moses. True, Fulton had run his steamboat down the Hudson a short time before I was born, but there were no regular steam ship lines, no railroads, and so when men wanted to travel they had to go in sail ships, afoot or on horse, just as they did in the days of Julius Caesar.

Well, I have lived to see men circle the globe in much less than Jules Verne's fanciful trip of eighty days. And last summer my son took me to the

Aero Club where I saw men flying through the air swifter than hawks or eagles. When my eyes first saw the light of day Byron still lived and was writing the poetry which makes him immortal; the author of our Declaration of Independence had two more years to live, while his friend Lafayette did not die until I was ten years old. My Aunt Deborah Kendall danced with Lafayette in Columbia Hall when he visited my father's home town, New Lebanon, N. Y., in 1825, and I remember how sad I felt when they told me of his death in 1834. I looked on Lafayette not only as a hero of our Revolution but as the friend and protector of Marie Antoinette; and in that day when the unhappy queen of France had not been dead so long she did not seem to me a mere historical personage, she seemed a real woman who had suffered the most frightful misfortunes. And so child though I was, when they told me Lafayette was dead it made me think of the Reign of Terror and the Tower and the guillotine and poor Marie Antoinette's head falling into the basket!

Yes, recollections which begin with things as they were in the time of Moses and end with flying ships, wireless telephones, radium and other modern miracles--which begin with days when Napoleon's wars had just ended and come down to the second year of the great war which is now devastating Europe and nearly all the world besides--Yes, such recollections may well be entertaining providing, of course, they are related in an entertaining way. I shall do the best I can but even though I fail to tell my story in a way that will interest my children, still shall I not regret the labor of writing. For the composition of these recollections will at any rate occupy my mind and prevent me from dwelling on the thought that I have lingered too long on the earth.

Young people do not realize the loneliness of old age. My children are good to me; they take from me at least some of the desolation of old age. But I know they cannot really like to be with me. How can Youth be congenial with Old Age? Almost all the men and women of my generation are dead. Never more shall I see the friends and dear ones of my youth and middle age. But before I join them in the next world, if there be another world, for a brief moment shall I live with them in memory. For the months I am writing these pages I mean to be young again, mean to be once more, in imagination at least, with the companions of my girlhood and young womanhood, some of whom have been dead and gone for more than sixty years. And in that way, my dear children, I shall feel repaid for the labor of this composition even if you do not care to read it.

Now then, to begin at the very beginning, let me tell you something of my parents and the place of my birth. My father's family lived in a small village in New York state, New Lebanon, a few miles from Pittsfield, Mass., but while still in his teens my father ventured on what in those days seemed a perilous journey--a trip to Tennessee. There were neither railroads nor steam boats to carry him and Indians, Tommyhawks and poisoned arrows were not then things which people only read about in romances; they were in that day all very real and very cruel, and so my grand parents were sad at heart when their son set forth for what they thought was a distant and savage infested wilderness!

My father liked Tennessee and decided to settle there. He there married my mother, Rebecca Rivers, daughter of Thomas Rivers, a Virginia planter who had settled in Tennessee. I shall give here an extract from a letter written by mother shortly after marriage; aside from the family interest I think this letter is interesting as showing the quaint, formal style of correspondence in those days. The letter, written to one of my father's sisters whom my mother had never seen, ran thus:

Nashville, March 14th, 1819.

SISTER CLARISSA:

We received your affectionate letter with emotions of real pleasure and I can scarcely pursuade myself I am yet a stranger in your family. You appear to think of me with affection because I am the being destined by Providence to be your father's companion, and who will participate with him in all his pleasures, one who will endeavor to solace him in all those disappointments and distresses which may occur during life. When I hear my husband speak of his maternal home, when he dwells with filial Love and fond recollections on the virtue of those characters who gave him birth, who formed his infant mind and who with parental caution reared him to manhood, would not my heart be void of all the finer springs of sentiment did it not glow with respect and Love for such parents? Yes, my sister, their son has inspired me with a profound veneration for them and a strong desire to become acquainted with them! . . . With regard to your interrogatories concerning the nativity of my family, etc., I will answer briefly and leave space for your brother. My father's name is Rivers, Virginia is the land which gave me birth; I was partly reared in North C. and Tennessee has witnessed the most important eras of my life. My love to papa, mamma and children and believe me your affectionate sister.

REBECCA RIVERS AVERY.

Following the above letter of my mother's is a post script written by my father in the course of which he says:

"Since I have formed a connection with one whose society fills the measure of my happiness it is with the greatest reluctance I leave home even for a day. I never thought it would be so much of a cross as, by experience, I find it to be. I now appreciate the anxiety I have so often witnessed in my kind mother in the absence of her affectionate husband."

This letter was not inclosed in an envelope; the custom in those days was to fold the paper in such a way that the address might be written on the sheet of letter paper itself. No postage stamps were used, but the figures "25" are written in ink above the address, meaning that the charge for postage was twenty five cents. The letter, yellow with age of nearly an hundred years, is in my "Letter" book where you may see it if you care to study the quaint handwriting of your great grand parents.

A good deal of ground belonged to our log cabin in Bolivar, Tennessee, where I was born January 19th 1824. In one field corn was planted, and in another field was a large sweet potato patch where I used to hunt for big potatoes. After the lapse of nearly ninety years I still remember what a delight it was to me when my father would "tote" me on his shoulder from the house to this potato patch and turn me loose to find a big potato. When a sweet potato is really big it makes a crack in the ground, as if it is eager to pop out; I would hunt first for these cracks in the ground and on finding them I would dig down with a stick and would feel proud and happy when my efforts were rewarded by the sight of a big potato.

We had cows and calves and horses and oxen on our place, from which you will easily guess that it was more like living in the country than in town. Boliver was a very small town. A few minutes walk were enough to bring you to where the town ended and the country began. It is not a large town even now--at least so I have been told; I do not know of my own knowledge, for I have not been there for seventy five years.

My father, Nathan Avery, was a physician of Quaker origin. I think the Quakers must have been good people. All I ever met were good, and I know that my father was good--he was kind and gentle and unselfish and loved by all who knew him. He had no carriage or buggy to drive in, or to take his family about, but he did have a saddle horse for use in visiting his patients, many of whom lived quite far from our home in Bolivar. This horse was named Salladin. I remember once my father lifted me up and put me on Salladin's back; I promptly rolled off his back down to the ground and screamed at the top of my lungs. When my father saw that I was not hurt he laughed at the fuss I was making--and that only made me scream the louder. I was Indignant. Insulted. Then my father begged my pardon and said he loved me and that he laughed only because I had rolled off the horse like a fat pillow and that he would never put me on Salladin again. I forgave him and loved him as before; I loved him as long as he lived--even more than I loved my mother. Somehow my father seemed nearer, closer to me than my mother; he seemed to understand me better. I know he was more indulgent. My mother was strict with me, as with her other children. Looking back on life after having children, grand children and great grand children, I know of course that there are times when strictness is necessary. But my mother went further than even now seems to me she should have done, and neither now nor at any time past in my long life has her memory ever been as sweet to me as has been the memory of my father. Later on in these pages I may give some instances of my mother's strictness which will explain this difference in the way I look back upon my father and my mother.

My brother Tom was some years older than I and could ride a horse well. My father often put Tom on Salladin and sent him five or six miles to carry medicine to patients. The first time father did this I was very unhappy and burst into tears.

"What on earth is the matter, Betsy?" asked my father anxiously "Betsy" was the pet name he used when I was a child. When I was grown I was called Elizabeth by everyone except my husband; he always called me Lizzie.

"Father, how can Tom ever come back? If you send him so far away I know he will never find his way home--Boo hoo, Boo hoo!" And I wailed aloud as if my heart would break.

My father was very patient and very sympathetic with me; he explained that after all six miles was not so very far and that my brother would manage to find his way back. After that, when Tom would set forth on these journeys to carry medicine to my father's patients I had more confidence and instead of crying I began to envy him his trips out into the big world--for that is what those horse back rides into the country about Bolivar seemed to me when I was a girl six years old.

Our kitchen was at least a hundred feet from our house. During all my life in the South it was the custom of the people to have their kitchens a long distance from the dwelling house. And all the negro servants had their cabins a long distance from what they called the "Great-us" (Great House). As I remember it, our house was far from being "Great." On the contrary, measured by standards acquired in later life, as I look back on it it seems very, very small. It contained only four rooms--two rooms on each side of a wide hall. The rooms were very large and the ceilings were high. But there were only four rooms and so, after living so many years in the big eighteen room mansion which my dear husband built for me in St. Louis, my child-hood home of ninety years ago seems to me rather small.

We had a number of negro slaves which my mother inherited from her father Thomas Rivers; I thought my grand father's name very beautiful and years after the log cabin home in Bolivar had become to me a mere memory I named one of my sons "Rivers" after his great grand father of Virginia.

One of the slaves which my grand father Rivers gave to my mother was old Aunt Sally; in the South all good old negro women were called "Aunt." We children loved Aunt Sally; she was good to us. Often after we had romped over the yard until we were tired and hungry we would run to the kitchen and beg Aunt Sally to make us an "ash" cake. You, my dear grand children, do not know the luxury of eating ash cakes. I will tell you how Aunt Sally made them. She took some corn meal, wet it with milk, then worked until the dough was smooth. When this was thoroughly done she divided the dough into small batches and rolled each batch into a round little cake. When these little cakes were all ready Aunt Sally would rake open the hot embers in the wood fire place, put the cakes on the brick hearth, then cover them with hot ashes and embers. This done, Aunt Sally would say: "Now run 'long and play, chilluns, till I calls you ter come git yo' cakes."

We would run out in the yard and play until we heard Aunt Sally crying to us to come quick, that the ash cakes were "good and hot," then you may be sure we lost no time running back to the kitchen; we knew from experience how delicious those corn cakes were. Aunt Sally would rake the ashes and embers off the cakes while I was given a gourd of cold water to pour over each cake as it came out from the ashes. The water did not make the cakes cold; Aunt Sally didn't leave it on long enough for that; just as quick as I poured the water over a cake she would wipe it off quickly with a clean towel. In this way all the cakes would be ready for eating in a couple of minutes and to this day I can remember how good they tasted as we ate them just after they came out of the hot ashes. No cake ever tasted so good to me as those hot ash cakes Aunt Sally made for me eighty eight years ago.

It was years and years before we came to use tin dippers; the only dippers we had in my childhood days were gourds. Everybody planted gourdseed and cultivated gourds as a household necessity. And whether it is really a fact, or only a notion, a fancy, a trick of my imagination, still it has always seemed to me that water never tasted so sweet and good out of a glass or tin dipper as it tasted when drunk from the gourds my mother had in Bolivar.

When I was eight years old I was taken on my first long journey. It seemed to me as big an event as a journey to the North Pole seemed to Dr. Cook. My mother wished to pay a visit to her mother at her home near Clarksville, Tennessee. Clarksville is even now only a small city; it was then, in 1832, only a village and to my childish imagination it seemed a frightful distance from Bolivar. Nowadays, on the railroad you can go from Bolivar to Clarksville in a few hours, but in 1829 that journey seemed to me like a trip to the end of the world.

My father put us in a wagon. There were five of us children, my brother Tom and my sisters Laura, Rebecca and Amanda, the last a baby in arms. I made the fifth child. My father drove the wagon which was drawn by a large bay mare. Brother Tom did not sit in the wagon with us; he rode Salladin and a negro boy named Jim rode a mule. Mother of course was in the wagon looking after us three girls and baby Amanda.

My father and mother were both very orthodox; they were Methodists and strictly obeyed the teachings of that sect. Such things as dancing were frowned upon as an invention of the devil. We had family prayers every morning and after he had read a chapter of the Bible father would kneel down on the floor and pray out aloud. All the house negroes as well as members of the family attended these morning prayers. My father invariably thanked God to bless our food and to make us thankful for what we had to eat. I remember as an instance of the perversity of childhood--or at any rate of my childhood, that I did not feel thankful to God for my food. I thought my father had earned the money to buy the food and that Aunt Sally had cooked it and so that *they* ought to be thanked. I said this once to my father and I remember to this day how serious he became and how hard he labored to make me understand that while he had bought our food it was the goodness of God which had enabled him to do so. I fear I was often disobedient and perverse and so caused my dear father and mother no little amount of worry.

Well, before setting forth on this great journey to Clarksville my father knelt in our little parlor--they did not say "Living Room" in those days--and asked God to bless our journey and to guide and protect us on the way. Then he arose, on his face a look of perfect peace and quiet and confidence. Never in my childhood, nor indeed in my later life either, did prayer seem to keep me from worrying, where there seemed to be cause to worry. And so it was always a little hard for me to understand how prayer made my father feel so quietly confident that all would be well. But to him God was very personal and very real; he believed his particular prayers were heard by a personal God, and that they would be answered providing they were righteous prayers, and providing further that the person who prayed was righteous and deserving of God's favor. As he believed all he read in the Bible, and all he heard in his church--and as, in truth, he was a good man and an upright, honorable citizen, my father felt confident God would answer his prayer and see that our journey was successfully and happily completed. And so it was with a smiling face that he lifted us children into the wagon and started for Clarksville with my brother Tom riding Salladin on one side of the wagon and Negro Jim riding his mule on the other side.

On this journey we had to cross a good many creeks; I thought them great rivers, and they were a little dangerous, because there had been so much rain and the water was running over the banks. I remember one specially big creek where the water was running so swift and seemed so deep that mother was afraid to cross it. Father, however, persuaded her to risk it and into the creek our big bay horse plunged. The water came almost up into the bed of the wagon, but we got across all right and I turned to my mother and said,

"Mamma, did we get across because father prayed God to take care of us?"

"Yes, dear," answered my mother, and she was firmly convinced that it was father's prayer which had saved us.

"But, mama," I said, "It wasn't deep enough to drown us. Even if father had forgot to ask God to save us we couldn't have drowned in water that shallow."

Mother said this was a very wicked thought of mine, and perhaps it was· but as I have confessed to you, my dear grand children, wicked, or raf' perverse, thoughts would pop into my head, try as I would to keep ther
I do not believe I have ever committed any really wicked deeds, b
can't control your thoughts as you can your actions. If it be really wir

to believe what we are told to believe, then I fear I have sometimes been wicked; for it has not always been possible for my mind to accept the dogmas which good religious men declare should be accepted.

At one of the streams we came to on that journey was a mill. My father took us children out of the wagon and carried us up some steep steps to the second floor of the mill where were many bags of corn waiting to be ground into meal. Putting each of us little girls on a bag of corn, my father gave us strict orders to remain seated on those bags until he returned. I am sorry to have to confess to you that no sooner was my father out of sight than up I popped and ran to a window to look down into the deep water below. I was there, my head sticking out of window, when my father came back. When he saw me he came quickly to my side, grabbed me and shook me hard; my father never slapped me or struck me, but he preached to me and quoted texts from the Bible, and told me about the Devil and altogether made me feel quite as uncomfortable as if he had whipped me. The Devil came to mean to me a very real and terrible person; I became afraid to be out in the dark lest the Devil might be lurking near and seize me and carry me off to the "bad place." My father never used the word "Hell." They told me the Devil dwelt in the "Bad Place," and that he would take me there if I was a bad girl.

Toward night of the first day of that journey we stopped at a little farm house; father went in to see if we might stay there overnight. Presently he came back to the wagon where mother and we children awaited him and said we would have to drive on.

"Why not stop here?" asked my mother. "It is nearly dark and the children are fearfully tired."

"I know it, but we must go on," answered my father. "It won't do to stop in this farm house. The woman who lives here is drunk."

"Drunk?" cried my mother, jumping out of the wagon. "I want to see her."

At that time I did not know what "drunk" meant, but I was curious to know what father meant, so I climbed out of our wagon and followed my mother in the house. And there I saw the first person I ever saw in my life who was drunk. It was an ugly sight. The woman was in a large chair, her feet pushed way out on the floor, her face red, her hair frowsy, her head wagging about as if her neck could not hold it up straight. Two ragged little boys were playing in the yard. For a minute my mother stared in silence at this sad sight, then she said to me:

"Let us go. I am sorry you have seen such a sight."

Without another word we went back to the wagon and my father drove on to the next farmhouse. There we were well taken care of; we had corn bread and milk and cold sliced ham for supper--that is, father and mother had ham. We children were never allowed to eat meat at night. But the corn bread and milk were filling and we were hungry enough to make it taste good. Oh, what a sauce is Youth and Health! No French *chef* could concoct a dish that would seem as good to me now as that corn bread and milk seemed to me in that farm house on the road from Bolivar eighty four years ago!

Next morning father ordered Jim to feed and water the big bay mare and harness her to the wagon. Jim went to the stable but in a few minutes came running back to the farm house, his eyes almost popping out of his head.

"Oh, Marse Avery!" he cried, "Yo' horse has done gone an' had a baby! "

Father and mother both ran out to the stable. It seems neither of them had expected the event so soon. Father thought the mare and her colt would not be able to travel, so he traded them off for a large strong horse which the owner declared was "as gentle as a sucking dove." That was the first time I ever heard the expression "sucking dove." I have often heard it since, but I confess I do not know to this day just how gentle is a "sucking" dove, or if in truth a dove ever does "suck."

We had not gone very far when we discovered that our new horse was neither gentle nor safe; once when we stopped at a farm gate my father handed the reins to Jim to hold, then went through the gate to the well in the yard to get a gourd of water for us children to drink. As father came back with the water a dog ran out and barked at him. Jim was holding the reins loosely as he did with our gentle old mare, but the new horse, the one who was as gentle as a "sucking dove" this bad horse gave a leap when he heard that dog bark, jerked the reins out of Jim's hands and started on a run down the road. My mother with my little baby sister Amanda in her lap screamed "Whoa! Whoa!!" but that only made the horse run faster and faster and presently the Wheels hit a tree, the wagon upset and spilled us all out on the ground! My father came running up, his face white, panting for breath and filled with the awful fear that he would find us dead. He picked us up one by one and felt our bones all over to see if any were broken, and when he found the bones were all right and that we were all right, except for the shake-up and excitement we had undergone, he kissed us all around and kept saying over and over again, "Thank God! Thank God! Only God's goodness has saved my wife and babies!"

At this moment he looked more closely at Baby Amanda and saw that she was unconscious; she breathed, but her eyes were closed and we did not move--*and her skull was mashed in!* When father saw this told Jim to get on his mule and ride as fast as he could for the nearest doctor. When the doctor came he said if the baby's skull was lifted up it might save her life, but my mother declared that no steel instrument should go into her baby's head. So all night long she sat with an unconscious baby in her lap, praying God to awake the baby and give her back her health. Father sat by her side watching and waiting. Toward dawn the baby did awake; she kicked out her feet, wriggled out and at last opened her eyes and demanded breakfast in so vigorous a manner as to relieve all doubt as to her consciousness having been restored. My mother was so glad to see the baby come out of that long stupor, she burst into a rapture of tears and thanks to God for his mercy. That baby lived and thrived and never seemed to suffer from having her skull mashed, although it was a long while before the skull rose up properly and became as good skulls should become. When this accident happened that baby sister of mine was just about a year old; she is now an old woman--that is if you call eighty five old. In this world everything is relative; I used to think a man of thirty very old, but that was when I was only sixteen. Now eighty five seems almost young to me, and Sister Amanda doesn't call it old. She is blessed with excellent health, goes everywhere by herself and says she hasn't begun yet to think of getting old. Of course this is all self-deception; in our hearts we know we *are* old. But we have fewer of the infirmities that usually accompany Old Age and our children are good to us and so Life is not altogether empty for us.

After the baby's recovery my father made the farmer take back his horse that was as gentle as a "sucking dove" and return our good old mare; and it was not very long before the colt was able to travel. Then we started again on our journey to Clarksville to visit my grand mother. This is all I remember of the journey, nor can I recall much of the visit itself. I remember that my grand mother did not seem to love me--at least, that such was the impression left on my childish mind. She never kissed or caressed me. She had another grand daughter who lived with her all the time and whose first name was the same as mine, Elizabeth. My grand mother loved the other Elizabeth. We both sat at the table with our grand mother and at every meal Grand Ma would give the other Elizabeth a spoonful of sugar or some jam or other dainty, but none of these "extras" did she give me. I never asked her for them, although I wanted them as much as my cousin did. A small thing to remember after eighty years, isn't it? But what seems small to us grown-ups sometimes seems very big and very important to an eight year old child. And so it is that now, after eighty four years, I still remember this little piece of unfairness, or perhaps I should say partiality, which my grand mother exhibited during my visit to her in 1832. You, my dear grand children, who live in an age when sugar is cheap and candy plentiful do not know what it is to hunger for candy and never have the hunger satisfied. When I was a child nearly a hundred years ago candy was scarce, at least it was scarce in our father's family and I never really forgave my grand mother for giving the other Elizabeth all the sweets when I was at the same table begging with my eyes, if not my tongue, for just a little bit for myself! Candy was so seldom given me in my childhood that whenever I got a lump of white sugar, or even a spoonful of brown sugar, I looked on it as a treat and regarded myself as a very lucky girl.

CHAPTER II

More pictures of early life in the South

In my childhood days, when we children came home from school an earthen vessel filled with clabber was put on the grass in our front yard and each child was given a spoon and an ash cake; and this was our supper. We never ate supper with the grown folks. They had things to eat which were not thought good for children at night. The earthen vessel containing our clabber was made of such stuff as our brown bowls are made of today. Mother had finer ware at our table but out in the yard the brown bowls were thought good enough for clabber.

When I was about eight years old my sister Laura (two years older than I) was taken sick with a bilious fever. As it was thought a doctor might be too anxious if he attempted to prescribe for his own child my father did not attend to Laura; he called in a brother physician and this doctor, following the custom of that day, gave Laura a lot of calomel; calomel was given for nearly every complaint, and often in large quantities--so large that frequently the patient became salivated. Well, that doctor's treatment salivated my poor sister. I remember seeing Laura put her poor little wasted fingers in her mouth and pull out her teeth. Then I saw a hole in her cheek. I can never forget the agony which overwhelmed my mother when she saw that hole in Laura's cheek. Mother rushed out of the room to keep Laura from seeing the anguish in her eyes.

This salivation killed my poor little sister. As I grew up I saw a number of persons who had been salivated but who were not killed by the holes in their cheeks were sewed up and the wounds were healed. But the face was left disfigured--and so I was set against calomel and made a solemn vow to myself that no child of mine should ever touch calomel. I do not think that physicians now give calomel so commonly as in my childhood days; I know it has never been given to either of the three sons whom I reared to healthy manhood.

As I grew to be a "big little" girl I became fond of reading and occasionally my mother gave me a novel to read. I remember to this day how I wept over the sorrows of Amanda in "The Children of the Abbey." I remember the title of another story, "Alonzo and Melinda," but I cannot recall what that book was about, as I can so well recall "The Children of the Abbey." In later life I tried to read "The Children of the Abbey" again and was quite unable to find it interesting, much less a story to cry over; but as a young girl I certainly did think this now quite forgotten story well nigh perfect. Another book which I found intensely interesting was the "Arabian Nights." I cannot now pretend to remember, certainly I cannot spell, the name of that one of the old Bluebeard's wives who put an end to his habit of killing his wives after living with them only one day; but I remember perfectly some of the wonderful stories with which she beguiled the old villain into forgetting to kill her. It seemed to me then, and it seems to me now after more than eighty years, that those Arabian Nights stories were wonderful in their style as well as in the romance and inventiveness.

Another book which I read while I was still quite a young girl was "Young's Night Thoughts." I thought the poetry of this book grand; here are four lines which I remember after more than three quarters of a century

> "Time in advance behind him hides his wings. And seems to
> creep decrepit with his age! Behold him when passed by!
> What then is seen. But his broad pinions swifter than the
> wind!"

I do not believe I understood the meaning of those lines when I first read them. Alas! I understand them only too well now. The child thinks Christmas will never come. To him a month seems long, a year seems eternity, "Time seems to creep," decrepit with his age. But to me at ninety-two, who am beholding time long passed by, his broad pinions seem flying by me swifter than the wind. I know that in the course of Nature not much Time is left to me, and that "swift as the wind" will Time soon put a period to my days.

I was given the Bible to read but one day I horrified my mother by saying I did not believe there was a devil.

"Why do you talk so? " she demanded.

"Because," I answered, "God wouldn't make such a bad thing as the Devil. Or if he did make him he would kill him and throw him into a ditch and cover him up so he could never, never get out."

My mother was shocked and bade me never to talk that way again, but it was in me and I couldn't help it. I questioned all I read, and many of the things in the Bible seemed to me either wicked or untrue. For instance, I refused to believe that Abraham sacrificed his son Isaac. But, I argued, if the story was true, then most certainly Abraham was *not* a good man and was *not* beloved by God. It was impossible that God could love a man who would murder his own son. So I argued. And again was my mother greatly grieved. Looking back at it now, I can see that I was disputatious; I did not understand the symbolism for the Scriptures, neither did I then understand how literally and how seriously the Bible is taken by many people. It was a book my mother did not wish to discuss; she accepted every word of it blindly and literally and was distressed beyond measure that I could not do the same. In some strange way we differed in many of our ideas and this led to an estrangement, or at any rate to a lack of sympathy, a lack of understanding between us which distressed us both, and which I could have given much to undo had I only known how.

Mother made her daughters go to bed very early; she said young girls who sat up late became sallow and wrinkled, consequently my sister Amanda (the sister whose skull was mashed in) and I were sent every night to our room with a piece of tallow candle three inches long, with orders to go to bed the minute that piece of candle was burned down to the socket. In those days there were no electric lights, no gas and often not even oil lamps; in our family tallow candles furnished the lights and we used them sparingly. I remember how my father, who was very fond of reading, used to sit at one side of a small round table which was called the "Candle Stand" because on it rested the tallow candle which lighted the room. My mother sat at the other side of the table reading or sewing, while we children crowded around as close as we could so that we too might get some of that dim light and read or study our lessons. In this day of brilliant electric lights people think they can't read by the light of one tallow candle, but I read by such a light during all my girlhood days and my eyes are still doing the good service.

A tallow candle requires to be "snuffed" every little while, that is the end of the burning wick has to be snuffed off; so there was always a pair of snuffers in the candle stick. We took turn about snuffing our solitary candle. Of course, during the operation of snuffing off the hard end of the wick every one had to stop reading, but we never minded this. It never occurred to any of us that we were suffering any inconvenience. On the contrary, we were very glad that we had candle to read by. I wonder what our spoiled boys and girls of today would say if every few minutes they had to stop their reading or studying in order to snuff off a little end of the electric light?

One dark, rainy day I went into our kitchen and on the table I saw burning a light which was not a tallow candle. Old Aunt Sally told me it was a "Potato" lamp. She had made it herself out of a large potato. The inside of the potato was hollowed out like a cup; the bottom of the potato was sliced off flat, so it would stand firm when placed on a table. Then lard was put into the potato and a cotton wick was put into the lard. Such was Aunt Sally's home made potato lamp. And I no sooner saw this specimen of her craft than I determined to possess one for myself. It did not take me long to make one and to hide it under my bed where there was little likelihood of its being discovered, because the cleaning of our room was my duty and my sister Amanda therefore had no occasion to look about the room too closely. Amanda always fell asleep sooner than I did and so, when our three inch tallow candle burned down to the socket, I would creep out of bed, get my potato candle from its hiding place, light the wick and then read for another hour or two until the potato lamp also was burned to the socket. Often I read thus until my feet were half frozen and my whole body stiff with cold. Of course, not supposing I would sit up, my mother allowed no fire in our room and thus I sometimes became chilled through and through. I remember one night, after the potato lamp had burned out and I got back into bed, I shivered and shook so hard that Amanda awoke and asked what was the matter?

"I don't know," I answered, "Only that I am very cold."

"Cold!" exclaimed Amanda. "You are a solid lump of ice." And up she jumped and ran to our father's room and told him I had a hard chill. Father came in with a lighted candle and, seeing me pale and shaking, he felt my pulse, looked at my tongue, then went out to get a stimulant which a moment later he made me drink. This warmed me and soon I stopped shivering and shaking and told my father that I was all right again. My conscience pricked me; I knew I ought to tell him I was not really ill, that I was shivering merely because I had been sitting so long in a cold room. But I feared if I confessed this, that my beloved potato candle would be taken from me, consequently when father went back to bed it was with the belief that I had had a hard chill, the kind of chill that comes from swamps and malaria.

About a month after the above episode my father happened to be out in the yard late at night and seeing a light shining in my window he came to my room to see what it meant. I was scrooched up on the floor reading by the light of my potato lamp. Now, as my father was himself very fond of reading he had more sympathy for me in such matters than my mother; he knew how hard it was to stop in the middle of an interesting book just because your three inch candle was burned out. So he did not scold me. He was not angry. But he told me how much older and wiser was my mother, how she knew better than I what was good for me and that I should repay her goodness to me by being obedient to her. My father's goodness, his gentleness overcame me. I felt terribly guilty and burst into tears as I promised to be good in the future. Then my father took my potato lamp, lard, wick and all, and placed it on the smouldering embers of the fire in his room and it quickly went up in a bright flame. That was the end of my potato lamp reading. As a reward for my future obedience my father refrained from saying a word of this episode to my mother. I stood in awe of my mother and his promise not to tell her was the one thing which consoled me for the loss of my beloved lamp and the hours of reading it afforded me.

When I was eleven or twelve years old my father decided to leave Bolivar and make his home in Memphis, Tennessee. We moved there about the year 1835; my parents lived there until their death; and Memphis was my home for nearly fifty years, until my dear husband took me in 1883 to live in St. Louis. My father and mother were buried in Memphis, and two or three years ago on what will probably be the last visit I shall ever make to my old Memphis home, I visited their graves in Winchester Street cemetery.

As we grow old we live more and more in the past; a thousand memories came rushing over me as I stood by those two graves--I, an old woman nearing ninety, could plainly see the little girl that once had been me--I could see that girl scrooched on the floor reading by the light of that potato lamp- and my father once more arose before my eyes and stood by my side telling me how I would make myself sallow and wrinkled! I wondered what my father would think could he have seen standing by his grave-me, his daughter, ninety years old! My father died before he was fifty four years old; if he could have seen me that day in the Winchester cemetery he would not have recognized that ninety year old woman as his daughter, as the girl he was so good and gentle to the night he found me disobeying my mother and reading by the light of that potato candle!

As I approached womanhood I began to understand my father's character and came more and more to appreciate his many good qualities. Often children do not appreciate their parents' unselfishness and goodness until they are dead and gone. My father had not one vice; he drank nothing stronger than coffee; he did not even use tobacco. To his family he was patient, kind and loving; to his friends he was generous and sympathetic. Everybody esteemed him and most of his patients loved him. Often he was summoned in the night to go to some sick person's bedside and no matter how dark or cold or stormy the night he always instantly obeyed the call.

While these traits of character made people love my father, they led to one unfortunate result: they caused him to be careless in exacting payment for his services. And when he did get his fees as like as not they slipped through his fingers much quicker than he had collected them. His amiability and love of helping his friends prompted him to give money, if he had it, to almost anybody who asked it. As I grew up my brother Tom and I often discussed this characteristic of our father and we resolved to fit ourselves for earning money, so as to be of help to the family. It was becoming apparent that our father would never make much money, and would not keep what little he did make. My brother decided he would be a lawyer; my forte, I thought, was teaching and I began a course of reading and studying that would qualify me for that profession. I soon learned that I was deplorably deficient in mathematics; to this day I don't know much about "figgering." But in literature, History, the art of speaking I developed some talent and I came to earn some money teaching those accomplishments. As illustrating my dislike of arithmetic I recall some doggerel which I wrote when I was about thirteen years old. The girls of the class above me were fond of singing a song some of the words of which I remember to this day. They ran thus:

> "Oh No, I never mention him.
> His name is never heard.
> My lips are forbid to speak

That once familiar word.
From place to place they hurry me,
To banish my regret.
And if a smile they win from me
They think that I forget!
Tis true that I no more behold
The valley where we met,
Nor do I see that hawthorne tree-
But how can I forget?"

One day when my teacher had given me a particularly difficult problem in arithmetic to work I made not even an effort to solve it; instead I spent the time I was supposed to be working on that problem in writing a parody on the song the girls in the class above me were so fond of singing. I have not seen that foolish parody of mine for seventy five years and do not know how it is that I am able to remember it, but I do--so curious are the kinks and tricks of the human brain. Here is what I wrote on my slate in our little school room in the winter of 1836, when Andrew Jackson was still president of the United States:

"Oh Yes! I often mention him.
His name is always heard
Old Steven Pike's Arithmetic-
I do detest the word.
From sum to sum they hurry me,
To banish my neglect.
And if they win a root from me,
They think that I reflect.
Tis true that I do now behold,
The slate that I cipher on,
And if it wasn't so plaguey cold
I'd cipher on and on!"

Just as I was finishing the last line of this doggerel my teacher came up behind me and looked over my shoulder and, seeing what I had done, said kindly:
"My poor little girl, I fear you will never know much about figures." My teacher proved sadly accurate in this prophecy; I learned so little about figures that during the short time I taught school I was careful to have nothing to do with the arithmetic classes; by turning them over an assistant I succeeded in at least partly concealing my deficiency in mathematics.
When my brother Tom was fifteen years old he stopped school and went to work; father bought him a mule and a dray and Tom's work consisted in

hauling cotton bales from the plantations around Memphis the steam boats on the Mississippi river. After the cost of the mule and dray was earned by this work and repaid to our father, Tom kept what he earned for himself. He did not spend his money foolishly, but put it by until he had enough to pay for his schooling in a High School. Twenty years later, when Tom was running for Congress, he was a distinguished lawyer; but his friends and political supporters delighted to call him their "Dray Driver" candidate. And when he was elected member of the lower House at Washington he was frequently called the "Dray Driver" Congressman from Memphis. This was not meant in derision or as a reproach; rather was it meant in affection and as an honor. My brother always so regarded it and when running for Congress would smile (he had an infectious, winning smile) and tell his constituents that if they did not care to elect him he could get along, that at any rate he could drive his dray again.

CHAPTER III

A Methodist missionary wants to marry me and take me to China. I decline and lose faith in Church dogmas. A bride's ruse to bring her husband, my cousin, to his senses. How my cousin made of his well a giant mint julep. My uncle Robert Rivers slays the murderer of his brother.

While I was still a young woman, long before I met the man I was destined to marry, my father fell ill of pneumonia and died after a short illness on the 5th of March 1846, in his fifty fourth year (he was born on the 8th of May, 1792). We owned the little house in which we lived in Memphis; mother owned a young negro slave named Charlotte, but father left us very little money and Brother Tom, young as he was, thought it his sacred duty to support our mother and her three daughters. At that time it was deemed a disgrace in the South to permit the women of a gentleman's family to work. Women had not then gained the measure of independence which they now have--a fact which caused me to do much thinking and finally to advocate votes for women forty years before the question received any general public attention. In a later chapter I shall tell how nearly half a century ago I rented the largest theater in Memphis and delivered a lecture on "Woman's Rights"; that act caused my friends to regard me with good natured toleration, as a queer crank; while those who were not my friends, and those who did not know me--the general public--looked on me either as a shameless woman or as a woman who had lost her reason. And yet I was not a crank, and I did have shame--or at least stage fright. To this day I remember how my knees shook when I stepped out on the stage of that Memphis Theater to tell the people why I deemed it unwise and unjust to rank women politically with convicts, lunatics and Indians. That was the first time I had ever spoken before a large audience and such was my stage fright, I would have abandoned the attempt then and there had I not felt it my duty to give my message to the people. I later addressed many other great gatherings of men and women and came, so newspaper critics said, to be an eloquent speaker. If this is true it is because my heart was in my message, and because I came to realize that an audience won't hurt a speaker even though it be hostile to his thoughts and doctrines. Indeed, I think my best speeches were delivered before hostile audiences; it seemed the more hostile people were to my principles, the greater energy I put forth in endeavoring to make them see the error of their ways.

But I digress; garrulity may be the privilege of Old Age but it is none the less tiresome for all that, and I must try to be more direct, more to the point. So to return to my brother and his efforts to support his mother and three sisters after our father's death.

The first offer of employment which Tom secured was a clerkship on a Mississippi river steam boat; he wished to accept it but our mother resolutely opposed the idea.

"But mother," said Tom, "What else can I do? Beggars mustn't be choosers. I *must* do something. If I don't, how are you and Bettie and Estelle and Amanda to live?"

"Your three sisters and I will manage someway," returned mother. "But any way, *your* life shall not be ruined on our account--and it would be ruined were you to become a river man. You must carry out your plan to be a lawyer. I know you can succeed in the law. Stick to it and soon you will be able to give us all a comfortable home. That is more than you could ever do as a poor river clerk." This last argument, perhaps more than the others, made my brother yield; he set resolutely to work reading law while mother looked about and secured several men boarders.

I think I have told you, my dear grand children, that my mother was a zealous Methodist. Well, because of this we were often visited by Methodist preachers and their long prayers wearied me; if they stayed to supper with us they would say a long "grace" at the table; and, as if this were not enough, they would have a long prayer just before leaving at night. I had been taught the Lord's Prayer which Jesus gave us and thought long prayers were unnecessary; Jesus Himself reprobated long prayers and made it plain that He thought a short prayer much the better. My mother, however, liked everything a preacher did, so I discreetly concealed my thoughts anent long prayers, and never ventured to get off my knees until the very last "Amen" had been said.

But after awhile some of the preachers began to annoy me in another way, especially a certain Brother F.; my mother called all preachers "Brother," not "Doctor" as is sometimes done today. She wanted me to do likewise, but I refused. I had one brother, Tom, whom I dearly loved; I did not love any of those preacher "Brothers," and especially did I find myself unable to love Brother F. Him, indeed, I heartily disliked. He had a way of watching me while he was talking to my mother, always on some religious topic. It seemed as if he wanted me to get the benefit of his religious discourse and feared I would leave the room if he did not keep his eye on me. At any rate, he did keep his eye on me and mother noticed it as well as I, and one day she said to me:

"Brother F. is preparing to go as a Missionary to China." I made no spoken reply to this, but to myself I said I devoutly wished he would make haste and go. Not understanding my silence, my mother added: "I'll never consent for you to go to China with Brother F."

"Go to China? With Brother F?" I exclaimed. For a moment I was too stupefied to say more.

"He wants you to go," said my mother. "He wants you to marry him."

"Well," I declared, by this time getting back the use of my tongue. "I wouldn't go with Brother F. if he were going to Heaven, much less to China."

I do not know that my mother repeated my message literally, but she did make him understand that I would not be his wife and after that, when Brother F. came to our home, I was permitted to remain in my room; this I regarded as a double blessing. For it not only spared me the discomfort of Brother F's presence, it also made it unnecessary for me to get down on my knees and bury my face in the seat of a chair while Brother F. indulged in his long prayers. A month or two after that talk with my mother Brother F. went to China and I never heard of him again.

The next preacher that wanted me was very different from Brother F. He was good looking and I liked him, but not enough to care to marry him. Indeed, not for a long time did I suspect that he was thinking of marriage. But one day when mother was not in the house this preacher took my hand in his and said:

"Little girl, would you like to live a long while and yet always be young?"
I said Yes, that I did not like the idea of getting old and wrinkled.

"Well," he continued, "You marry me and you will be Young as long as you live." I did not know what he meant until he reminded me that his name was Young, Samuel Young. I told this good preacher that while I liked him I did not love him, and so that I would have to grow old as other people do.

In the first chapter of these *Recollections* I told you, my dear children, something about my father's family, but on reading over what I have written I find I have told you nothing of my mother's family. I fear I can not say as much good of them as of my father's people. My father came from good old Quaker stock, from ancestors who were religious and law abiding. But some bad things were said of my Rivers kin--you remember that my mother was a daughter of old Thomas Rivers of Virginia. It was a legend in the Rivers family that the men were all brave and the women all chaste; I thought this division unequal. The men ought to have some of the chastity and the women some of the bravery. When my grand father Rivers moved from Virginia to Tennessee he was considered a rich man, that is he had some seventy five or eighty slaves and a large plantation. He sold his land and negroes, came to Tennessee, bought land, built cabins for his slaves and became a prosperous planter. One of the stories my grand father told on a Rivers kinsman will illustrate what was said to be a family failing with the Rivers men--and incidentally will tell how in this particular instance a Rivers man was induced by his wife to forswear his habit of making love to pretty women.

My grand father said that this cousin of his, also named Thomas Rivers, was a very young and handsome man when he brought his bride to his plantation in Virginia. For a time all went well and the bride was as happy as a bird in a gilded cage. Then the young husband had to go away on a long business trip and while he was gone something happened to betray to his bride the fact that he had been a little promiscuous in his attentions to handsome women. Only a few days after the young husband set forth on his journey the lonely bride on that Virginia plantation heard an unusual noise on the broad verandah in front of the house--a sort of wail, then a whimper and a cry. Running out to investigate, she saw on the verandah in front of the door a basket whence was issuing that unusual cry. It took but a moment to stoop down and uncover that basket. And then appeared to the bride's startled gaze the pink face of a new born baby. Pinned to the shawl in which the baby was wrapped was a paper on which were written these words:

"Thomas Rivers: This is your child; you are better able to care for it than his mother. Jane"

The young wife sat down and stared at the little pink face in the basket, then she burst into tears and wondered what on earth she should do. An old black Mammy, who had been the bride's nurse when she was a baby, came running out to see what ailed her young mistress. And when she saw the baby and was told what was written on the paper pinned to the shawl, that old black Mammy advised a scheme which was really almost Machivellian.

"Laws, Honey, don't you cry" said the old Negro slave when her young mistress moaned out that she would never live with her husband again. "Don't you go talk that way. Marse Tom don't keer no more for that thar baby's mother than he keers for the man in the moon, an' he don't keer for the baby. Men don't love babies that ain't born of their own sho' nuff wives. I knows men, Honey. You jus' listen to me, an' do de way I ses and Marse Tom he gwine love you more'n ever.

Then she explained her plan which the young bride thought so good that she carried it out to the letter. The old Black Mammy kept watch on the front gate about the time her Master was expected home--some two months after the baby finding episode; and the moment she caught sight of him coming up the road she rushed to the cabin where the baby was being cared for by a woman who had a child of her own and so could give the white baby milk, took the baby to the bride's room, put her young mistress to bed and lay the child beside her. The curtains were pulled down, then Mammy withdrew and was in the front hall when the Master of the House arrived.

"How is your mistress?" was Thomas Rivers' first question.

"Thank you, Marse Tom. Miss Lucy is doin' pretty well, just 'bout as well as kin be expected."

"As well as can be expected?" exclaimed Mr. Rivers. "Heavens!! What is the matter? Is she sick? "

But without waiting for an answer, he hurried to his wife's room and, seeing his young wife in bed, rushed to her side. My darling Lucy! Why didn't you write me you were ill? What is the matter? Where is the doctor? Why is he not here? "

"I do not need him now," murmured the bride.

"Have you needed him? Was he here? What did he say was the matter?

"Something very serious," replied the bride solemnly. And as she spoke she turned back the white spread displaying the pink face of that new born baby. "See," exclaimed his young wife. "See! This is what is the matter! It is this that has made me so unhappy, so wretched, so perfectly miserable!"

For a moment Thomas Rivers was as dumb as though struck by a thunderbolt. Then he burst out:

"Great Heavens! Whose baby is that? Who is the father of that child? I shall kill him on sight. Tell me who the scoundrel is. "

"Thomas, if I tell you, you won't believe me, and I won't tell you unless you promise not to kill him. I love him, at least I once did. I know not how I feel towards him now. "

"Great God!" exclaimed Thomas Rivers. "That I should live to hear you utter such words. You love the scoundrel! You beg me to spare his life! Well, I won't. I shall shoot him as I would a dog. "

"No, Thomas, No you must not do that. It would kill me were you to do that--because, Thomas, *you* are this baby's father."

Thomas Rivers was almost stupefied. He saw that the baby was a full nine months child--and he had been married less than five months. Was ever in all the world such a lame excuse? Did ever a wife before make so silly an excuse? *His* child? And they married only five months! How she must love the fellow, to try so hard to shield him! "Oh, who would have believed this of my Lucy!" he cried, "of the girl I entrusted with my heart, my happiness, my name, my honor!" And out of the room he rushed, determined to hunt down the man he imagined had wronged his wife. But before he had time to mount his horse Lucy came running out on the verandah. Thomas Rivers stared at her, amazed. He almost believed he was living through a frightful dream. Lucy had run down the steps in her usual girlish way; she did not in the least look like a woman who had just gone through the ordeal of ushering a baby into the world.

"What does all this mean," demanded the husband. "How old is that baby? Though you have ruined my life I do not wish to see you suffer. You should not run down the steps so soon, you should not even leave your room so soon. "

"Why not, Thomas? I have not been ill--only unhappy. I told you the baby is yours. But it is not mine. See here." And she handed him the note that had been pinned on the baby's shawl; "This is all I know about your baby. If any explanations are to be made you must make them. I have none to make."

Thomas Rivers made no explanations, but after that he did make a good husband, my grandfather said after that lesson he behaved himself fairly well--that is for a Rivers.

As I have said, the Rivers men bore none too good a reputation when it came to drink and women. Another of my Rivers cousins, Dick Rivers of Tennessee, had the great sin of drinking too much peach brandy. He was not a steady drinker, but he took "spells" of drinking about once a month. When under the influence of drink he seemed in a good humor with all the world, and sometimes did queer things. One of the queer things he did was this: after becoming unusually "mellow" under the influence of an unusually liberal indulgence in his favorite peach brandy, Cousin Dick ordered his houseman to blow the cow's horn which was used to summon the slaves from the fields; when the slaves came trooping up to the house they found their Master out in the yard by the side of the well. Close at hand stood a keg of peach brandy, also a bag of brown sugar.

"Knock open that keg," he commanded. It was done. "Now, empty the brandy into the well." That, too, was done. The slaves never dared question Cousin Dick's orders, no matter how strange they were. "Now, sweeten it, you rascals!" was the next command. And in went the bag of brown sugar. This done, the bucket was let down into the well and soon Cousin Dick was ladling out well water, flavored with brandy and sugar, to his astonished slaves.

Some of my Rivers kin who were much nearer to me than Cousin Dick furnished food for much talk in our family. They have been dead and gone so long--the last of them more than sixty years--that I do not think I do harm in telling of their conduct, which after all was not really disgraceful--at least not judged by the standards of their day. Sixty years ago drunkenness was more common than it is now; it did not then do any particular harm to a gentleman's reputation to have it known that he got on sprees.

My mother had three brothers, all younger than herself. Their names were Robert, Thomas and John Rivers, usually called Jack Rivers. While I was still a very young girl an awful tragedy was enacted by my mother's brother Robert Rivers, who lived on his plantation on the Tennessee side of the Mississippi River some twenty miles north of a little town called at that time "Mills Point," but which is now known as Hickman, Kentucky. Uncle Robert Rivers' brother Thomas, a doctor, also lived at Mills Point, and was fond of playing cards and drinking mint juleps. He did not play with regular gamblers, but with men in his own station in life--lawyers, doctors and business men. These men made bets that were not large but which nevertheless seemed to arouse their interest and make them as keen to win as if thousands were at stake.

One night while Uncle Thomas Rivers and his friends were playing cards and drinking mint juleps a lawyer named Ferguson said something which my Uncle thought intimated that he, Ferguson, believed my Uncle had cheated at cards--and quick as a flash my Uncle slapped Ferguson in the face. Ferguson was furious and fell upon my Uncle with deadly hatred. The other men succeeded in pulling them apart and it was thought the affair would end there. But Ferguson brooded over the blow my Uncle had given him until he persuaded himself that only blood could wipe off the stain and restore his honor. And so next morning as my Uncle Thomas Rivers was going to his office, holding his little eight year old son by the hand, a bullet from a gun stuck through the crack of a log stable struck my Uncle and he fell to the ground exclaiming, "My God! I am killed" He expired almost as he uttered the words; at the same moment Ferguson rushed out of the stable crying, "I am avenged! My honor is redeemed."

Hickman, or Mills Point as it was then called, was a small place. The noise of the pistol shot was heard by many people and soon a crowd gathered around the body of my Uncle and his slayer who stood, gun in hand, looking down at his victim. The town had no jail but Ferguson was arrested and taken to a vacant house and there locked up and a guard placed in front of the door. In the mean time Uncle Thomas' body was taken home for his lonely young wife to weep over. She had heard the shot which killed her husband and never after that cruel day did she hear a gun shot without a shiver running through her body.

My Uncle Robert Rivers was notified the next day of the death of his brother; he was deeply attached to Thomas. Faulty as were the men of the Rivers family, they had deep feeling; they loved kindred and friends and were good to their slaves. On hearing that his brother had been murdered, Uncle Robert Rivers took two negro men and got into a skiff and rowed up the river to Mills Point. Before starting he armed himself with a dagger, a pistol and a shot gun. On landing at Mills Point he first went to his dead brother's house, looked on the pale, still face and wept over him with the weeping widow. Then he started to the house where Ferguson was locked up; he saw the murderer through the window and the sight of him so stirred Uncle Robert, nothing could restrain him. He smashed in the window and climbed through it into the house. Ferguson saw him and broke through the door, across the hall and smashed through a window on the opposite side of the house and ran for his life. Uncle Robert followed in close pursuit and, coming within pistol aim, took deliberate aim and fired. Ferguson was hit, but not mortally; he fell to the ground; Uncle Robert went up to him; Ferguson begged for mercy but my Uncle was merciless; taking aim again, again he fired and this time Ferguson was instantly killed. In a very few minutes a large crowd was on the scene. Uncle Robert faced the crowd, a grim look in his eyes. The local paper which related the affair said my Uncle said to that crowd only a dozen words, and that those words were spoken in as low and calm a voice as if he were asking some one to hold his horse, nevertheless the crowd opened a passage for him and made no effort to detain him. These are the words which the newspaper said my Uncle spoke:

"Gentlemen, I am a small man, but I defy a regiment to take me."

With that he walked straight back to his dead brother's house, ordered his two negro men to carry the body to the skiff, and soon was on his way back to his plantation where my Uncle Thomas, the doctor, then was buried. Uncle Robert supposed the Sheriff would come sooner or later to arrest him; when he expressed this belief to his friends and neighbors they swore they would never let the Sheriff arrest him. Every body in the county knew and loved Uncle Robert; everybody thought he did right to avenge his brother's murder. Whether the public expression of this sentiment deterred the Sheriff from seeking to arrest my Uncle I do not know, but it is a fact that the matter dropped right there. My Uncle was never arrested and never prosecuted for killing Ferguson.

A year or two after this tragedy Uncle Robert Rivers studied law, moved to Texas and there won great fame as a lawyer and an orator. I have kept to this day a Texas paper's account of Uncle Robert's death in which is given an instance of his wonderful eloquence. A woman, who had killed a man for aiding another man to run off with her daughter, was on trial for her life; Uncle Robert was her lawyer. Now, like his brother Thomas, the Doctor, Uncle Robert was fond of card playing. Seeing which, a friend felt prompted to caution him.

"See here, Rivers," he said. "That murder case of yours is to be tried tomorrow. Better not get into a game tonight. Go home and look up your law books."

"Law books be hanged!" replied Uncle Robert lightly. "My client's a woman and a mother. That's better than law books. That's all I need."

And the event proved him right. The fact that his client had killed the man was not denied; Uncle Robert did not question the facts; on the contrary he stated them plainly and so eloquently pictured the feelings of a Mother robbed of the very offspring of her body--That Texas newspaper says the Jury listened with rapt attention, tears in their eyes. And they brought in a verdict of Not Guilty without even leaving their seats.

My dear Children, I have unbarred the bad qualities of my Mother's Rivers kin, but I want you to know that they had many very good and noble traits. They were not only talented, but generous, openhearted, true to their convictions. My Aunt, sister to that Robert who so fiercely avenged the death of his brother Thomas, told me that Uncle Robert Rivers at twenty one was one of the handsomest men God ever created. And not only handsome, but brilliant, talented and as tender hearted as a girl. When his mother was ill Uncle Robert would care for her lovingly; there were slaves to wait on her, but he would wave them aside and lift her in his arms and himself carry her out to her carriage, or would sit by her bedside and read to her. When a busy man does this for his mother it shows his heart is good.

When my brother Tom married on Dec. 27, 1852, our uncle Jack Rivers wrote him a letter which I have now in my book of "Old Letters." That letter gives a better idea of what sort of man Uncle Jack was than could be given by pages of description, so I will insert it here:

DEAR TOM:

I believe you have forgotten me since you have a little wife to fondle on, but you are like all the balance of the world, confound them! so soon as they get married old Jack Rivers may go to the devil! I want to see your wife worse than anybody in the world, that is the truth I swear. I know I would love her, couldn't help loving Tom Avery's wife some. I am going to Memphis soon to see you all, from there to brother Ed's. I want to see him one more time before he starts to Heaven. God, Tom, how we all will be scattered in the next world! And here I am most forty five years old--Good Lord, it nearly kills me to think of it. If I knew how to get religion, damn my old coat if I wouldn't get it! ! ! Let people say what they please, it is the safe side of the question, but it is hard for a Rivers to go to Heaven (I mean the males), just as hard as for a camel to go through the eye of a needle and I am afraid, Tom, you have too much Rivers blood in you. Our great, great, great grand father down to your old Uncle Jack was fond of liquor and all kinds of sporting. Now that you have a wife one you would butt your brains out before you would make her unhappy, let me give you a little friendly advice. If you don't choose to take it, some twenty years hence you may wish you had. It is this: Run from a bottle of brandy, a pack of cards and a race horse as you would from the devil!

You know, Tom, I have been the worst drunkard God ever made, and all my brothers loved the cursed stuff too well. Long after he was a father Jones Rivers disliked the taste of it, never drank unless it was a social glass with a friend; yet how was it with him? He is now a first rate drunkard A moderate drinker is the most dangerous sort--take three drinks a day for a few years and then fifty a day won't be enough. Look at cousin Robert Rivers; ten years ago I was with him several weeks in Orleans. He was a temperate man. When I was in Memphis last I saw him--drinks a hell of a site of liquor. No man is ever safe that drinks any at all. The appetite for it will increase. You will say I am crazy. Maybe I am, but the cussed, infernal stuff has made me see trouble in this world; no woman likes to see her husband take a dram. You will be a mighty happy man if you will guard against these vices of the Rivers blood.

JACK RIVERS.

That letter, written by one who knew, seemed to me a powerful sermon against alcohol; I got my brother to give me the letter so I could preserve it and show it to my sons. It has spoken to them, a voice from the grave, and has, I am happy to believe, played some part in making them sober, temperate men.

CHAPTER IV

Adventure with a ghost, and with Indians. I fall into the Smoke House lard.
Why I still read my Bible. My first poem.

My mother was a very little girl when her father sold his Virginia plantation and emigrated to Tennessee. My grand father set his negroes to building log cabins for them to live in, but he rented for his own family an old house that had been used by early settlers as a fort against Indians. My mother told me her father had barely gotten his family settled in that old Fort of a house before they were told the place was haunted, and from that time on things happened to make my mother believe there was a "haunt" over the place. For one thing, she said, her little sister while in the yard saw a dog; the dog ran up to her and shook himself against her and sprinkled water on her dress. And the very next day a neighbor called to tell them to look out for the ghost of a little wet dog!

The other ghost was that of a negro man who had been killed in the Fort by the poisoned arrow of an Indian. My mother never saw the ghost but she told me it was frequently seen by a young man who visited the family. A Miss Sally Henderson, a relative of my grandfather's, was with them at the Fort and this young man, who was courting Miss Henderson, frequently remained all night at my grand father's house, rather than ride back to his own home in the night and run the risk of meeting Indians. (In those days Indians were in many parts of Tennessee.)

This young man, while asleep one night in the Fort, felt a breeze of cold air on his face; it awakened him and he saw the black face and wooly head of a negro man bending over him. The young man tried to seize the negro but his fingers gripped only the thin air. He leaped out of bed to grapple with the negro, but he grappled only thin air--and then the young man realized it was a ghost he had seen. This was the story he told next morning, and I tell it to you, my dear grand children, so you may form some sort of picture of the times and doings of my grand father's day. I do not believe an ordinarily intelligent young man of this day would imagine he saw ghosts; and if he did imagine such a thing he would hardly wish any body to know it. But in that day, now more than a hundred years ago, and in what was then a frontier land, among Indians, even educated people indulged in some queer fancies. I think my mother was quite a grown girl before she came to cease looking with awe on the "ghost" of the little wet dog that sprinkled water on her little sister's dress.

Sally Henderson afterward married that young man who saw the negro ghost, but before she married she had an exciting experience. It happened one day when she was some distance from the Fort gathering black berries, in a field near the edge of a forest. So busy was Sally filling her bucket with the black berries, she did not see or hear the Indians until they were right upon her. There were ten or a dozen of them and they seized the girl and forced her to go off with them through the forest. Sally knew her friends would try to rescue her and, with what always seemed to me great presence of mind, she immediately began carrying out a plan calculated to give her friends a clue to the place the Indians were taking her. She slipped the skirt of her frock down on the ground, then took it in her hand and from time to time slyly tore it to pieces and dropped the pieces as she walked along. Occasionally she managed to hang a small piece on a bush or on some of the underbrush through which the Indians were forcing her to go. Miss Henderson thought this would enable my Grand father and his men to follow her--which is exactly what it did do. And three days later my grand father and his posse of armed men came upon the Indians while they were asleep--most luckily; for it enabled them to capture the whole band without firing a shot. The Indians had not harmed Miss Henderson. Apart from the fright she had been given, she was none the worse for the adventure. And it seemed that she had not even been much frightened. Either she had unusual nerve, or those Indians must have been unusually amiable in their demeanor. Certainly, few young ladies of this day could go through such an ordeal and not faint or scream or do something silly.

This grandfather Rivers of mine called himself a Christian but he did not practice the customs of good Christians, as my father did; Grandfather Rivers never said grace at the table. He declared there was no sense bothering God three times a day about the food we ate, but once a year he asked God to bless his smokehouse and the fruits of his fields. My father, I remember, said of this habit of Grandfather Rivers that it was most ungodly and unchristian.

Speaking of my Grandfather's "Smoke House" reminds me, my dear children, that perhaps I should tell you what a Smoke House is, or rather was; for now-a-days they are not so common even on farms as they once were. And of course, you who were born and have always lived in the city know nothing at all about Smoke Houses. Well, in my girlhood days people in the country raised great numbers of hogs. The negroes were very fond of hog meat. They said ham and bacon were very "strenthen"' (strengthening) and where there were many slaves there was always a big Smoke House--that is a house where the hog meat was cured. Usually the Smoke House was built of logs; the chinks between the logs were nailed up by what were called "clap boards" and were daubed with mud so as to be air tight. Inside this log house was no floor, only the earth, and in the center was dug a hole as big around as a flour barrel but not so deep as a barrel. Overhead were "scantlings"--timbers that reached across from wall to wall --and big spikes were driven into these scantlings. With the approach of

Winter the hogs were killed and cut up into hams and shoulders and jowls, and these were hung from the spikes in the scantlings after they had been properly salted. Then a fire was kindled in the hole in the center of the floor and was smothered in such a way as to make a dense smoke. Never was the fire allowed to blaze.

When I was a little girl I was often sent to the Smoke House to see if the fire was smoking or blazing; I was not to go into the Smoke House, but peep in and report to some grown member of the household who would go and fix the fire right, in case I reported it was blazing instead of smoking. Not only was hog meat kept in Smoke Houses, but barrels of sugar, molasses, apples and lard were kept there, the barrels of lard buried in the earth almost to the tops of the barrel so as to keep it cool and prevent its becoming rancid. It was my mother's custom to send the cook every morning to get what food stuff was needed for the day and often I went with the cook. The barrel of lard buried in the earth was covered with boards. One morning while the cook was busy getting out flour, rice, sugar etc I got into trouble; I was skipping and jumping about, first in one place, then in another, until in an unlucky moment I hopped up on the narrow boards that covered the buried barrel of lard and began to dance a jig. Result: the boards tipped up and I tipped in, down into that barrel of lard until only my head remained in sight. Had I tumbled to the bottom of the sea I would not have been more frightened. I screamed at the top of my lungs, which caused my mother to come running out to the Smoke House. On seeing my predicament she cried to the cook to pull me out, the cook dropped her tray of flour, thrust her arms down into the lard barrel, seized me by the arms and in a moment had me out in the yard where the cleansing process began. I shall never forget it; I remember as if it were yesterday how I was put on a stool and how that old black Mammy set to work scraping the lard off my body. My screams ceased but not my tears, I sobbed bitterly, for to me it seemed as if I were ruined for life.

"Don't cry, Honey," said the cook consolingly. "I'll get you scraped off purty soon, den you c'n go git yo' white frock and be as purty as eber. An' dis lard'll make powerful nice soap, so dere ain't no harm done at all."

Under Cook's treatment I soon stopped crying, but to this day I have detested lard--have never used it in my kitchen when butter was available. And I dare say it was that Smoke House episode of eighty five years ago that turned me against the stuff.

After my Grand father Rivers built a handsome home not far from the Fort where he lived on first coming to Tennessee he moved his family into that home and lived as became a Virginia gentleman. In the sitting room was a large mahogany sideboard on which always stood a decanter of peach brandy and near by a sugar bowl filled with lumps of loaf sugar--not such lump sugar as you have, my dear children; the sugar of that day came in loaves the shape of a cone or pyramid, about eight or nine inches long, and as hard as flint. It took an axe to break up one of those eight inch long loaves of sugar. The Houseman had standing orders, whenever he saw a gentleman riding through the front gate up to the house, to run at once into the garden and get a bunch of peppermint and proceed to make a peach brandy toddy for the visitor. It was the custom of my Grand father, and of other gentlemen of that day, to give strong drink to all visitors, even to young boys. Luckily it was not thought right to give strong drink to girls. Had the women of that time consumed as much alcohol as the males of the family their children could scarcely have failed to be drunkards, if not idiots. A doctor once told me that where both the father and mother are alcoholics the children are very apt to be imbeciles. I have hated liquor all my life and even as a young girl wondered how the men of the Rivers family could be at once brainy, cultured, talented, and also weak enough to poison themselves and their friends with whiskey and brandy! I remember once quoting to my Grand father the lines from the Scriptures.

"Wine is a mocker! And strong drink is raging! It biteth like an adder, it stingeth like an asp. Who hath sorrow? Who hath contentions' Who hath redness of nose? They that tarry long at the wine!"

My Grand father only laughed, but I thought then--and I think now--not even the literature of Greece or Rome contains a sentence comparable with this from the Jewish Bible. I have always thought that we Christian people do not really appreciate the Jewish race, or the fact that from that race we have a book worth all the others written my man. It were better for the world to lose any thousand books ever written by man than to lose the Jewish Bible. I studied the Old Testament when I was a girl, and now that I am past ninety two I still find comfort and interest in reading those wonderful pages. From this, my dear Children, do not imagine it is religion that prompts what I am now saying; I can not say that I think God had anything to do with the Bible; it was written by men; it is a story of men, of the Jews of Antiquity. But that only makes the book more wonderful--it is wonderful that such men as the ancient Jews should have produced a work of such imagery, of such power, of such appeal to all the human emotions.

I am fond of reading the New Testament, too, but it is the Old Testament to which my eyes more often turn and I think every orator, every man of letters, quite apart from any spiritual or religious feeling, would do well to read often and long in the pages of the old Jewish Bible.

Although the men of my mother's family were what is called a little "wild" in the matter of women and drink, they had good hearts and in money matters were the souls of honor. The men of our own immediate family were decided improvements on the generation before them--they drank less and were less given to admiring other women unduly. My brother Tom in particular had the best heart of any man I ever knew. As an instance of his goodness of heart let me tell you an incident that occurred during my childhood. Tom was seven years older than I, and was a close student; he was trying to read Homer in the original Greek and Virgil in Latin, while I, who knew nothing of either Homer or Virgil, wanted to talk to my brother and persisted in interrupting him until at length, his patience exhausted, he slapped me on the cheek.

The slap did not hurt me physically but it hurt my feelings terribly; I felt it was an insult and burst into tears. My brother tried to sooth me but the more he tried the more I cried.

"I did not mean to hit you," he said penitently.

"But you did hit me," I sobbed.

"I know I did," he answered contritely. "That is what distresses me, that I--a great big boy--should hit a little girl. I am a brute, that is what I am." He thought a moment, then his face lighted up as if he had found a way out of the difficulty. "I'll tell you what we will do," he said. "I am a big boy. Big boys can fight. But little girls can't fight. So we will go out into the yard, I will lay down on the ground in the snow and you can pelt me with snow balls until you think you have punished me enough."

This struck me as a grand plan. I wiped my eyes and my brother took me by the hand and led me out into the yard. Then he lay down in the snow and I pelted him with snow balls until my hands were half frozen. When at last I stopped my brother got up, kissed me and we returned to the house as good friends as ever. I doubt if many brothers would have been so kind. I think the average boy would have said: "You are such a nuisance, you deserved a slap. And I'll give you another if you don't run along and let me study my lessons."

My dear children, let me now tell you how near your grand mother came to being a poet. I was twelve years old when I wrote my first, and I may say also my last, poem. The theme was good, at least it so seemed to me when I wrote it. I had a beautiful young girl fall in love with a handsome young soldier. Before the day set for the wedding arrived the young soldier was killed in battle; the poem moved on swimmingly until this untimely period was put to my hero's life, then I made the heroine give voice to her despair in the following lines, which are the only ones I remember after all these years:

> "Oh Carl! Oh Carl! She cried,
> And in her wild despair
> She tore from off her hide
> Her long and jetty hair!"

Just as I penned these last lines of my one and only "poem" my brother Tom came into the room where I was writing. He looked over my shoulder and read in silence until he came to these last four lines, then he laughed aloud. I tried to cover up the paper but he snatched it from my hands, held it high above my head and exclaimed:

"Don't tell me you wrote this. It is impossible that any little girl could write such poetry. You borrowed it from Homer--or perhaps Shakespeare. 'Fess up,

Betsy. Didn't you copy this out of Shakespeare?

"No, I didn't. I wrote it myself. Give it to me."

But he held it tight and held it above his head as he spouted out those last four lines.

"'She tore it off her hide'--that is good," he cried. "I never saw anything like that before. Only a born poet could conceive a line like that."

By this time I saw Brother Tom was making fun of me and began to cry. Brother was instantly all contrition; he handed the paper back to me and said he didn't mean to hurt my feelings, that the lines were really very good, considering I was only a little girl and wouldn't I forgive him? I did forgive him, but I realized that the lines were not good, even for a twelve year old girl-- and so I tore them up and never tried to write poetry again. My brother advised me to write a story and I forthwith began one about a little girl with a bad stepmother who treated her so unkindly that she ran away from home. My little girl went through a dark forest with tall, towering trees until she got so tired she could walk no further; I put her down on the gnarled root of a tree to rest. And for all I know, that little girl is sitting on that root yet, for I never knew how to finish the story. I have since written a number of stories, and several novels, which the critics said were not without merit, but certainly that first story was an ignominious failure, almost as complete a failure as my first and only "poem" which, as you can judge from those last four lines, is saying it was a failure in the superlative degree.

As both my father and mother were strict Methodists they required their children to go to Church with them every Sunday, and after church my father would question us about the sermon. This caused us to listen more attentively than we might otherwise have done, for none of us cared to have our father look at us in that serious, hurt way which he had whenever our talk showed we had not paid attention to the preacher or had not remembered what he said. In our younger days we also went regularly to Sunday School. Miss Ann Kesterson was our teacher. I became devoted to Miss Ann and my personal devotion prompted me to a degree of attention to her instruction which mere love of the subject would not have done; Miss Ann told my mother I knew my Bible lessons better than any of the others in the class. This greatly pleased my mother, and in turn that made me study still harder, so that I came to be a really good Bible scholar, and to this day the Bible affords me more pleasure, and occupies more of my time, than any other book in my library. I fear, however, I do not now read it, and have not read it any time these last seventy years with the faith and reverence which Miss Ann Kesterson taught me to read it when I was a little girl. Miss Ann believed in the Bible "from cover to cover," and accepted its words literally. I did, too, when I was in her Sunday School class eighty years ago; but as I grew into womanhood, while appealing more and more to my intellect, to my appreciation of their great moral truths, to the wonderful literary skill with which they reveal those truths, the Scriptures commanded less and less of my unquestioning Faith until at last, had poor Miss Ann lived to see the change in my religious convictions her amiable soul would have been overwhelmed with horror. Miss Ann, like my mother and father, imagined that one who did not believe literally in the Bible as a message direct from the Deity would, when dead, go at once and permanently to a literal Hell No matter how correct one might be in all one's relations with others no matter how sweet, loveable, generous one might be, yet Hell was the sure result of non-belief in the Bible. Such was Miss Ann's belief, and not for the world would I have owned to her the doubts which began to come to me even before I left her class. It would have distressed her and it would have distressed my parents, to believe that after my death I would have to suffer for all Eternity the fires of Hell. There may be people today who believe such things, but I ceased to believe them while I was still in my teens. It seemed to me preposterous to imagine that a *good* God would create a human being with the power to feel and to suffer if He knew before creating that being that its fate was Hell for all eternity. They told me God was both good and all wise and so it seemed to me even while I was still in Miss Ann Kesterson's Sunday school class that there was a flaw somewhere in the belief of the people about me, that a good God would not send any of his creatures to a Hell--and I came then to the opinion I still hold, viz. that the Hell we mortals get is of our own making and that we get it on this earth and not in a future life.

The Church where Miss Ann taught me my first knowledge of the Bible was a large frame building; it was plainly furnished--wooden benches, ordinary glass windows (not beautiful stained glass such as I see in the Methodist church near where I now live and to which I occasionally now go), and not a sign of an organ. On one side of the pulpit was what was called the "Amen Corner." Every time the preacher said anything particularly good or pleasing the dozen or more men in the Amen Corner would cry out as with one voice, "Amen, Amen!" I never saw a woman in that Amen Corner, nor did my father ever sit there. He always sat beside my mother and his children.

When in Memphis on my last visit to friends and relatives in my home of long ago, I tried to find the church of my girlhood days; the old frame building no longer exists. In its place, on the same spot, stands a handsome brick church and I attended services there and tried to realize that the little girl who had attended Miss Ann's Sunday school class on that same spot eighty years before was the same person who, old and wrinkled, now sat in that brick church and mused over by gone days! I could see the old wooden church with its rude benches and plain windows; I could see the men in the Amen Corner and could hear them lustily groaning "Amen! Amen!" And then I could see my father and mother and by their side a little girl with round face and bright eyes and rosy cheeks.

Was it possible that little girl was I? No; it did not seem possible that I was ever so young and so pretty. I have been old so long, it is hard for me to realize that I was ever young. Ah, what a glorious thing is Youth! But since even you, my dear children, you who are now so young--since even you will some day be old, let me tell you that Old Age has its compensations. So do not worry when the gray hairs begin to whiten your heads. Provided you keep your health you will find much to make *Life* worth living even when you are old.

CHAPTER V

Death of my parents. Early poverty. My sisters and I teach school. Brother Tom gets into politics. How I got the opposition Leader to support my brother.

My mother died on May 30, 1847, just fourteen months after my father's death on March 5th, 1846. My mother had pneumonia and was ill only a few days. I do not think the doctors of that day knew how to treat pneumonia. They gave my mother hot whiskey toddy to make her sweat, and when she did not sweat as freely as they thought necessary the doctor bled her. Was not such treatment enough to kill her even if she had not been ill of pneumonia? I have always thought so.

On my last visit to Memphis I had myself driven out to Winchester cemetery where are buried my father and mother, and while standing over their graves I bade them a last farewell. I am too old to travel and shall probably never visit Memphis again. If there be another Life the next time I am near my parents will be after I, too, have passed into the Great Beyond and when I can stand--not over their graves--but by their sides and greet them and take them by their hands.

Should that day ever come I wonder if in this old woman long past ninety they will recognize the young and fairly good looking girl that was I when they died in 1847?

After mother's death brother Tom felt as if the weight of the world was on his shoulders. We had no money and Tom felt responsible for the support of his three young sisters. He did his best for us, but he himself was very young and his best was not very good; there were days when we had hardly enough to eat. On such days Charlotte, our negro woman, came to the rescue. "Doan you worry, chilluns," she would say. "I knows a lady what want some work done. I'll work out today an' bring you back fifty cents."

Food was then much cheaper than now; Charlotte's fifty cents bought enough food to keep us from starving. A bushel of sweet potatoes cost only twenty five cents, and for twenty five cents you could buy a bushel of corn meal. In our poorest days we lived on sweet potatoes and corn meal hoe-cakes. Brother Tom was too proud to let us keep boarders. I think, too, he did not like the idea of boarders in the house with three pretty young girls; we three sisters were all very young, and Tom thought us also very pretty. So he frowned down my suggestion that we take in boarders. Then I said I would like to teach school. Being young and in good health, baked sweet potatoes and corn cakes might do for our food, but what about clothing? We were anxious to get black gowns as mourning for our parents, and to get dresses of any kind money was needed.

When I spoke of this to our brother, he said:

"Never mind, Betsy; I am thinking of a plan to make money enough to take care of you and Estelle and Amanda without your going to work."

As this was not a positive refusal, I went to some of our father's friends and told them of my desire to teach a little school. There were no public schools in Memphis in those days. Our friends, because of this--and perhaps, too, because they knew how badly we needed money--approved my plan and soon our little dining room became the school room of some twenty or twenty five little boys and girls. I had read that Milton ate in his kitchen, and I thought if so great a man as the author of *Paradise Lost* did not disdain to eat in a kitchen, we could afford to do it too. So our dining room became a school room and my two sisters, Estelle and Amanda, assisted me in the work. The pay we received was very small but it helped us greatly. Each child paid eight dollars for the school season of five months, which made about a dollar and a half a month per child. As we had on an average from twenty to twenty five scholars our little school brought us in about forty dollars a month--not a brilliant result, but it seemed brilliant to us then. It was so much more than we had ever had before; it sufficed us to buy those black dresses. It did not enable us to buy three pretty bonnets, so we bought one bonnet and took turns in wearing it. By and by, after saving some of our earnings, we bought two more bonnets and then for the first time after our mother's death, we all three went to church together.

As time passed I could see that brother Tom, who at first feared his sisters might do something to compromise the dignity of his family, lost that fear and began to trust us. Even our youngest sister, Estelle, (now living in Memphis with my other sister, Amanda, both well on toward ninety) was ever quick to resent attempted familiarity from any man. When our Methodist church gave a Fair to raise money to repair the church, Estelle was appointed to serve as "Post Mistress." A little place was curtained off and called the "Post Office." This little Post Office had one chair and a small table on which the letters were to be written. Each letter cost twenty five cents. My sister was to stand at a little window in the curtained off Post Office, deliver the letters and take in the twenty five cents.

The little window was just about large enough to be a frame for my sister's face as she looked out at customers who came for letters. A young man named Lawrence B.--of a fine family, but given to pertness and flirting with girls who permitted such things--came up to the Post Office window, looked in through the little window at sister Estelle and said:

"Miss Stella, nobody can see us. Give me a kiss as well as a letter!"

Estelle, whom we called "Little Spitfire," she was sometimes so high tempered, looked at young Lawrence B., scorn and anger in her brown eyes, as she said:

"I didn't know you were such a fool! ! Stand away from the window. There is no letter here for you."

That young man never tried to flirt with my sister again.

When Brother Tom received his license to practice law he obtained almost immediate recognition as a man of eloquence and ability. At a public meeting where were many of the most prominent people of the city he seized the chance to speak; the speech was short but it was to the point and so forcibly, so eloquently delivered that it fairly brought down the house. "Who is that boy"' I heard people in the audience ask. "He doesn't look much more than a boy," others said. And one man replied, "Well, all the same he is a Cicero, a Sucking Cicero! "

It is now some seventy years since that night, but that expression "Sucking Cicero" still lives in my memory; it was often used after that meeting in referring to my brother and so widely and favorably did that speech make Tom known, he was soon afterward put forward for the Office of Clerk of the Criminal Court of Shelby County, the county in which the city of Memphis was located. This office paid a good salary, enough to lift us all out of the mire of poverty and shut the door in the face of the hungry wolf that seemed so determined to enter and devour us. Tom told us after he got the nomination that if he was elected we should do no more teaching; he would have enough money to buy us all the nice frocks we wanted.

While running for that office our brother not only had to go all over Memphis making speeches, he had also to attend meetings out in the county, but he had come to have confidence in us and no longer feared to leave us in the house alone. On one occasion when Tom returned from a two or three days electioneering trip over the county he got home about ten o'clock at night and asked if we could give him a bite to eat. Now, we three girls were rather stingy to ourselves in the matter of food; we felt that it was necessary first of all to look decently dressed, so as not to shame our brother who was then so much in the public eye. Consequently, the greater part of the little money we had went for articles of wearing apparel and when Brother was away we lived on potatoes and hoe-cakes. Not expecting him that night, we had only a scant supply even of potatoes and hoe-cakes--no molasses nor cheese nor tea or coffee. Poor Brother Tom nibbled at the hoe cake we set before him a moment, then looking up he exclaimed:

"My God! Children, I don't believe you get enough to eat!"

"Oh yes we do," we all three cried in chorus.

"How comes it then that you have nothing but a potato and a hoecake in the house?"

We sisters looked at one another, at a loss how to answer this question. Finally I said:

"Don't you know, Tom, we never eat suppers? Have you forgotten our mother told us suppers give one indigestion?"

"No, I have not forgotten, for she never told me any such thing. And any way,

I'm not going to have you starve in this fashion. You wait and see what I do to you when I get to be Circuit Clerk!"

He never waited till then to get us something to eat. The very next morning he sent Charlotte out to the grocer's and when she returned it was with butter, cheese, coffee, eggs and bacon--luxuries we had seldom seen. I felt that Tom had pretty well stripped himself in buying these things, so as he was about to leave after breakfast I took our last three dollars and laid it on the table and said in a careless way:

"Brother, I wish you would take this money and order out a load of wood today; there's hardly enough to run the kitchen stove another day."

Tom hesitated a moment, then picked up the money, put it in his pocket and went down town. In due time the wood came, but it was bought on credit (as I intended it should be) and the money was used by my brother for some of his pressing needs. Of course he did not tell us then that he so used the three dollars, but after his election he confessed not only to so using my three dollars but to having been forced to borrow from his friends.

After Brother Tom had canvassed the county he turned his attention to the city and made speeches every night in one or more halls in Memphis. He told us he found much opposition in Memphis and almost lost hope of success. Some men said he was too young, others that he was too inexperienced to fill so important an office; some, in derision, repeated the phrase "Sucking Cicero," and the "Boy Orator." His friends called him the "Dray Driver" and this reference to the days when he earned his first money hauling cotton on a dray to the steam boats on the Mississippi river won for him many voters among the working classes.

Every objection urged against him made our brother work all the harder. In North Memphis was a large number of rough laborers; this part of the city was called "Pinch" and the voters in Pinch invited our Brother to attend a social gathering given by some workingmen's Union. They had heard of his three sisters and asked him to bring them, too. Tom did not like the idea of taking us among such a crowd, but I told him at least one of us ought to go and finally he consented to take me. I was glad to do anything that would help him win.

The men of "Pinch" were very attentive to me; it is some seventy years since that dance but I have never forgotten how that night I longed to be a wall flower, but how I was not allowed to sit out even one dance. The men were honest enough, but their rough, sweaty hands, their awkwardness, their clumsy efforts to compliment me--all made me wish I was back in our poor but cozy little home. At last, seeing that as long as I remained in the hall l would be forced to dance, I made a great fuss about my head, said it ached me horribly and that I simply had to rest. The wife of one of the men came to sympathize with me. I begged her to show me to a room where I could be quiet until my head ceased aching. In truth, my head did not ache at all, but head aches have ever been handy excuses for a woman and on this occasion a pretended head ache saved me from further dances with those honest but rough, sweaty men of Pinch.

On our way home that night Brother Tom whispered in my ear: "You have done splendidly. I know how you feel, but luckily I don't think those fellows know. You made them think you were having the time of your life. It will make them feel kindly toward me."

A few nights after that "Pinch" episode Tom said he wanted to take me to another party; I made a wry face but told him I would go. Tom laughed. "I believe you'd go to the devil for me, wouldn't you, Little Sis? "

"Yes, I would," I answered plainly.

Tom laughed again. "Well," he said, "You don't have to go to the devil this time. You don't even have to go to Pinch. This party is among a different set of people. Some of the nicest men and women in Memphis will be there. I want you to look your best and be especially nice to a Mr. Shepheard who will be there."

"Why especially nice to him?" I asked. "Who is Mr. Shepheard?"

"He is the head of a big wholesale house--very influential in the party," replied my brother. "And I am sorry to say he rather leans against me. I'll get a friend to introduce him to you. If he asks you to dance, be nice to him."

I said I would do my best and that evening my brother pointed Mr. Shepheard out to me. He was a large and somewhat rubicund looking man, and seemed old in comparison with my slim, youthful brother. When this oldish, rubicund looking gentlemen was finally introduced to me and invited me to dance, I accepted with a smile. After dancing a while, I assumed a serious look and said to my partner in the dance:

"Did I understand your name aright? You are Mr. Shepheard?"

"Yes."

"Oh Mr. Shepheard!" I exclaimed with a still more serious face. "I am *so* sorry."

"What do you mean?" he asked. "Why are you sorry? Don't you like the name?"

"Oh, yes. Shepheard is a fine old name. But I heard something very bad about Mr. Shepheard tonight and after I met you it seemed so hard to believe it could be you. Is there another Mr. Shepheard here tonight? "

"N-O! I don't believe there is. But what did you hear bad about me? I can't guess what you mean."

Of course I knew his curiosity was aroused but I pretended to be sorry I had spoken, now I knew what I had heard referred to him, and not to any other Mr. Shepheard.

"Please forgive me for mentioning it," I said contritely. "I thought of course it must have been about some other Mr. Shepheard. I wouldn't ever have mentioned it had I dreamed it was about you."

"Dreamed what was about me?" demanded the mystified Mr. Shepheard.

"Dreamed that *you* could do such a thing. You don't look like that sort of a man, you are such a delightful dancer and such a charming gentleman."

"In Heaven's name, Miss Avery, what are you talking about? If some scoundrel has been slandering me, tell me his name that I may go to him and horse whip him!"

At this I smiled and told him the bad thing I had heard about him was that he was doing all he could to defeat my brother. And was not that bad, about the "badest" thing he could do? "I think so," I concluded. "For you must know, Mr. Shepheard, my brother, Tom Avery, is one of the best men who ever lived and he is a brainy man and will make the Court the best clerk it ever had."

Mr. Shepheard looked relieved. "Well," he said, "Tom Avery certainly has a beautiful sister, and a bright one, too, and I'll be hanged if I don't support her brother for that job of Circuit Clerk."

We parted good friends and the next day a big bunch of roses came to me with a card from Mr. Shepheard saying he wanted me to know he had not been merely "talking", that he was going to do everything in his power to elect my brother. After my brother was elected Mr. Shepheard began calling on me and I really acquired a liking for him, but not in the way he wanted and I felt conscience stricken when at length the affair came to such a pass that Mr. Shepheard made me a formal proposal of marriage. I had not intended to allow my zeal for my brother's success to cause me to mislead a man into thinking I could marry him. And yet apparently this was what had happened in the case of the big wholesale merchant. I told him I could not think of marrying at my age (I was not yet twenty); I said my brother had declared he would never marry as long as he had young sisters to protect and that I felt I too should remain single so as to look after Estelle and Amanda. Thereupon Mr. Shepheard said he would wait twenty years if I wished to postpone matrimony so long, and would promise then to have him! Twenty years! That looked to me then longer than a century now looks and I felt like giggling over the proposal. I put my handkerchief up to my face and tried to conceal my merriment; Mr. Shepheard thought I was crying and essayed to console me--it was a very trying experience and I was greatly relieved when at last he gave up the attempt to change my answer and took his departure. It is no doubt unusual (and in bad taste) for a woman to tell of the marriage proposals she receives; but poor Mr. Shepheard has been in his grave more than a half a century and nothing here said of him can do any harm. So far as I am aware, he has no descendants. I never saw him again and do not believe that he ever married.

CHAPTER VI

My marriage. My husband and I agree that slavery is wrong. We free our slaves and send them to Africa.

As an instance of my brother Tom's temper I will tell you, children, what he did to an ill bred Shop keeper from Cincinnati. This Cincinnati man had only recently come to Memphis and he was advertising great bargains in order to attract trade from the old stores of the town. All the world loves a bargain. I put in my purse a ten dollar bill, the only bill and all the money I had, and went with a woman friend to that Cincinnatian's shop in quest of bargains. In those days there were no "$4.99" bargains; pennies were not in circulation. Five cents was the smallest amount one could spend. My purchases amounted to $3.75. I handed the shop keeper my ten dollar bill, he gave me a hand full of silver and I started for the door, counting my money as I went. By the time I got to the door I had finished counting and found I had only $5.25 instead of $6.25. So I went back to the merchant and told him the change he had given me was one dollar short.

"We never make mistakes in this house," returned the man haughtily.

"Nevertheless you have made one this time," I answered. "I handed you ten dollars. My purchases cost $3.75. You should have given me back $6.25, whereas you only gave me $5.25. Here is my money. You can count it and see for yourself."

The Shop Keeper merely glanced at the money, then said: "You may have only $5.25 there, but I do not know how much you may have in your purse. We have made no mistake. We never return short change in this house."

"Do you think," I demanded, "That a lady would hide a dollar out of the change you gave her and then claim you had not returned the correct amount?"

"No. I do not think a lady would do that."

This reply, of course, was sufficient notice that neither honesty nor courtesy was to be expected in that shop, so I walked away without another word. That night when I told Brother Tom what happened he exclaimed, "The base born cur!!" That was all he said and I did not dream he thought further of the matter, much less that he would trouble himself about it. But that afternoon, meeting an intimate friend of Tom's, he laughingly asked if I had heard of my brother's bad behavior?

"My brother doesn't behave badly," I declared. "He will get after you for slander if you are not careful."

"Heaven forbid that he should get after me!" exclaimed Mr. B. solemnly. "After what he did this morning I'll do anything to avoid offending him. He's too dangerous a man, Miss Avery."

"What on earth are you talking about?" I demanded. "What has Tom been doing to make you talk such nonsense?"

"Nonsense? That Cincinnati chap doesn't think it nonsense. Tom went into his store this morning, called the proprietor out from behind his counter, then caned him so hard, the cane broke in two pieces. The fellow threatens to sue your brother for damages but no jury will ever give him any. If he ever has the nerve to bring suit the jury will be only too glad to show what it thinks of a man who insults a Southern lady."

Mr. B's prophecy proved correct to the letter; the episode became the talk of the town for a few days; and so general was the approval of my brother's action, the Cincinnati shop keeper not only did not think it worth his while to bring a suit, but his store lost the better class of custom and not long after the proprietor "pulled up stakes" and returned to Cincinnati.

My two sisters, though both were younger than I, married some years before I did. At the time of my marriage I was nearly twenty six years old, but the man I married was well worth waiting for. Indeed, my dear grand children, no woman in all the world ever got a better husband than mine, for no truer, nobler, more unselfish man than Minor Meriwether ever lived. We lived together nearly sixty years and not once in all that time did I ever know him to do a mean thing, not once did we ever have even a little quarrel. In these days of quick and numerous divorces sixty years of happy companionship with one husband is a record that may merit at least passing mention. Even after more than four score years had whitened my hair and chiseled wrinkles in my once smooth face my dear husband seemed never to see them, seemed to think me as beautiful as in the days of my youth and to love me as much as on the day he asked me to be his bride.

At the time of our marriage Minor (throughout these *Recollections* I shall, in speaking of my husband, call him by his first name) was earning only seventy five dollars a month, but that did not frighten me a bit. "I can live on less than half of seventy five dollars," I said.

Minor smiled. "Exist, perhaps; but not live," he replied. "However, don't worry, Dear. I shall soon make more than seventy five dollars a month. And, whatever I earn, half of it shall be yours. If you attend to your duties, which I trust in time will include looking after several children, I shall consider your work equal to mine and, therefore, that you are entitled to an equal part of my earnings."

We began Life with this understanding, and we carried it out to the end; half of the real estate Minor accumulated was deeded to me and he also gave me half of his accumulations of stocks and bonds. I think this perfect trust did much to smoothe the way and make our long married life a happy one wholly devoid of contentions and quarrels. And I can truthfully say my husband's trust was not misplaced or abused. I saved my money as carefully as he saved his, neither of us ever spent more than we had and never, even during the long four years war between the States, did either of us go in debt. There were times when we had very little money, but during such times we got along on a very few things. And it was always a comfort to know that however modestly situated we might be, we owed no one a dollar and need ask no landlord's leave to stay on the face of the earth. For a home was one of the first things we bought--a modest one. But it was a home, and it was ours. Both Minor and I had during all our lives a horror of paying rent; and, apart from one or two temporary instances, while awaiting the completion of some new home of our own, never in all the sixty years we were together did we live in a rented house.

Minor's father, Garrett Meriwether, was a man worth knowing. He owned a large plantation and a number of negro slaves and, for that day was deemed rich. But he belonged to that rather limited class which uses its wealth solely to advance the welfare of the undermost strata of Society. Long before negro slavery was denounced in New England my husband's father in Kentucky preached its abolition and set about devising ways and means to secure freedom for the Blacks. His plan was to get the Southerners to send their slaves to the African Republic Liberia; he earnestly believed that an All-Ruling Providence designed that the negroes of the South should return to Africa and there Christianize and civilize their savage cousins. He did not approve of setting them free in America; he urged that they could never be equal to the Whites, either socially or intellectually, and that consequently friction if not disaster, would result from permitting them to live in America as freemen.

So ably and so persistently did Garrett Meriwether urge this plan that he won to its support a number of rich slave owners who then, moved merely by intellectual and moral convictions, voluntarily divested themselves of, for that era, large fortunes. I remember one instance, that of a Mr. James Tyrell of Virginia, who freed seventy five slaves and was on the point of shipping them at his own expense to Liberia when he changed the plan at the Slaves' earnest request, and consented to their going North and living in a free state there. The Negroes declared they would rather remain slaves in America than be freemen in Africa filled, as they heard, with wild beasts and still wilder men.

Garrett Meriwether not only educated his negroes to fit them to live and do missionary work in Liberia, but he educated his sons to think it best that they should live by their own labor and not by the labor of slaves. Thus it was that Minor while still a beardless boy, instead of living the life of a rich man's son, worked his way through College and, on leaving College, began at once to earn his own livelihood. When you remember, my Children, that all this took place, not in the Sixties when Slavery was universally condemned, but way back in 1840, twenty years before the War between the States--way back in a time when to speak of Slavery as other than a Heaven-ordained institution was the Hall mark of a weak brain, if not of a treasonable one--When you remember all this it will help you to understand how remarkable a man was your Great-grandfather and how far in advance of his day he was! Your grandfather, my dear husband, did not in the least object to his father's views; on the contrary, he shared them and willingly put aside the easy life of a rich man's son and set about making his own way in the world. His first work was cutting a tunnel through the Cumberland Mountains in Tennessee. As a Civil Engineer your grandfather attained eminence even when he was in his early twenties. As I write these lines I have before me a Memphis newspaper of May 28th 1853, containing an account of the completion of a specially difficult engineering work in the Mountains; a paragraph in that article reads:

"Minor Meriwether is destined to rank as one of the best Civil Engineers in this country; the accuracy of his work on this great tunnel is recognized as a triumph in railroad engineering. Although not yet twenty four years old this brilliant young engineer has succeeded where older men failed. He first laid down the lines on the surface of the mountains, then transferred to a depth of several hundred feet through shafts and ran horizontally into the mountain from each end of the cutting. In running these direction lines from either end young Meriwether executed his work with such scientific accuracy that the center lines met exactly and cover each other the whole length of the tunnel. Pennsylvania, Maryland and Virginia for twenty years have been endeavoring to penetrate the inexhaustible wealth of the Mississippi valley by means of a tunnel; they expended twenty millions of dollars in the effort and failed. Now the work has been accomplished by the energy and talent of the engineer in charge, a young man of twenty four who began the work when little more than a boy."

I do not know that the reporter who wrote that description of the completion of the tunnel--the long tunnel on the railroad between Nashville and Chattanooga has correctly described how Minor ran his lines and did his work, but I do know that he correctly describes the impression made on the public opinion of the South in 1853 by the doing of such a task by such a youth. The art of railroad building was not then developed as it is now; the Simplon, The St. Gotherd, the Mt. Cenis and the other great tunnels of the world were then not even dreamed of; engineers did not then have the instruments of precision for making surveys which they now have, neither did they have the wonderful machinery modern engineers have by means of which they have been able to pierce the Alps and the Pyrenees and the other great mountain chains of the world. Judging, not by the standards of today, but by the standards and facilities of 1849-1853, the piercing of the Cumberland mountain chain in Tennessee by a youth of twenty two (he was twenty four when it was completed) is a feat of which Minor had a right to be proud; it is a monument to his memory and you, my children, must see that monument if ever you go to my native state. You will see it a few hours after the train starts south from Nashville and begins to climb up into the mountains; over the north entrance of the tunnel was placed a tablet in stone on which an inscription was carved telling how this great work was done by your grandfather sixty five year ago; his name, carved in large letters, may easily be read if the train stops for water just before entering the tunnel. It did this the last time I went that way--but that was in 1878 and since then no doubt the time tables of that road have been changed.

When Garrett Meriwether was told that Minor and I were engaged to be married he placed two chairs side by side in front of him, then he called us and asked us to sit in those chairs before him. We did as he wished, whereupon my future father-in-law said:

"Miss Avery, I am thought to be rich; it is true that I have what some people might call a fortune But that does not mean that my son here is to go through life playing the role of a rich man's son. Has he told you this?"

I answered that Minor had told me something of his father's plans and opinions.

"And what he told you has not affected your purpose to become his wife? "

"Of course not, why should it?" I was a little nettled. Minor's father smiled gravely. I can see him now as he looked at me, seemingly trying to read my very soul. What he read must have satisfied him, for presently he said:

"Your answer pleases me. Nothing could be more foolish, as well as unwise, than to marry for money, or even to care for money. Yet many men and women do it. The negroes on my plantations have been in the Meriwether family since their ancestors were brought from Africa to Massachusetts and thence sold into Virginia. They are attached to our family and we are attached to them; it is my purpose to set them free. I think that is best for them, and I think it best for my son here that he should live by his own labor rather than by the labor of slaves. It is right you should know all this before you marry Minor. He will not be rich but he is a good boy; he has brains; he will always earn enough to provide his wife the comforts as well as the necessities of life. If this will satisfy you, Minor will make you happy."

How well Garrett Meriwether knew his son! That interview took place some sixty six years ago but I remember it as if it were yesterday--those two chairs side by side, Minor in one, I in the other; and before us in another chair that grave, kindly eyed man, so shrewd, so just in his judgment of his son! Even through all the storms and stress of War Minor did provide for me even more bounteously than his father promised he would; and after the War his abilities enabled him, not indeed to make me rich, but to make me more than comfortable, to live in a large mansion and to travel over America and Europe when I felt like getting out and seeing the world.

Not long after that memorable interview with Garrett Meriwether, and before his plans regarding his negroes could be carried out, he fell ill and died after a very short illness. His will left no direction as to freeing his slaves and so Minor was not legally obliged to give them up. But to my dear husband duty and moral convictions were more compelling than any mere statute law and he religiously carried out his father's wishes. He sold enough land to provide the money needed to buy the slaves clothing for a long journey, then he put them on a steam boat and took them to New Orleans whence he shipped them to Liberia in Africa. During many years after that voyage to New Orleans and Liberia those negroes wrote to their former master telling him of their new life and plans and hopes and frequently expressing their gratitude for what he had done. In truth, did your grandfather not deserve gratitude? All this happened many years before the War between the States. No one then thought of freeing the negroes; to give away a slave in 1850 was like giving away a thousand dollars-- few people did such things, and those who did were regarded as the victims of absurd and rather expensive convictions.

After getting his slaves off to Liberia Minor left New Orleans on a Mississippi river steam boat and came to Memphis where I lived. And there we were married in January 1850. My two sisters had married several years earlier, so had my Brother Tom; he died many years ago, but both my sisters are living. They reside in our old home town, Memphis, Tennessee, and although long past eighty both are still well and able to get about.

Minor's work at the time of our marriage was that of railroad building and our first home was in Winchester, Tennessee. Before we left Memphis, a few days after the wedding, my dear, good Brother said to Minor:

"As you have sent all of your negroes to Africa I am going to give Betty a negro girl to wait on her, and don't you let any of your anti-slavery notions upset this arrangement. I don't want my sister to do house work when she can have a slave do it for her."

Minor laughed. "I am your sister's husband, not her master," he said. "If *she* believes in slavery enough to keep a slave, that is *her* affair."

I did not believe in slavery; on principle I was as opposed to it as Minor. But I considered the times and country in which we were living; it was difficult, if not impossible, to hire a white maid--and I thoroughly agreed with my brother that I did not wish to do domestic drudgery if there was a way to get it done by a servant. The upshot of it all was, Tom gave me a fourteen year old negro girl named Evelyn and Minor promised to suppress his inclination to set her free and ship her off to Liberia. Evelyn was jet black and had a pile of black wool on her head which she called "Har" (Hair); she was a lively girl and I remember as if it were yesterday how she giggled when Brother Tom first brought her to me.

"Evelyn, this is your Mistress," said my brother. "You will call her Miss Betty."

The jet black slave grinned and showed the whitest teeth I ever saw. "I'se monsus glad to be yo' slave, Miss Betty," she said. "I sho' is. Mammy tole me how lucky I wuz jest soon as Marse Tom tole her he dun bought me fur you an' dat I'se to go trabblin'. I'm powerful glad I'se goin' trabblin', Miss Betty. I do so wants ter see sumthin', an' besides I wants ter git away from Mammy. She do beat me so."

"What do you do bad to make your mother beat you?" I asked.

Evelyn grinned and showed her big white teeth again.

"Laws a mussy!" she exclaimed. "My Mammy doan' wait till I does sumfin bad--she jes beats me caze she likes to be a beatin' somebody all de time."

As Evelyn looked so jolly and amiable I thought her mother too severe in her treatment of her; before long, however, Evelyn did some astonishing things and I was compelled to revise my judgment, as will be related later.

CHAPTER VII

My husband builds railroads and tunnels in the mountains. The King of Crow Creek. Curious customs of the early Tennessee mountaineers. Why we bought two slaves and sold one.

Winchester, Tenn., as I remember it, was a pretty place; the views of the mountains were fine and I greatly enjoyed riding horse back up to some peak and looking out over the picturesque country. I enjoyed, too, riding over the mountain to where Minor was making his surveys and planning to have the railroad tracks laid. On one of these trips I went quite a distance, a several days journey in all, and stayed with Minor at the home of an old mountaineer who was called the "King of Crow Creek"--his farm of several thousand acres abutted a stream called Crow Creek, and the old mountaineer was the patriarch and ruler of all that valley, hence his title of King of Crow Creek. I fancy the life of the patriarchs of old was about as was the life of our host that summer in the Cumberland mountains. His home was Liberty Hall; if any traveller happened by at the noon hour he was asked to "Light and look at his saddle." This was the local idiom for "Get down, tie up your horse and have dinner with us"--Alight and look at your saddle: in riding about those mountains it was necessary to tighten the saddle girths. And equally was it necessary to loosen the girths to let the horse breathe more easily and get more rest, when you stopped for your dinner. It was all very simple when you understood what it meant, but the first time Minor and I were asked if we wouldn't "Light and look at our saddles" we did not even suspect that we were being invited to stop for dinner. However, the hospitable old King of Crow Creek quickly made his meaning plain to us, and we did "Light and look at our saddles" and kept looking at them for several days--at least we remained several days and greatly enjoyed every minute of our stay.

The King of Crow Creek had been married a number of times, and by each wife he had had a number of children. The result was, his home resembled an institution rather than a private home. There were never fewer than thirty or forty persons gathered around his table, and when travellers happened by, the number was even larger. The "King" was some sixty years old, but very sturdy and strong. Although lacking in bookish knowledge--he could sign his name to a check, that was all the writing he knew--he had a world of native sense and shrewdness and ruled his tribe as firmly as did the patriarchs of old. His word was law to all his sons and grandsons, and to all the women-folk of his family. Many of the children were born out of wedlock, but the King made no distinction between them and the others whose parents had remembered to comply with the marriage law of the land.

"Taint their fault" the old Mountaineer said to me one morning after breakfast, as we sat on the broad verandah running across the front of his house. "That thar gal," pointing to a little tot not yet five years old, "Is jes as much my boy Tom's gal as ef he'd 'membered to get married. Why then shouldn't I treat her same as 'tothers?"

Why indeed? I observed that all the family treated that little tot exactly as if she were legitimate, instead of illegitimate, and I uttered no argument to prove that they were doing wrong. In that long ago day, and in that mountain country, the law was often disregarded, in more ways than one. For instance, the women smoked big, black cigars, when they had any to smoke--which was not often. And when they had no cigars they smoked pipes, just the same as the men. Also they drank whiskey freely. The first morning of our stay at the "King's," while I was sitting on the verandah I saw one of the King's daughters walk up to a flour barrel that stood in a room next to the wide center hall, take off the lid and stoop down and get something out of the barrel. To my surprise, that something was not flour, but a bottle of whiskey. The girl explained that she had hidden the bottle in the flour to keep her brothers from finding it. They had been drinking too much, she said, and so it was advisable to hide the bottle.

"What are you going to do with it? " I asked.

She seemed surprised at the question.

"Why, I'm getting it out to take a drink," she answered. And forthwith proceeded to put the bottle to her mouth and pour a goodly portion of its contents down her throat.

Many years afterward, in 1878, when the yellow fever was raging in our then home city, Memphis, we fled from the fever and took refuge with this same King of Crow Creek. Tho' far on in his eighties he was still stalwart and strong and still the undisputed master of his domain; he still chewed tobacco and squirted the juice all around the chair in which he sat; the flour barrel was still used as a hiding place for the whiskey bottle; there were still little tots playing on the place whose fathers had neglected to wed--little tots who were great grand daughters and sons of the King; the mountain country was still wild and sparsely settled, in spite of the fact that the railroad which Minor had built had been running through the place for thirty years. And so during our refugee days there in the summer of 1878 it was hard for me to realize that thirty years had slipped by since Minor and I had first ridden into that valley of the Cumberland mountains. Everything looked so exactly the same, I would not have believed more than a few weeks had elapsed since our first visit had it not been for our three big boys, the two eldest nearly grown. When I looked at my three sons, almost men, and remembered that when first I rode up to the door of the King of Crow Creek I was a bride of only two months--why of course then it was easy to realize that many years had elapsed, even if everything did look just as it had looked in 1850.

I thoroughly enjoyed those horse back trips with Minor; I was interested in his work and took the greatest interest in seeing the railroad grow, in seeing it get longer and longer every day; in seeing the tunnels, at first barely more than little dents in the sides of the mountains, gradually grow and grow until they pierced through to the other side and the light shone through from the other valley, telling us the big work was nearly done. Yes, looking back at those months among the Cumberland mountains after the lapse of more than sixty years I can still say that the life of the bride of a civil engineer is not without its interests, even its excitements. I enjoyed it to the full--partly, I admit, because I was in love; I was a bride with a husband to be proud of, a youth of twenty four (Minor was two years younger than I) with more brains than many a man of twice his years, doing the job of a big man! No doubt that helped make my Winchester days seem so happy, and brought to my heart a feeling almost of sadness when at last the railroad was finished and we went to Memphis to live. But the sadness soon left me. Minor's salary had been raised to a pretty good figure long before we left Winchester and the first thing he did on coming to Memphis was to buy four acres on the eastern edge of the city. On this ground he erected a pretty little cottage which we called "Sunny Home."

Sunny Home had a large front lawn in which I planted flowers. In a garden in the rear of the house we planted all sorts of fruits and vegetables. We had a cow and Minor had for his special use a fine saddle horse named Charley which was given to him by the President of the Railroad Company as a token of the President's personal appreciation of the work he had done in building the road.

Minor hired a negro named Henry to take care of Charley and cultivate the garden. As much will be said of Henry before I finish these *Recollections* I will describe him to you. He was the slave of a very dissipated young man, a man who drank and gambled until both ill health and poverty overcame him. The little money he received from Minor for Henry's services was about all the money this broken down, dissipated young man had. Bad as was this young man, Henry was devoted to him; he declared his master was always good to him. "He is good to everybody," said Henry, "good to everybody except himself." Henry often went to see his young master and sometimes actually wept over his sufferings and his poverty.

One day on returning from a visit to his master Henry told Minor his young master wanted to see him. Minor called to see what was wanted and learned that the young man's desire was to sell Henry for $900.00.

"Henry wants to live with you," said the young man. "He likes you and he knows I won't live long. I need money badly and Henry is a good negro. He will be worth more than nine hundred dollars to you."

"Perhaps so," said Minor, "but I do not believe in slavery. Neither did my father believe in it. I promised him to do my little toward getting my countrymen to see the evil of owning slaves."

"Admit it to be an evil," returned the young man. "You can't end it by denying yourself Henry's services. If you don't buy him someone else will, and I can't bear to think of putting him in the power of a bad man, of a man who may mistreat him. Yet I must sell him. I am in absolute need of money."

This argument made an impression on Minor. It was only too true that his refusual to buy the boy might condemn him to suffer abuse and cruelty from the man who did buy him. Minor knew *he* was incapable of mistreating a slave.

"I'll think it over," he told that young man at last. "I'll talk it over with my wife."

And that night he did talk it over with me. The result of it all was, Minor consented to buy Henry and keep him for five years, then set him free. "Henry," he said to me, "is now seventeen years old. When he is twenty two I shall give him his freedom. But he is not to know of my intention for the present. It might cause trouble. He would boast of it to others, that would make them envious and their masters would think me a mischief maker."

I shall relate later how Minor did set Henry free but how he refused his freedom, or at any rate insisted on serving Minor, being his devoted body servant throughout all the four long years of the War. From the first Henry loved his new master. His face glowed with pleasure when told the papers had been signed and he bowed and scraped and said over and over again, "Thanky Sir! Thanky Sir! You'll find me a good boy, Marse Minor. You'll nebber have no troubble with me. But you'll let me go see my young master 'long as he lives, won't you?"

"Yes indeed, Henry," Minor told him. "He thinks a great deal of you and I shall want you to go to see him."

And thus it came to pass that in spite of our anti-slavery notions we had two slaves, Evelyn and Henry. Never were two negroes less alike in their mental and moral character, as well as in their physical make-up. Henry was yellow; Evelyn was coal black with a pile of kinky wool on her head. She was careful never to go out of the house without a calico sunbonnet on her head. One day when I asked her why she was so particular about that bonnet she answered:

"Laws a mussy, Miss Betty, you doan want my har (hair) to burn red, does yo'?"

"No," I said, although to me red would have seemed prettier than black, kinky wool. "No, Evelyn, but what makes you think the sun would burn your hair red?"

"Caze everybody ses so," she replied. "Please doan ask me ter take no chances, Miss Betty. I doan want my har ter burn red."

I laughed and let her take her calico bonnet. She was a useful girl. She milked the cow, did the cooking and cleaned up the house. If ever I attempted to do any work about the house, sweeping or dusting or the like, Evelyn would run up, take the broom or duster out of my hand and say: "Laws a mussy, Miss Betty, dat ain't no work fer a lady. Dats nigger's work. Gib dat broom ter me. "

Minor and I thought ourselves lucky to have two such good servants. But little by little Evelyn began to show traits that foreboded trouble. For instance, it was her duty to feed the cow, milk her and always keep fresh water in her tub; it was Henry's duty to feed Charley (the horse) and keep water in his trough. Every morning when Henry brought Charley around to the front, for Minor to ride him to town, Minor would ask if fresh water had been put in his trough, and usually Henry would answer, "Yes sir!" But now and then he would say, "Oh Marse Minor, I plum' forgot dat water!" And off he would run to remedy his omission.

Now, it was my habit to ask Evelyn if she had given the cow fresh water and never once did she fail to say, "Yes'm de tub's 'most full of cool water." At first I believed her, but once a few minutes after she had made that answer something called me out into the back yard, and then I saw that the cow's tub, instead of being "mos' fuli of cool water" was as dry as a bone! In spite of my arguments and entreaties Evelyn seemed incapable of telling the truth, then, too, she did the most cruel things--not from anger or spite, but sheer love of seeing animals suffering. When I remonstrated and asked why she tortured poor innocent little kittens or dogs or chickens, she laughed and showed her white teeth and said it did no harm, that chickens, "and sich like" had no feelings. Among our household pets was a beautiful Maltese cat which used to sit at my feet in the dining room waiting for her saucer of milk and bread. One morning Tabby came mewing to me as if she was unusually hungry.

"I know why dat cat's so monsus hungry," grinned Evelyn. "She's dun gone an' had six kittens. I'se seed 'em in deir place out in de coal shed."

I made no comment and thought no more about it until some days later when, happening to look out of my window, I saw some little kittens in the yard below trying to crawl along, dragging their hind legs and mewing as if in great pain. As I gazed on the piteous spectacle the mother cat approached, seized one of her babes by the scruff of its neck and ran off with it. At this moment Evelyn came into my room and noting that I was looking at the kittens, she exclaimed,

"Laws a mussy, Miss Betty, dem kitten's got deir backs broke. Dey can't walk a bit. "

"What happened to them?" I demanded. "It is strange that all of them should be hurt in the same way."

"Oh no, Miss Betty, it ain't strange at all," grinned Evelyn. "I dun throwed 'em out of de window, all at de same time. Dat's what broke deir backs."

"You threw them out of the window?" I cried, horrified at the girl's cruelty.

"Sho', Miss Betty. We ain't got no use for so many cats about de house. Dat's why I tried to kill 'em. "

I have seldom been tempted to strike a person, but certainly was tempted to strike that negro girl that day at Sunny Home. But restraining myself, I turned from her in anger and disgust and called to Henry to take the poor maimed kittens and put them out of their pain by drowning them at once. Henry gently picked up the poor little things and as he turned away to carry out my order he looked reproachfully at Evelyn. "You good fur nuthin' gal, You!" He said. "You sho' ought ter be 'shamed of yo'self!"

Not long afterward I was passing the kitchen door and heard Evelyn laughing loudly. Looking through the open door I saw the girl down on her knees, rocking herself backward and forward, convulsed with laughter.

"What is the matter?" I asked.

"Oh Miss Betty, doan you hear 'em? Jes listen to deir squealin'!"

"To what squealing?" I did hear a faint, far away sound as of an animal squealing. But I was at a loss to guess whence the noise came.

"Why, it's a rat, Miss Betty. I set de trap last night and dun ketched a great big rat. Doan yo' hear him squealin'? He's dar in de bake oven! "

"What! In the stove?" I cried.

"Sho', Miss Betty. I made up de fire and het de stove an' now dat rat he sho' is purty nigh dead. At fust he made an awful noise but he's mos' baked by now and I reckon can't squeal no mo'!"

I was aghast and well nigh sickened and rushed out of the room. Plainly Evelyn enjoyed the suffering she inflicted. She was not a fool; she knew she could have put the rat trap in a tub of water and thus caused death without pain but she preferred to torture the rat and see it suffer. No argument, no reproach, no command had the power to cause Evelyn to desist from such conduct. She would giggle and say "Laws, Miss Betty, dey's only rats!" and straightway go and do some other cruel thing.

I talked with Minor about this trait in the girl's nature and he exhorted me to continue my efforts to make her understand the enormity of her conduct; I did try--with what success I shall relate presently. But first I wish to tell you of a little present Minor made to me shortly after we began to live at Sunny Home. I have already told you, my dear grandchildren, that Minor had Charley to carry him to town, but I had no horse to carry me. One day I said:

"Minor, it is a long way to town, nearly two miles. It tires me to walk so far. I wonder if you will ever be able to buy me a buggy?"

Minor looked serious. "Perhaps some day," he answered. "But it will not be for a long time. I have not quite paid all on this home yet."

"How long do you think it will be?" I asked.

"Oh, I should say in not more than four years."

There the subject was dropped. And I thought no more about it. Then about a week later when Minor started to town in the morning he told Henry to accompany him, that he had some work for him to do. And that afternoon Henry returned to Sunny Home driving a large iron gray horse with a flowing tail and a pretty mane, drawing a nice carriage. I ran out to the gate to see what it all meant and Henry handed me this note from his Master:

Darling Lizzie: This Rockaway and horse are yours to use as you please. Henry is a good driver; The horse, who is named Selma, is very gentle.

MINOR.

Had Minor sent me a ton of gold he would not have pleased me more than he did by sending me Selma and that "Rockaway." Henry also was jubilant and begged me to get in the carriage and see how I liked it. Not much persuasion was needed. In a few minutes I had run back to the house, put my bonnet on, and was in that Rockaway on the way to Minor's office. I wanted to thank him and tell him what a darling he was. I wonder if there are such things now as a Rockaway? Perhaps not. Nowadays everybody seems crazy about automobiles or flying machines. My son has automobiles, two of them--a big touring car and a small car for just two people--a Roadster I think he calls it. I have been in both of them. They are very nice. I like them all right, but they don't compare with the Rockaway Minor gave me. That was exactly the thing I wanted. The rear seat held two people comfortably; the front seat also held two people and the one by the driver could be turned so as to face to the rear. For the next eight years that Rockaway played a part in my life, as you will see if you have the patience to go on reading these *Recollections*. When General Sherman drove me out of Memphis I went in that Rockaway, my children and my goods and chattels piled up around me--but that story comes later. I must now return to Evelyn.

Evelyn was always cheerful; she seemed happy and ever willing to serve me. I taught her to sew and she was very vain of the appearance she made in her new frocks. She would come into my room and stand before the mirror and admire herself and ask me if she wasn't the finest dressed nigger gal in Memphis? One day shortly after my Rockaway was given to me Evelyn stopped the sewing she was doing in my room, looked up and said:

"Miss Betty, ef you wuz ter go ter town an' bode in a bodin' house, stead ob libbin' here, which ob us niggers would you take, me or Henry? "

I carelessly replied that I would take Henry because he could drive my Rockaway.

"I kin drive jes as good as Henry," said Evelyn. "I kin harness Charley up jes as good as Henry, I kin do ebery thing Henry kin do, an' sides dat I kin sew, which Henry can't do. So why won't you take me, Miss Betty?"

"Oh very well, I'll take you then, when I leave here and go to boarding," I answered carelessly, hardly knowing what I said. I had not the slightest idea of going to any boarding house and really did not realize what the girl was saying. Very soon was this conversation to stand out in vivid colors.

Our bed room opened on a lattice screened porch and the door usually remained open. Late that night I was awakened from a sound sleep by a noise on that porch and to my amazement I saw a great blaze of fire just beyond our door. I awoke Minor and both of us rushed out with buckets and pitchers of

54

water and worked hard to put that blaze out. Had it had five minutes more lee way our efforts would have been in vain; the house would have burned to the ground. As it was, only the porch burned. When we at last had the blaze extinguished we went back to bed, but not to sleep, excitement killed sleep. And so we lay there trying to puzzle out how that blaze had started. As soon as day broke Minor went out and made a close inspection. On the ground, up against the wooden latticed porch lay pieces of kindling wood, half burned. The same suspicion came at once to both Minor and me, the suspicion that Evelyn had had a hand in this affair.

"You send for her," said Minor. "Say nothing of your suspicion but keep her busy here. I want to examine her room."

Evelyn was sent for and Minor left our room; in a quarter of an hour he returned looking very grave and told Evelyn to go to her work in the kitchen. Then turning to me Minor said:

"It is evident that, for some reason, Evelyn wanted to burn this house down."

"Why do you think so?" I asked.

"I found her trunk packed. Everything in the world she possesses is safely stowed away in her trunk. *She* was ready to escape the fire."

"Why on earth should she wish to do so fiendish a thing?" I asked.

"That is what we must try to find out," Minor replied and called to Evelyn to return to our room. "Evelyn," he began abruptly and sternly, "why did you do it? You piled the kindling up against the house. You set it afire. Come. Tell me why you did it."

"Laws a mussy Marse Minor," broke out the girl glibly, "I never wanted ter burn de poch down. God knows I nebber did."

"Don't lie!" commanded Minor sternly. "I have been to your room. I saw your trunk, all packed to take out when the fire got to you. None of your things would have been burned, but we would have lost everything. Why did you do it?"

After thinking a minute Evelyn answered with a grin: "Marse Minor, I'll tell you jes how it happened, ef you won't tell my Mammy. Mammy, she'd beat me plum ter death."

"Tell me the truth and I won't tell your Mammy. But mind, if you tell me a single lie I will turn you over to your Mammy and have her beat you until you can't stand."

"Well, Marse Minor, hit's jes dis way. Miss Betty, she dun tell me ef she wuz ter go ter town ter bode in a boden house she'd keep me 'caze I kin dribe de kerredge as well as sew. And Marse Minor, hit's powerful lonesum out here so far frum town. I lubs ter see de folks on de streets en I lubs ter walk 'long en see deir fine close en hab 'em see my close."

"And you were willing to burn me up, and burn Miss Betty up, just to get a chance to live in town and show off your fine clothes?" demanded Minor grimly.

"Laws a mussy Marse Minor, I warn't gwine ter let you an' Miss Betty burn up. I wuz a stayin' wake on purpose for ter wake you up. I wouldn't a burnt you an' Miss Betty not fer nuffin' in de worl, caze I jes lubs Miss Betty an' I lubs you too, Marse Minor!"

Believing that she was telling the truth, Minor ended the interview without further questions, and sent the girl back to the kitchen. Then he turned to me and said:

"She is a hopeless case. That girl has no more comprehension of the enormity of her act than has a Hottentot of his acts. As a rule negroes are tender hearted and kind, but Evelyn is a monstrosity. We must get rid of her. There is no knowing what she might do. She is capable of putting poison in our food. I will consult with your brother as to what is the best course to pursue."

Brother Tom's advice was to sell Evelyn to someone who would work her in a corn field. "Such negroes," he said, "have no business in a white man's family. Her place is in the cotton field, plowing, hoeing, doing rough, hard work. That is what is needed to keep her out of mischief."

Minor followed this advice and sold her to a cotton planter the very next day. When a man came for her and she was told to get her things together a fearful scene ensued.

"Don't let that man take me away," she screamed. "I doan want ter go wid him. I wants you ter keep me, Miss Betty."

I was so distressed I could not speak; I knew not what to do or say. Minor released my skirt from Evelyn's clutching fingers and said to her sternly:

"Your Miss Betty is afraid of you. You cannot live with her any longer. She fears you will do something dreadful. Behave yourself and this gentleman will be kind to you, but if you try to set his house on fire or do other bad things, he will punish you severely."

Evelyn again clutched my skirt. Her new master, a big powerful man, forcibly pulled her away and lifted her into his wagon and drove away. I never saw her again but I heard from her new master that she turned out to be a good field hand, strong and willing to work and seemingly jolly and contented. She married a big black man who beat her regularly once a week and made of her a docile, well behaved woman.

56

CHAPTER VIII

Brother Tom elected to Congress, 1861. My husband in the Confederate Army.
Battle of Shiloh. Soldiers camped out in my front yard. Stirring scenes.

About two months before the birth of my first child I was walking along a
street in Memphis when a little brown skinned negro girl of twelve or thirteen
standing at the gate of a little house said to me:

"Oh Lady! Please buy me! I aint got no Mammy nor Pappy nor home to live
in. I'd lub to live with a pretty lady like you. Please, Lady, buy me!"

This unusual request interested me; I stopped and took a good look at the girl,
then began to talk to her. She had a pleasing face, kindly eyes and a gentle
voice. Her skin was not black like Evelyn's; it was a pleasing brown and the
wool on her head was nice and soft.

"Where is your mother?" I asked.

"She's dead, Lady, an' I doan know what become of my Pappy. The lady
whar I belonged was monsus good ter me but she took sick an died so quick she
had no time ter gib me ter a nice lady like you. Dey sold me 'long wid de odder
niggers an' de man what bought me said he didn't have no use fer a little gal
like me an' he tole me ter say he'd sell me cheap ter anybody what wants a little
gal like me."

I was so pleased with this little girl that I wanted to take her home with me.
When I got home I told Minor about her and the upshot was that he paid
$560.00 for Louise (that was her name) and when our first child was born
Louise was as much delighted as if the baby had been her own. She tenderly
nursed it, rolled it over the lawn in its little carriage, rocked it to sleep--in short
she was a treasure. Her fate was cruelly tragic, as I shall relate presently.

During the years just before the outbreak of the War between the States, my
brother Tom became a well known man not only in his state of Tennessee, but
in the country at large, for he served in Congress a number of years and his
ability and eloquence won for him more than a local reputation. When he retired
from Congress he acquired a large law practice; his wife bore him two sons and
a daughter and altogether he was a happy man. My sister, Mrs. Lamb, also had
a happy family; her husband was an excellent man, prosperous in his business,
and their six children gave them great joy. Perhaps I should add that some of
these six were not born until long after the war, but three came before the War,
so that at the outbreak of that great cataclysm my sister Estelle with her husband
in the army and three little children on her hand certainly had all she could
attend to. My sister Amanda had married a wealthy man named Trezevant and
she too was prosperous and happy. When we looked back at the days when food

was scarce in our home, and no money to buy any, we felt that Fate had indeed been kind to us.

After the birth of our second son, Rivers Blythe Meriwether (we had named our first boy Avery), Minor thought it best to rent out Sunny Home and take our boys to a home with a large yard and shade trees to play under. Accordingly he purchased five acres of fine wooded land with big forest trees, in the outskirts of Memphis, and there erected a comfortable home with stables and out houses, a garden and a big, beautiful lawn. The two little boys delighted to play on that lawn and under the big oak trees; Minor rode into town every morning on his big bay horse; Henry drove my Rockaway; Louise looked after the two children- -in a word, we were all as happy as birds. Then the unexpected happened. A world of trouble fell upon our beautiful Southland and for many years Life ceased to be the peaceful, uneventful thing it had hitherto meant for me--it came now to mean storm and stress, anxiety and trouble, hope and despair.

When news of South Carolina's secession reached Memphis everybody was stunned; Tennesseeans did not want to quit the Union. They grieved when they heard of South Carolina's action and, although they strongly opposed Lincoln and the Republican Party, they did not think it wise or necessary to secede. When the question was put to a vote Tennessee decided against Secession by a majority of 67,000. Minor was one of those who opposed Secession. When the movement to quit the Union was defeated by this decisive vote Minor was delighted and thought the trouble ended.

Then, as it seemed, out of a clear sky clouds gathered; Lincoln issued a call for 75,000 men to coerce South Carolina and instantly every man in Tennessee, those who had opposed Secession as well as those who had favored it, resolved to stand by South Carolina in resisting Lincoln's army of invasion. The proposition to secede was submitted again to the people and this time it carried by a larger vote than that which had previously defeated it. When not long after that Minor came to tell me and our two baby boys goodbye my heart sank within me. He was dressed in grey, a leather belt girded his waist, two pistols were stuck in the belt; he looked very brave and very handsome, but *he was going to war!* And the terrible fear came to me that I was never to see him again! I knew little of battles. I had a vague idea that when thousands of men stood off and shot at you with pistols and rifles and cannon there was little chance of your coming home alive, and so I entreated Minor not to go.

"If I listened to you," he said, "If I stayed at home like a woman you wouldn't love me. You couldn't love a coward. I must go. And you needn't worry. I shall come back. You have our two boys to comfort you. Be brave. Remember, I am going to fight for you and for the South that we both love so dearly. Lincoln's legions have already started to invade South Carolina. We must drive his mercenaries back North where they belong!"

And off he rode, accompanied by Henry, my carriage driver. I tried to smile and follow him with my eye as long as he was in sight, but tears blinded me and I went back into the house and gave way to sad forebodings. It was some comfort to me, however, to know that Henry was with my husband. Not only was Henry a good servant who would look after his master's comfort and health, but he was so gay and happy that I knew his presence would have a good effect on those around him. Minor had recently given Henry his freedom, but the faithful fellow refused to leave us; and I may as well say here as elsewhere that during the whole four years of War he stuck close to my husband, following him in good and in bad fortune with a loyalty that was beyond praise. There was no time during those years that Henry could not have deserted Minor; he could have gone over to the enemy's lines, or he could have returned to Memphis. And in either place he would have had a hundred times more comfort and ease than was possible for him in the Confederate army, pursued and harried as it was most of the time after the first year of the War. But the idea of seeking his own ease never seemed to occur to Henry; he declared that he loved "Marse" Minor and meant to serve him as long as he lived.

For a while I had no news of my husband and his faithful servitor; then we heard that they had been in a terrible battle. Anxiously I awaited further news-- had Minor been wounded, perhaps killed in that battle? Then came word that he was safe, not even a scratch, and I breathed easily again. I was destined to go through this suspense of waiting news of the outcome of a battle many and many a time during the next four years; and it was always a frightful suspense. But never was it quite so frightful as it was that first time a month or so after he left me in Memphis. Afterwards I came in a degree to believe that Minor was not destined to die in battle--and though he was in the army the whole four years and fought in many pitched battles, not once was he wounded, this Fatalistic belief in his destiny helped me wonderfully. But it took me sometime to school myself in that belief and so it was that in the outset the sudden change in my fortunes, the change from a happy wife with her husband by her side to love and protect her, to a wife and her husband off at War, often surrounded by enemies, fleeing before them, two babies to look after--such a change and such a contrast did indeed at first quite unnerve me.

After the battle of Shiloh Minor was made a Major and granted a furlough and never did I know happier days than those he spent at our home with me and his two boys on this, his first visit after joining the Army. Avery and Rivers never tired talking about their "Big sweet Soger Papa" and when he came home on that first furlough they sat on his knees and made him tell about his fights with the Yankees. On the first day of the battle of Shiloh the Confederates had the best of it; they would have won a decisive victory had not Gen. Grant received heavy reenforcements and thus become able on the second day to withstand the assaults of the Southerners. But on that first day it was a Southern victory and the Confederates in the ardour of pursuit penetrated far beyond Gen. Grant's lines. Henry told of the things he had picked up in the suddenly vacated Yankee tents.

"Laws, Miss Betty," he grinned, "The way we gobbled up dem Yankees' things would hab done yo' heart good ter see. Dey sho' does hab lots ob good tings ter eat--twice as much as our soldiers hab! But Laws, Miss Betty, dey can't fight like we'uns do. You ought ter see 'em run!"

It was curious to note the negro's attitude toward the Northern soldiers; they maintained that attitude to the end, long after the Federal armies were heralded as Emancipators of the blacks. Though they pretended to be fighting to free the negroes the best negroes, such as our Henry, to the end loved their Southern masters and had only scorn and contempt for "dem po' white trash Yankees!"

Henry captured a sword and pistol at Shiloh; the pistol he proudly kept stuck in his belt; the sword he gave to Avery, our first born boy. When Minor and Henry returned to the Army after this first furlough it was many a long month before we saw them again; and after the Yankees captured Memphis even Minor's letters stopped coming to me. It was thus a sad day for me when the Union gun boats rounded the bend in the Mississippi and the soldiers in blue marched through our streets and hung up their flag over the City Hall. All Memphis seemed sorrowful and mourning. I drove into town and saw the streets thronged with women and children; all seemed as if at a funeral--it *was* the funeral of our hopes; we felt as if chains were encircling us. While the soldiers were marching past us little Rivers suddenly stood up in the Rockaway and, pointing a broom handle which he carried in his hands at the marching troops, shouted:

"Watch me shoot the Yankee! ! Bang! Bang!"

I trembled with fear lest this would be resented and jerked the youngster to his seat, but the soldiers only laughed and cried back "Bully for the little Reb!" I thought if all the Yankees were like these men that we would not much mind going back into the Union.

When General Grant occupied Memphis (he came after the Gun Boat soldiers took possession), he brought with him an army of, we were told, some eighty thousand men. A line of pickets was thrown all around the city; it was directly in front of our fence (we lived beyond the city limits), and near our gate was what was called a "picket post" composed of fifteen or twenty men who stayed there night and day. They cooked their rations there and made free use of our garden as long as it contained any vegetables for them to take. Knowing their power, and fearing to anger them, I made no remonstrance; so long as they did not steal my little boys I was content.

Louise, the young negro girl mentioned in a previous chapter, was now eighteen and married to a good, steady man named Hense; she and her husband lived on our place and worked for me, as did also an old negro named Lewis. Uncle Lewis belonged to my sister's husband, Mr. Lamb; he was off in the

Army and my sister had gone to Clarksville, so Uncle Lewis came to me and said:

"Miss Betty, my white folks done run off an' left dis old nigger all alone an' if you doan disagree I'll come lib wid you."

I did not "disagree" and so, although I had no earthly use for him, he was so good hearted and amiable I let him live on the place and he came in time to be very useful. Uncle Lewis drove me about in the Rockaway and one day he took my two boys out for a ride. When he returned his eyes were gleaming.

"Miss Betty," he said, "I'se been insulted. You knows I'se a preacher as well as yo' driber. Dem dirty Yankees knows as I'se a preacher ob de Gospel, but you tink dey has any respect for dat? No, Miss Betty, dey aint got no respect for de Lord nor any de Lord's servants."

"What did they do to you, Uncle Lewis?" I asked.

"Dey made me stand up in de kerridge an' den dey purty nigh stripped me ob all my close--dey run deir han's in my pockets and kept a feelin' under my shirt as ef dey thought I was a thief. I doan want to dribe by dem Yankee lines no mo', Miss Betty."

After that we were cautious how we drove near the Northern soldiers. Hense also hated the Yankee soldiers, but his feeling grew out of the way some of them treated his wife. Louise, as I have said, was a comely negress, bright and shapely, and not black like Evelyn--her color was a light brown. The soldiers liked her looks and had a habit of hanging around her kitchen. One day Hense came to me and begged me to try and make Louise behave.

"'Stead ob slappin' deir fool faces," said Hense, "Louise jes laughs when dey kisses and hugs her. It makes me bilin' mad, Miss Betty."

I told Hense I would see what I could do. I was afraid to speak to the soldiers, but I called Louise to my room and told her she must not let any soldier hang around the kitchen. "I don't want them here on my own account," I said. "And you oughtn't to want them on your account, Louise. Hense makes you a good husband, but you can't keep him if you let those white men play with you."

Louise promised to behave, but she was fond of admiration and let the soldiers stay around her as before; then one day Hense came to me holding his head as if he feared it would tumble off his shoulders

"Oh Lordy, Lordy!" he groaned, looking at me despairingly. "See what dat girl's gone an' dun, Miss Betty. See dem two holes in my face!"

I looked and saw two small holes in his right cheek. From each hole blood was oozing.

"How did you get hurt? " I asked.

"I tole Louise I wasn't gwine stan' her conduc' no longer an' she up and sassed me and said, 'How you gwine hep it, Mr. Hense? You aint my Master. No nigger's gwine master me.' When she gib me dat sass I ups wid my han' an' fetch her a good slap on her face. An' what you spose dat gal dun den, Miss Betty? Why, she grab de carbin knife and struck me on de jaw, struck me twice an' made dese holes here."

I stopped the holes with cotton and camphor and gave him some cordial and kept him quiet until he recovered his composure. When finally he went away he said dolefully that he never expected to see Louise again, that she had packed her trunk and he believed she meant to run off with one of "dem nasty, Iyin' Yankee solgers." Poor Hense's prophecy was only too literally fulfilled. Neither of us ever saw Louise again. When we went to her room both she and her trunk were gone and from that day Hense began to pine; he lost his appetite and seemed listless and without any more interest in life.

Some people make the mistake of thinking an humble negro is incapable of deep feeling; this is not true. At any rate, I know few white men could feel more deeply the loss of a white wife than Hense felt the loss of his comely brown-skinned Louise. He could read fairly well and after his wife disappeared he would sit out in the sun all day long pouring over the Book of Revelations; its mysteries still further confused his mind; he began to think the world was coming to an end and that Judgment day was close at hand. Uncle Lewis prayed and sang several times a day with Hense, exhorting him to be a good Christian and forgive his wife for running away from him. It was not long after this that the newspapers of Memphis published an account of the death of Hense's wife. It seemed she was living in a room with a white man; one night piercing screams came forth from that room and the next moment Louise rushed from the room and fell to the ground, her throat cut from ear to ear! Her murderer escaped and his name was never learned. All this so upset poor Hense, I feared he was going to lose his mind and was glad when one of his cousins took him to the country to live with him there in his log cabin.

One day a soldier from the Picket Post by our front gate came to our door and said to me:

"Your little boy has been playing out by the gate; I heard him say you have a Yankee sword and that you had hidden it on top of your book case. Now, I don't care a rap how many swords you have on your book case, but a lot of our fellows might feel differently about it. If they heard of it they might make trouble for you."

"What must I do?" I asked.

"I will take it away for you, if you wish."

I pointed to the book case and told him to take the sword which Henry had brought back from Shiloh; he did so, and no doubt this soldier's kindness saved me great trouble. I knew of instances where women were thrown in prison for having a weapon in their homes.

A few days after this sword incident I saw two soldiers leading our cow out of the back lot and it worried me greatly. Milk was the chief article of food of my two little boys. What could I give them in place of milk? This question bothered me all day. Then towards night, when the children began to clamor for their supper, a bold plan occurred to me. I took my two little boys by the hand,

Avery the elder, carrying a tin bucket in his hand, and we three marched down to the Picket Post by the gate. Around a smouldering fire were a dozen or so soldiers.

"Good evening, soldiers," I said politely. "I have come to ask you to be kind enough to give me some milk for my children's supper. Our cow is a fine milker; she gives nearly a gallon at a milking, night and morning. A quart will do for my little ones."

For a moment there was a dead silence; the men stared at me but spoke no word. I began to fear my boys would go to bed supperless. Then one of the soldiers broke into a good natured laugh.

"Of course the little Rebs shall have some milk for their supper," he said. "What do you say, Boys?"

"Sure, let 'em have some," cried a chorus of voices.

"Gimme your bucket, Sonny," said the first speaker; little Avery stared at the big bearded soldier as he handed him the tin bucket. The soldier patted the child on the head. "I've got a little shaver at home," he said, "a boy just about this one's age. I guess his mother would feel bad if he couldn't get any milk for his supper. Just wait here, Marm. I'll be back in a minute."

We waited by the gate and very soon the soldier came back with the tin bucket full of milk.

"Thank you so much," I said gratefully. "May I have some every day? "

"Sure you may. Bring your bucket every morning and evening. I'll fill it for you."

From that time on the big bearded soldier kept us supplied with milk; true, it was the milk of my own cow, nevertheless I felt very grateful. Had those soldiers not been kind hearted they could have kept all the milk for themselves and my two little boys would have had nothing but dry bread for their suppers.

CHAPTER IX

Mrs. Hickey pursues me with a carving knife. The Soldiers' Saloon. My interview with General Grant. He gives me protection from the Hickey woman. How General Grant looked and behaved when he was Military Commander of Memphis.

In order to escape seeing so much of the soldiers, who were fond of visiting my kitchen out in the yard (as I told you before, the kitchen was always in a house to itself, fifty or a hundred feet distant from the living house), Uncle Lewis closed up the Kitchen house and we did our little cooking in the back room of our dwelling. Across the road from our home lived a rich man and his wife, a Mr. and Mrs. Hanover. They had only recently bought the place, some twenty seven acres, with a beautiful lawn and a grove of fine forest trees and a lake on which swam a lot of geese and ducks. Mr. Hanover was from Missouri where, it was said, he had made a fortune selling supplies to the Union Army. He and his wife seemed friendly to me and when they learned that my two servitors, Hense and Louise, were gone and no one but old Uncle Lewis on the place to help me, Mr. Hanover came to see me and ask what he could do to help me.

"How would you like to have a well behaved white man and his wife come and live in your yard?" he asked. "They might be some protection for you. It is not a good idea for a young and good looking woman to live alone on this place, with a lot of soldiers camped out at the front gate."

"I am well aware of that," I answered. "But what can I do? I am thankful I have even old Uncle Lewis to stay near me. I do not know where I could find a white couple to come to me. If I knew of one, I would be glad to let them stay in the kitchen house."

"Well, I have the very couple for you," replied Mr. Hanover. "I have no room in my house for Hickey and his wife and you have a room in your yard that is going to waste. I'll let Hickey come here. The arrangement will help us both."

"Who is Hickey?"

Mr. Hanover explained that Hickey was his gardener and a very trustworthy man. The next day Hickey and Mrs. Hickey and their small son came across the road to our place and took possession of the Kitchen house out in the yard. As soon as I laid eyes on Mrs. Hickey I felt that if I had seen her first, before agreeing to Mr. Hanover's plan, never would have I let her step her foot on my place. She was a large, raw-boned woman with fierce black eye brows, a dark skin, sharp nose, red at the end, and projecting, somewhat decayed teeth over which the lips never quite closed. Her whole aspect gave me the feeling that she was ill tempered and mean. Her boy was hardly more prepossessing than the mother; his hair was red and frowsy, his eyes lowering and sullen, his brows frowning. I resolved to keep my distance from them and give no pretext for trouble.

Two weeks went by and the Hickey woman kept so quiet that I began to reproach myself for the harsh judgment I had formed of her. In the outset Hickey went every day to work for the Hanovers, but after ten days he stopped going to the place across the road and loafed about in my yard under the trees, smoking his pipe and chatting with anyone who cared to join him. Then one day as I sat on my porch I saw Hickey come running out of the yard room, his wife close behind him; she was pursuing him and though he dodged about behind and between the trees she finally caught him and began to beat him with her fist as hard as she could. "Stop! Let me alone! I won't stand this!" yelled the little man, but Mrs. Hickey paid not the slightest heed to his cries. She continued beating him until exhaustion stopped her, then the little man meekly crept back into the yard room where he and his wife were staying. Ten or a dozen soldiers witnessed the performance and they laughed immoderately at the spectacle of a woman beating her husband.

A few days after the episode just described the Hickey woman asked Uncle Lewis to lend her my little wagon, saying she wanted to go into town and fetch out some groceries. Uncle Lewis had come to fear the woman and did not dare refuse her request, or even to tell me of it. The first I knew of it was when I saw her driving up that afternoon. And then we discovered that she had gone to town to get, not groceries, but a barrel of whiskey. One of the soldiers helped her roll the barrel into the yard house and that evening over the door of the yard house appeared a sign bearing these words:

"THE SOLDIER'S SALOON"

This was frightful, but I still feared to protest--the woman's temper was so violent and I was so unprotected, so entirely surrounded by enemies. All next day a stream of soldiers was flowing in and out of the Yard House and their conduct and language grew more and more boisterous. In the midst of it all the Hickey woman came to me, a newspaper in her hand and pointed to an article on the first page she said with a coarse laugh:

Hey you seen this, my foine leddy?"

The item she indicated was an order issued by Gen. Grant decreeing banishment for any person found corresponding with the enemy.

"But, Mrs. Hickey, this place belongs to me. You must leave once if you will not obey my orders."

"Obey your orders?" she screamed. Her face became hideous with fury. "I'll show you how I'll obey your orders. I'm here helpin' the soldiers, giving 'em a drink when they are cold and thirsty. Your husband is a rebel, doing all he can to shoot loyal soldiers. I'm goin' to stay right here, and the 'Soldier's Saloon' is going to stay, too."

"You are not going to stay, Mrs. Hickey. You must leave at once". "It's *you* who are going to leave at once," she yelled, and running into her room, she returned in a moment with a carving fork in her hand. "Now git!" she commanded. "Git quick before I jab this in your heart!"

With each "Git" she brandished the fork and came closer to me; I dared not turn and run; I feared the Virago might stab me in the back. So I retreated backward, keeping my eye fixed on her all the time as she kept advancing toward me. Old Uncle Lewis saw my predicament; he grabbed my two little boys and ran for the gate. When I reached the gate I seized my children by the hand and fled with them across the road. The Hickey woman made no attempt to pursue me beyond the gate; she stopped there and seemed well pleased with the situation as well she might be. For she was in complete possession of the yard and house and also the Kitchen room occupied by her and her husband.

"Keep offen' this place in the future," she cried to me as she leaned on the gate looking across at us on the other side of the road. "This place is no good for rebels."

I went at once to see Mr. Hanover and told him what had happened. He said he had wondered why Hickey had quit coming to work; he said he had not known that Hickey was a drinking man and suggested that I spend the night at his house and that next morning, before Hickey had time to get drunk, he would go over with me and see what could be done. I accepted this plan and next morning went with Mr. Hanover to my place to see what we could do. As we passed the door of the "Soldier's Saloon" we saw the red head Hickey boy already at work serving drinks to soldiers. Hickey, a pipe in his mouth, was reposing under a tree; the Hickey woman was sitting on my porch rocking herself in my favorite chair. Mr. Hanover called to Hickey to come to us; he came promptly and Mr. Hanover told him he was surprised at his wife's disgraceful behavior.

"If you can't make her behave herself, Hickey," concluded . Mr. Hanover, "why, then you both will have to leave."

At these words the Hickey woman bounced down the steps, rolling up her sleeves as she came, and glared at Mr. Hanover as she said:

"Me lave this place? The loikes of me lave on account of a Johnny Reb's wife? I'll have you know, Mr Hanover, I'm a perfect loidy and trooly loyal, and it's not for a loidy like me to be run out of my home by a rebel."

Mr. Hanover was a large man; no doubt he could have whipped the woman had he tried. But he did not want to get into a row with a woman. His face turned red but he controlled himself. Turning to Hickey he said: "Hickey, as it was I who induced Mrs. Meriwether to let you come on her place it is my duty to see that you either behave or leave. Since your wife will not behave, will you take her away at once?"

Before the man could speak his wife elbowed herself in between him and Mr. Hanover.

"Keep your mouth shut, Hickey,' she said to her husband as she pushed to the front. Then turning to Mr Hanover she screamed: "I'm running this place and I ain't goin' to let any man drive me away. This foine loidy here's been writing to rebels and that's against orders. Gen. Grant will never send me away to make place for a female spy. I'm going to see Gen. Grant tomorrow."

Perceiving nothing was to be gained by further parley, Mr. Hanover and I withdrew to talk the situation over. I said I would appeal to the military authorities but Mr. Hanover said anything would be better than that. My husband being a Confederate officer Gen. Grant would be prejudiced against me; I had nothing to hope in that direction. I was about to yield to this argument when one of the Picket Post soldiers came to us where we were talking the matter over, not far from my front gate, and said:

"Why don't you go see Gen. Grant? That woman is getting a wagon ready now to drive into town. She will see Gen. Grant and the Lord knows what lies she will tell on you. Better beat her to it."

"Do you think Gen. Grant will listen to this lady when he knows her husband is a Confederate officer?" asked Mr. Hanover.

"Of course he will listen to her." replied the soldier. Gen. Grant is a gentleman and he knows a lady when he sees one. Several of us saw Mrs. Hickey drive this lady off with a carving fork. If you wish you can tell Gen. Grant that the soldiers here will back up your story."

In view of this soldier's words Mr. Hanover said he thought it would be best after all for me to go to Gen. Grant, accordingly Uncle Lewis got out my Rockaway and off we started for town accompanied by the friendly Union soldier. Gen Grant's headquarters were on Beale Street in the home of a friend of ours, a Mr. Hunt. Two soldiers with guns on their shoulders stood at the front gate, but they readily permitted us to drive in. At the front door of the Mansion stood two more soldiers, also with guns on their shoulders. Uncle Lewis drove the carriage to a place designated by the soldiers and waited for us there; in the meantime Mr. Hanover and the friendly soldier and I were ushered into a room which in happier days I had known as Mrs. Hunt's parlor. It was now the waiting room; a little man in an office coat met us at the door of this room and bade us be seated. We all took seats and sat as still as mice. Presently the silence was disturbed by the entrance of two boys of about ten and twelve years of age, these boys gave us a curious look, then walked on into the General's room. The little man in the rusty office coat observed the surprise we felt at the way those boys intruded on the great Union General without even knocking on his door.

"Fine boys, eh?" he whispered. "They are the General's boys. Uncommonly fine boys. No such boys in this part of the country, eh?"

"I have never seen any like them," I replied. I thought my own two boys a million times finer and better boys than those two sons of Gen. Grant, but that was not the time or place to argue the question.

In due time our turn to see the General came and we were ushered into his presence. He was seated at a table, a cigar in his mouth but no smoke coming from it; it was not lighted. I took a seat at the far end of the room, as at the moment I entered he was engaged in conversation with a lady whose skirt of flowered muslin was ruffled up to her waist and was so bellied out by its enormous hoop skirts that it over-flowed from her own seat and quite covered the legs of the Union General. The friendly Union soldier sat beside me and we both could overhear the talk between Gen. Grant and the lady in the flowered muslin dress

"And, General," she was saying as we entered, "We were all so awful glad when you and your army came to Memphis. We were almost starved before you came, you couldn't get flour or bacon or anything else good to eat. Don't believe what some folks tell you about the people being sorry you came. The real best people of the city wanted you to come."

Gen. Grant took the cigar out of his mouth and seemed about to speak; then, apparently thinking better of it, he replaced the cigar between his lips and continued to present to the lady a silent, impassive face. Whereupon the beruffled lady arose to go.

"Good bye, General," she said, "I am so sorry not to see Mrs. Grant this morning; her dear little boys are quite the finest little fellows I ever saw, though perhaps I hadn't ought to say it to their own father. Good bye, General!" And out she bounced, leaving Gen. Grant, as I thought, distinctly relieved by her going.

"Hadn't ought!" That told the tale. She was no Southern woman. No matter how illiterate a Southerner may be "Hadn't ought to" is not one of the mistakes he ever makes, whereas sometimes even educated Northerners make this mistake.

As the beruffled "Hadn't ought to" lady walked out of the room I arose, thinking I was next. And then to my surprise the two Hickeys came in.

"I will hear these people first," said General Grant quietly. Whether he knew the Hickeys and my business were the same I did not then know, and I have never been able to guess since. I only know that I subsided into my chair again while Gen. Grant sat at his table, the cigar still between his lips, his face still passive and inscrutible; and Mrs. Hickey poured forth such a stream of lies as I had never heard before. She began by saying to Gen. Grant as she indicated her husband:

"This is my man. He's a true Union man, General, he ain't no rebel. He rented a place from a rebel loidy who's trying now to drive us away because my man here won't go jine the rebels and fight agin' his country. So my man and me, we have come to get an order to make that rebel loidy leave us in peace in the house we rented. She's a Secesh woman and writes everyday to her man in the rebel army."

The Hickey woman rattled this, and much more of the same sort, rapidly as if she had learned a speech by heart. Gen. Grant's impassive face gave not the slightest sign of what, if any impression her story was making. Mrs. Hickey seemed to feel that he was indifferent; to arouse his interest she pulled out a dirty handkerchief and rubbed it in her eyes and blew her nose and declared in a whine that she didn't know what in the world she would do if she were made to leave the house "she had rented."

Whether this show of emotion moved Gen. Grant or not I do not know; I only know that as Mrs. Hickey dug her dirty handkerchief into her eyes Gen. Grant slowly took the cigar from between his lips and uttered a brief sentence.

"Stay in the house," he said. Then replacing the cigar in his mouth, he relapsed again into impassive silence.

Mrs. Hickey mumbled her thanks and got up to go. As she passed out she shot me a triumphant glance. My heart sank within me but I had no time to say a word to her even had I wished to do so. Gen. Grant was looking at me and by a nod of his head indicated that I was "next." Obeying his look, I approached and stood before him and stated my case as briefly as possible, and as I finished I beckoned to the friendly Union soldier and added: "General, this young man is one of your soldiers. He was on my lawn when the Hickey woman drove me away with a carving fork. It is true that my husband is a confederate officer but-"

"That does not matter," interrupted Gen. Grant. "What is your name?" I gave it and stood almost breathless, not knowing what to expect. Gen. Grant wrote a few words on a piece of paper, then looking up added: "Take that to the Provost Marshal."

I did not look at the paper; I did not know what Gen. Grant had written on it, whether he had decided for or against me. But I thanked him and withdrew from his presence. Once safe in my Rockaway I pulled the paper out of my pocket and read it and showed it to Mr. Hanover. It was very brief, but very much to the point:

"To the Provost Marshal:
See that Mrs. Minor Meriwether is protected in her home.

U. S. GRANT"

That was all; but it was enough. We drove at once to the office the Provost Marshal, in the residence of a friend of mine, Mr. Mat Galloway, on Madison Street. Mr. Galloway was on Gen. Forest's staff and Mrs. Galloway had been banished from Memphis as a punishment for the fiery "Secession" editorials which her husband had written as Editor of the Memphis *Avalanche*. The

Provost Marshal made his headquarters in Col. Galloway's home. I handed him Gen. Grant's note; the Provost Marshal read it, then asked what I wished him to do I explained what the Hickey woman had done and what a dangerous woman she was. The Provost Marshal laughed.

"Dangerous to you, perhaps. But not to me. I'll send a man with you who was once a Chicago policeman. He knows how to manage big Irish women."

Calling an orderly he directed him to get Big Bill Clanahan and order him to go with me. A few minutes later I was on my way home again, accompanied by one of the biggest soldiers I ever saw, a tall stalwart fellow with a hand that was literally as big as a small ham. When I looked at Mr. Clanahan's hands I knew that all he needed to reduce Mrs. Hickey to subjection was to lay those hands upon her arm and tell her to go! As we drove into my yard and by the "Soldier's Saloon" the red headed Hickey boy was, as usual, on his job, serving drinks to soldiers; Mrs. Hickey was on the front porch in my rocking chair. She gave me a defiant grin, evidently thinking she was fixed my home for life. Hickey as usual was sitting under a tree smoking his pipe.

"Where is the man?" asked Sergeant Clanahan. I pointed to Mr. Hickey. The big Sergeant called to Hickey; he lounged lazily toward us, he, too, evidently thinking they were firmly entrenched. When Hickey stood beside the Rockaway the big Sergeant took out his watch. "Your name is Hickey?" he demanded. Hickey nodded head. "Well," continued the Big Sergeant, "you have just one hour pack all your things and get off this place."

For a minute Hickey stood stock still, speaking not a word, seemingly stupefied by what he had heard. Then he started on a trot toward the house where his wife was sitting. When Mrs. Hickey heard what the Sergeant had ordered she leaped out of the rocking chair and came bounding toward us.

"Lave this place in an hour?" she screamed. "I'll have you know this is my place. I saw Gen. Grant this very day. He's give orders to make this Secesh loidy let me alone."

Big Sergeant Clanahan looked down on the Hickey woman, a smile curling his lips as he said:

"I don't know what Gen. Grant told you, but I do know what he ordered me to do. If your things are not ready in an hour, out you'll go without your things. Get busy!"

He was so big and so cool and the hands of his watch kept moving even while he spoke--the Hickey woman quailed and cowered before him. She knew her game was up; she, too, noted how enormous Sergeant Clanahan's hands were. She had no desire to have those hands laid in anger upon her and so she proceeded at once to get her belongings together.

It was thus that the "Soldier's Saloon" was abolished and that I was permitted to return to my home on Kerr Avenue in the outskirts of Memphis.

CHAPTER X

My brother a prisoner. General Sherman's soldiers' brutal behaviour. My life in danger. I flee to my laundress' cabin for protection. The Yankees confiscate my property. I appeal to General Sherman. His insulting manner. He banishes me from Memphis. A two years pilgrimage begins. In a "Rockaway" drawn by my faithful mule Adrienne.

Not long after my interview with Gen. Grant I heard that a steamboat full of prisoners from Johnson's Island in Lake Erie would land at Memphis the next morning; my brother Tom, as brave a Southern soldier as any of the hundreds of thousands who fought for the Confederacy, had been a prisoner of War for several months on Johnson's Island and, hoping that he might be among those on that boat, I drove to the city early and waited until the steamboat landed. As the boat approached I could see it was crowded with prisoners and to my delight my brother was among them. I was the first person to run across the gang plank; a crowd of other citizens, eager to see loved ones, followed me closely and soon we were all embracing and shaking hands and talking and crying and laughing--all at the same time. While Brother Tom was holding me close to his side and telling me how glad he was to see me, one of his friends snatched my younger boy Rivers from my arms saying:

"I must show this little fellow to our men!"

And off he started, pushing his way through the crowd, each man trying to get hold of the child and give him a kiss. I tried to follow them, I was uneasy lest my darling boy should become lost from me, but Brother Tom pulled me back.

"Don't be uneasy," he said. "Our boys won't hurt your baby. They'd cut off their arms first. It's so long since any of us have seen a child, we sorter want to make over him."

The boat had pushed off from the landing a few moments after I ran across the gang plank, so as to keep any more citizens from crowding on to see their prisoner friends; it kept steaming up and down the river in front of the city. When afternoon came and still the boat continued to steam up and down the river I became anxious to get off; my children were getting very tired and I knew it would take me a long time to drive way out to our home. I sought the Captain and begged him to let us land. He replied gruffly that he had not invited any Rebels to come aboard his boat, that since they had come without an invitation they would now have to wait his pleasure before going ashore. I said:

"Captain, you ought not to be too hard on Rebels. Remember that Washington was a rebel."

"We are speaking of rebels of this day, not of Washington's day," was his answer, and I deemed it wise to drop the subject.

It was quite dark before the Captain finally turned his boat inshore and although I was very tired I was glad to have had a whole day with my brother, and with our brave Southern soldiers. Those brave fellows were sent to some distant prison and it was long before I saw my brother again.

One day the friendly soldier who had helped me get rid of the Hickeys came to me and said that Gen. Grant was going to Vicksburg and that Gen. Sherman was coming to take charge of Memphis. "You'll find Gen. Sherman's soldiers a tough lot," was my friendly soldier's final statement. I asked why? He said it was because Sherman's army comprised so many foreign mercenaries, men who came from Europe to enlist in the Northern armies merely because of the money and loot to be had. I do not know that this is the correct explanation but it is a fact that many of Gen. Sherman's soldiers were downright barbarians; they seemed to delight in terrorizing women and children, as well as in fighting men. They sat on my porch and in my hearing would talk of what they meant to do as soon as they had the rebels well whipped. Each had his place picked; rebels would have to go to work; their homes and their property were to be enjoyed by their conquerors; all Union soldiers were to live like rich gentlemen and have their pick of Southern girls. As for the brats of rebels, why the sooner the breed was exterminated, the better; when they talked about exterminating the "brats of rebels" I looked at my two little boys and shuddered.

One night a bullet came whizzing through my door and lodged in the wall just above my bed, and after that we slept on the floor thinking that there we would be more apt to escape any bullets that came through the room. On one occasion when two of Sherman's soldiers were sitting on my porch talking of what they meant to do with the rebels' property and the rebels' wives, one of the men asked me what I thought of it all? For the moment I was off my guard and answered spiritedly that I supposed Yankees were liable to do anything, that I would not be at all surprised if they did steal private property and mistreat women if they found they had the power! One of the two soldiers was a German; he hardly spoke English, but he understood English and my answer angered him. He drew out his pistol and held it at my head.

"Dat is Secesh treason!" he growled.

The other soldier grabbed the pistol out of his hand.

"You fool!!" he exclaimed. "Put up your gun. We ain't fighting women."

The next day this soldier warned me not to anger a German soldier again. "They are the biggest damn fools in the world," he said. "And they don't mind shooting a woman any more than they mind killing a cat. Fellows like me are fighting to keep you people in the Union. We ain't got anything against you women, but them damn Germans are so rough, I'm ashamed of them."

This man's language was certainly more profane than it should have been, but he meant it in a friendly spirit and I thanked him for it. Indeed, I came to believe what he said was quite true. The German soldiers I saw were as a rule rough and brutal in their manner to women. "Bull Run" Russell, the London *Times* War correspondent, relates in his "Diary" that Seward told him thousands of savage Germans "come over here and join our army; and they plunder and destroy as if they were living in the days of Agricola!" I resolved to heed the advice of that friendly soldier and thereafter no matter what the provocation I spoke no word that could reasonably anger any Union soldier. But even so, my position soon became dangerous and unbearable.

One night as I sat on my porch two soldiers came and sat on the steps within ten feet of where I sat rocking my younger boy to sleep. For a while they talked between themselves, and such language! I hope never to hear such vulgarity and profanity again. But worse was to come. After a while one of the men struck a match and held it before my face.

"Damn me if she ain't pretty!" he exclaimed.

The other soldier followed his comrade's example; after he had struck a match right in front of my face, he too exclaimed that I was good looking.

"Well, Jim, I see where I'm going to roost here all night," said the first soldier. "What do you say?"

"Suits me down to the ground," replied the other.

For a moment I was dumb; luckily, in the dark they could not see how frightened I was or I could not have worked the ruse I did. Pulling myself together, resolving to do and dare anything for the sake of my two children, I was presently able to say in what at least appeared to be a calm voice:

"Of course you gentlemen want supper before you go to bed?"

"We sure do. Damned handsome of her to invite us, ain't it, Jim?"

Jim agreed that it was handsome. I said pleasantly:

"I know how hungry you soldiers get. I don't like to see men go to bed hungry. Would you like fried ham and eggs? I am afraid that is about all I have on hand."

"That's good enough for us, Ma'am. Fried ham and eggs and coffee."

"Oh, of course. I'll make some hot coffee."

And I arose and walked out to the kitchen, my two boys close by my side. Once in the kitchen I told Uncle Lewis how the men behaved and what they had said. He was scared nearly to death. "Don't you fear, Uncle Lewis," I said. "They won't hurt you. But I must run from here as fast as I can. I shall go out through the garden to the road back of us and walk to Aunt Sallie's cabin and sleep there tonight. In the morning you come to me and tell me what those men do."

Aunt Sally was my laundress; she was a good old soul and I knew I would be safe in her cabin. It took but a minute to run through the garden out onto the road; then we had to walk about a half a mile. Every few steps I would turn, fully expecting to see the sky reddened with flames from my burning home. I feared those men might be mad enough to burn the house when they found how they had been tricked, but no flames lighted my way and at last I and my two little ones safely reached Aunt Sallie's cabin where we spent the night. Early next morning Uncle Lewis drove the Rockaway over for me and we went into the city to find some place to lodge. Uncle Lewis said the men stayed all night in my house, both of them sleeping in my bed; and it seemed time for me to move into the city where I would be less exposed to such intrusion.

I owned property in Memphis; it was the rent of this property which had enabled me to keep my little family supplied with food. On going to town that morning I learned to my consternation that Gen. Sherman had confiscated my rents and that thenceforth my tenants would have to pay their rent to the Provost Marshal. Supposing that Gen. Sherman had done this on the mistaken supposition that the property was my husband's, I took my title deeds and drove to the General's headquarters on Rayburn Avenue in the Southern part of the city. There, under a large awning, I found Gen. Sherman sitting at a small table. Several officers were standing about him. I gave my deeds to Gen. Shaman and stated my case, and specially called his attention to the fact that the houses had been acquired by me long before the war and were mine quite independent of my husband. Hardly more than glancing at my title deeds, Gen. Sherman whirled around and looking me over coldly, demanded:

"Why did you let your husband go in the rebel army?"

I answered that I could not keep him out of it.

"Did you try?"

"Yes, I did."

"Still he went?"

"Yes, he went. He said only a coward would stay at home when his country called him."

"His country?" repeated the General with a sneer. "Why, he is fighting against, not for, his country. Why did you let him do it?"

This was too much; it was the third time he had demanded of me why I let my husband go to the Confederate army.

"General Sherman," I said as calmly as I was able to speak under the circumstances, "by all the laws you men have made, and by all the religions you men do teach, we women have been brought up to obey our husbands, not to rule them. I had no power to keep my husband out of the army."

"Well, you ought to have done it. I won't give you back your property as long as your husband is in the rebel army."

I made a last appeal; I told him that while my rents meant only a pitiful trifle to the great United States Government, to me and to my two little children they meant existence itself, that we had absolutely nothing else to live on. Gen. Sherman looked down at his shirt front thoughtfully for a moment, then he said:

"I would give you a set of shirts to make for me if I had not already given the order to a woman who says I have robbed her of everything she has. No, I don't need more shirts and I can do nothing for you. You oughtn't to have let your husband fight in the rebel army."

I felt this as an insult not only to me, but to the womanhood of the South, I saw that Sherman took pleasure in the pain he had power to inflict. Hastily pulling my veil over my face to hide the tears that came to my eyes, I hurried out of the monster's presence. This interview with Gen. Sherman took place late in the year 1862; I am writing these lines in 1916, fifty four years afterward, but not one word of that interview have I forgotten, not one detail of that picture has faded from my memory. Sherman has been dead many years and according to the old maxim, of the dead we should say nothing unless we say something good. Well, I can say nothing good of Gen. Sherman. Gen. Grant led armies over our fair Southland; but he did not insult women and children. My interview with Grant caused me to have an almost kindly feeling toward him. But never shall I feel kindly toward Sherman's memory, no, not though I live another ninety two years!

Fearing to return to my home after the conduct of those two soldiers of Sherman's, and having no money with which to rent a house in Memphis, I told Uncle Lewis to drive me to the home of a friend named Lanier, a wealthy Memphian who lived in a beautiful home in the heart of the city. Mrs. Lanier was an old friend of mine and she agreed to care for me and my two children until some plan could be arranged. I was anxious to go South, inside the Confederate lines, where I could see, or at least hear from my husband. Mr. William A. Blythe, a dear friend of both my husband and brother, advised me against this plan. Mr. Blythe argued that if I went south I would have no home, no permanent abiding place, that I would have to follow the Confederate Army in its various fortunes and even under the most favorable circumstances seldom would I be able to see my husband.

"What then am I to do?" I said. "I dare not go back to my home. Those Sherman soldiers are dangerous."

"I agree thoroughly as to that," answered Mr. Blythe. "It won't do at all for you to go back there. But Sherman will probably be leaving Memphis soon. The next Commander will be more humane. He will restore your houses to you, then your rents will enable you to live comfortably here in town. In the meantime you can stay here with the Laniers."

I agreed to follow Mr. Blythe's advice but, alas! We both were reckoning without considering Gen. Sherman's implacable nature. Shortly after I went to the Laniers, Gen. Sherman issued an order to the effect that he would banish ten rebel families from Memphis for every one of his Gun Boats fired on by the Confederates. Of course our brave soldiers did not stop firing on the enemy because of Gen. Sherman's cowardly threats against women and children. And I was among the first ten who were ordered out of the city. When the order came it was very peremptory; I was given one day to leave. Uncle Lewis was sick in bed. I begged to be allowed to wait until he was well enough to drive my Rockaway. The corporal who brought me the order of banishment laughed in my face.

"You don't suppose," he said, "that Gen. Sherman can change his orders on account of sick niggers? The order is to git out of town within twenty four hours. If you are found inside the Federal lines after tomorrow you will be thrown in prison.

"You mean the Irving Block?"

The corporal nodded. "Yes," he said, "the Irving Block. I see you have been there. Well, you know what sort of a place it is. You don't need my advice to git out of this town as quick as you can."

No. I did not need his advice; I knew the Irving Block well. It was an old office building on Second Street which Gen. Sherman had converted into a prison. It was crowded and dark and unsanitary.* I decided to make the best of it and start South at once. The Yankee corporal gave me a list of contraband goods which I was forbidden to take into the Confederate lines. Among these articles was quinine. I asked if I might not take a small quantity of quinine so as to be able to care for my children in case they had chills or fevers? The corporal roughly replied it was none of his business if rebel children got sick; orders were orders; if I took any quinine, however little, and it was discovered I would be thrown into prison. Gold, silver, powder and shot were also contraband; so also were flannels and gray goods that might be made into uniforms for Confederate soldiers.

*The Irving Block still stands in Memphis, opposite this building in 1862 was a small park called "Court Square." Big oak trees were in this park and squirrels played about the grounds--a pleasing sight for the poor Confederate prisoners to gaze upon, from their iron barred windows across the street. That little park with its trees and squirrels is still (1916) there and a few months ago some of the Daughters of the Confederacy erected in "Court Square" a bronze tablet bearing this inscription:

PRISON HISTORY OF MEMPHIS

The building opposite, known as the IRVING BLOCK, was used as a prison by the Federal Government from 1862 to 1865. Much needless suffering was imposed upon the prisoners--so much, that President Lincoln ordered an investigation of the conditions there. Both Confederate soldiers and citizens of high rank were within its walls. At the close of the war, April 1865, about twelve hundred soldiers and one hundred citizens, both men and women, were incarcerated there.

There's no stigma on it
This our Confederate story--
Never a prouder Nation lived
In whom her sons could glory.

Erected by Confederate Dames in 1915.

76

I had heard that on one of the roads going South a very amiable negro woman was stationed to examine ladies who passed the lines, and that this negress was often made more amiable by the present of a five dollar bill. I had a small pistol and was anxious to take it with me for protection, so I prepared myself with a five dollar bill intending to try its power on that amiable negress. My plan was to smuggle that pistol, also several other small contraband articles through the lines and stop the first night at a farm house some fourteen miles out of Memphis. Our friend Mr. Blythe was not in the city the day I had to leave; I therefore wrote to him, telling him what had happened, and inclosed in my letter the key to my husband's bank box in the Union & Planter's Bank of which Mr. Fred Smith was cashier. In that box were $1,300.00 in gold and I asked Mr. Blythe to pay the taxes on all my property. Before starting for the Army Minor told me, no matter what happened, to pay my taxes; if all taxes were paid I would have a good chance to get my property back. But if my property was sold for taxes, then I might never get it back again. It was because of these admonitions of my dear husband that I was careful to send Mr. Blythe that key to my box containing the $1,300.00 in gold. I also requested him to look after poor Uncle Lewis until he got well.

And now, my dear Grand children, I must introduce you to a member of my family who from this time on until the close of the war was destined to be my constant companion. I refer to Adrienne, our mule! Adrienne was no ordinary mule. She had lots of horse sense and was as gentle as a kitten. When allowed to graze on the lawn my children played about under her feet and pulled her tail; Adrienne was always careful to lift her feet slowly and gently so as not to hurt the children. I had a horse for my Rockaway but when I found that Uncle Lewis was too sick to accompany me and that I had to drive I left the horse in Memphis and chose Adrienne to take me on my pilgrimage through Dixie Land. Never shall I forget that pilgrimage. Every day and every incident of it is as fresh in my memory now as when it happened more than half a century ago. I can see before me now that broad, jolly negress at the picket lines who searched me, can see the expression on her face and hear the words she spoke when she found that small pistol where I had thrust it in the bosom of my corsage.

"I'se monsus sorry, Lady," she said softly, "monsus sorry indeed to hab to bother a lady 'bout dis little ting, but I'se ordered to confi'scate all sich tings."

Then I made the little speech I had all ready turned over in my mind, at the same time slipping in her hand the five dollar bill. I said I was alone with two small babies, no man to protect me and the roads full of rough people, stragglers from both armies. Little as this pistol was it might scare off bad men if any troubled me. I concluded by saying:

"Surely the great United States Government has no use for a little thing like this!"

"Laws, Honey," whispered the amiable negress laying my pistol on the table and slipping the five dollar bill into her pocket, "Laws, Honey, I ain't gwine ter be hard on no lady dats trabblin' all alone, deed I ain't! I knows dese times ain't fittin; to trabble widout some kinder protection."

"Then I may keep it?"

"Sho', Honey, only be quick about it--put it back whar you had it, den no one's gwine see it."

The few other trifles I so much wished to take with me were also amiably overlooked by the amiable negress who searched me and I regarded my experience with her as a good omen. As I was about to tell Adrienne to move on, after my search, two rough looking men on horseback rode up by my side and began to question me. Which way was I going? Why was I leaving Memphis? Whom did I expect to see in the South? I replied as briefly and evasively as I could. I did not like these men's looks and when they began to rail at Yankees and abuse them for their villainies I became suspicious and left them as quickly as I could.

I was not accustomed to driving; the roads were very bad, not having been worked since the beginning of the War, and I feared every minute a wheel would slide into a gully or get knocked off on a rock or a root and then that we would all be overturned and perhaps killed. I depended far more on Adrienne to take us on safely, than I depended on my skill as a driver. We jogged on very slowly between wasted fields and through lonely forests, for a long time seeing not a human being. The farm houses in that region were deserted; there were no cattle, no fowls. Just as we emerged from a lonely lane between two fields with broken down fences and entered a woods my good, faithful Adrienne of a sudden seemed to go crazy. She leaped high into the air, her body quivered, her feet kicked out wildly. Never before had I known her to act so strangely. I was frightened, fearing she would smash the carriage against a tree or upset it in a gully and crush my children. My one idea was to get her still long enough to permit me to grab my babies and run. Once safe on ground, Adrienne might wreck the carriage if she wanted to. So I leaped to the ground, caught the bridle close to the mule's mouth and called in despairing tones, "Whoa Whoa! !" Adrienne paid not the slightest attention to me but kept kicking and rearing in that extraordinary fashion. Then, chancing to look down at the ground, I saw a thousand little winged things flying about poor Adrienne's legs and body. They were hornets!! The unlucky mule had put her foot in a hornet's nest! Snatching my bonnet from my head I fanned the tormenters away and after a while the poor beast regained in a measure her composure.

It was almost dark when we arrived at the farm where I planned to stay all night, and you can imagine my feelings when I tell you that instead of seeing a little cottage set in a pretty yard all I saw was a heap of blackened ashes! Not a living thing was on the place! The last time I had been on that farm it was alive with poultry and cattle and the master and mistress were there eager to give me a welcome. The contrast now was painful. I was about to drive on when I saw an old negro man crossing the field toward me; as he neared I recognized him as old Uncle Ned who belonged to the owner of this farm. I stopped long enough to hear Uncle Ned's story of what had happened.

"Fo' days ago," said the old negro, "some Yankees from Memphis come a ridin' up to de house an' axt Marse Jim whar could dey water deir horses, an' Marse Jim he tole 'em of a little branch furder down de road. Dem Yankees rode on down to de branch and was a waterin' deir horses dar when 'long come some Bushwhackers an' begun firin' on dem Yankees. An' dey killed two' ob 'em befo' dev spurred up deir horses an' gallp away. Well, Miss Betty, dem ar Yankees took de notion dat Marse Jim he sent 'em to de branch special so de Bushwhackers could shoot at 'em. So dey come back to de house from de branch an' tuck Marse Jim an' stood him up against de house an' tole him ter say his prayers, case dey wuz gwine ter kill him. Marse Jim's Ma got on her knees an' tole dem Yankees Marse Jim wuz innercent, dat he nebber had no spicion at all about no Bushwhackers. But dem Yankees wuz so mad dey wouldn't listen ter a word she said. Dey jes pinted deir guns at poor Marse Jim and shot him dead. Den dey set fire ter de house and gallop away leaving Marse Jim's Ma layin' dere on de ground, her arms around her po' boy an' mose as dead as he wuz."

The old man wiped tears from his eyes. Tears filled my eyes too. As I drove away from that once happy home the whole world seemed to be growing dark; once it had all seemed so bright and gay; once humanity had seemed good to me. Now it seemed to me as if I were surrounded by demons. Surely no demon could be any more cruel than these soldiers of Gen. Sherman!

A mile or more beyond the burned farm house I halted Adrienne before a small home and asked the woman who came to the door if she could take care of us over night?

"I can give you and your children a bed," answered the woman, "but I ain't got any feed for your critter, not a bundle of fodder nor an ear of corn. The soldiers have used up all my feed."

I was thankful for the little this woman could do for me, consequently I climbed out of the Rockaway, lifted out my two boys and dragged myself into the house; my strength seemed all gone. The woman looked at me and said:

"You do look plumb used up, but a night's rest will set you up. My old man will 'tend to your mule. You lay down and rest until I call you for supper."

I fell on the bed she pointed out to me and felt as if the weight of the world was on me. The woman, perceiving something of my condition, questioned me as to what had happened. "Whar did you come from;" she asked. "Did the Yankees drive you out of Memphis?"

"Yes."

"The mean, cruel devils! What were they afeared of you for?"

"I don't know."

"And they don't know either. They did it just for devilment!"

The woman was tall and slim and quaint looking. Somehow her sympathy affected me. I burst into a passion of tears! Whereupon the slim, quaint old woman began to walk the floor and wring her hands, crying all the while: "Oh! What devils they are! To treat a poor young woman so cruelly! What good does such deviltry do them?"

I tried to explain what had happened but I could not. Sobs choked my throat!! I seemed all of a sudden to realize the desolateness of my position, alone in the world with two little children, driven from pillar to post, my husband off in the army, I knew not where--surely it was a pitiable situation. I became filled with self pity and cried as if my heart would break. And the harder I cried the more the old lady walked the floor and wrung her hands and called Gen. Sherman's soldiers devils for mistreating a poor young woman like me! Then in the midst of all this hub bub a sudden change came over me. The comic aspect of the scene suddenly appealed to me. I began laughing, but I did not stop crying. I was fully conscious of the absurdity of my conduct but I could not help it. The old lady took it all in a very tragic way, becoming more and more excited as she witnessed my condition. And to cap the climax, my two boys, perceiving that their mother was in trouble, set up deafening howls which, luckily, served to bring me to my senses. I subdued my hysterical laughter, dried my tears and begged the slim, quaint old lady not to worry. It was true Gen. Sherman had driven me out of Memphis, but that was all there was to it. My husband and friends were in the South and soon I should meet them and all would be well.

When the tension was relieved the old lady set about cooking some hoe-cakes and baking some sweet potatoes and soon we sat down to supper that quite made us forget our woes. After all, misfortunes are easily forgotten. It is the small things near to us that demand our attention. I was hungry, my children were hungry. And so, in the satisfaction of eating those hot hoe-cakes and baked sweet potatoes we quite forgot our troubles and became in truth almost happy. So wonderful, so buoyant, so resilient is Youth!

Immediately after that supper of hoe-cakes and potatoes we all went to bed; the day's events had made me dreadfully tired and I fell fast asleep almost as soon as my head touched the pillow.

NOTE BY THE AUTHOR'S SON, LEE MERIWETHER.

St. Louis, May 1951

When Gen. Sherman was military commander of Memphis in December 1862 he announced he would banish from the city the wives of ten "rebel" officers if the "rebels" fired again on one of the Union Gun Boats on the Mississippi.

By "rebels" Sherman meant the Southern patriots who were fighting for their country's independence. The patriots of course continued in every way they could to repel the armies that came from the North to burn Southern homes an kill Southern men and inflict hardships upon Southern women and their babies.

So Sherman compiled a list of the wives of ten Confederate officers and notified them to get out of Memphis within 24 hours, or be imprisoned during the duration of the "Rebellion."

Mother's name was on that list; she thought when Sherman knew she was about to have a baby he would remove her name from the list, or at any rate would permit her to remain in her home until the baby arrived. But when mother saw Sherman and explained her condition, he looked at her coldly and said:

"I am not interested in rebel wives or rebel brats; if you are in Memphis day after tomorrow you will be imprisoned for the duration of the rebellion."

Mother hurriedly piled a few clothes and blankets on the back seat of her "Rockaway," put my brothers, Avery, five, and Rivers, three, on top of the blankets and drove her mule "Adrienne" through the slush and snow of Mississippi until she reached Columbus. There she paused to let me be born on Christmas night 1862.

Gen. Sherman's treatment of women and children was as stupid as it was vile it did not shorten the war by a single day. On the contrary, it prolonged it, for it increased the South's desire for independence and caused it to fight longer than it otherwise might have done.

My mother wrote me a letter on January 10, 1863, 17 days after I was born I did not read that letter until I was ten years old, then it inspired in me a contempt for Sherman that I still feel for him 95 years later.

My mother's father's brother, John Avery, resided in Cleveland, Ohio; he was as ardent a Northerner, as my mother was a Southerner. He regarded Sherman as a good as well as a great man. While I was Uncle John's house guest in Cleveland in September, 1881, Gen. Sherman called and Uncle John introduced me to him. Sherman reached out his hand to take mine, but the memory of what he did to my mother 18 years before made me revolt at the thought of touching his hand. I turned on my heels, packed my grip and left at once for Memphis. There I said to mother:

"I never want to see your Uncle again."

But time heals most wounds. I later came to be fond of Uncle John and his children, my cousins. But there is not enough time in Eternity to make me like or respect the memory of General Wm. Tecumseh Sherman.

(EDITOR'S NOTE: The letter referred to by Mr. Meriwether is herewith incorporated in his mother's Memoirs. In many respects the letter is a most remarkable one and should by all means appear in connection with the above note of her son.)

"Columbus, Miss.
January 10, 1863.

MY DARLING LITTLE LEE:

You were born on Christmas night, 17 days ago, and are too young to read this letter now, but when you are a big man you will read it and understand what trouble I took to bring you into the world.

The Yankees captured Memphis and General Sherman, the city's military commander, published a proclamation seven weeks ago, saying he would banish the wives of ten Confederate officers if the "Rebels" didn't stop shooting at his gunboats on the Mississippi river. Of course our brave soldiers kept on shooting Yankee gunboats whenever they could, so Sherman drew up a list of ten Memphis women to be banished. I was on that list.

I knew you were coming soon and thought this might cause my name to be taken off the list, or at any rate, my banishment would be delayed until after your birth, for it was very cold and no time for a woman with two little boys, and a third one on the way, to be wandering through the slush and snow of Mississippi. So I went to Gen. Sherman and told him my condition. He merely looked at me coldly and said:

"I am not interested in rebel wives and rebel brats. If you don't leave Memphis in three days you will be locked up in the Irving Block as long as the war lasts."

The Irving Block opposite Court Square in Memphis is a terrible prison, jammed full of Memphians, eight or ten people in a room. I couldn't bear the thought of being there for months, maybe years, with Rivers and Avery--and with you when you came. So I put your little brothers and some clothes and blankets in my Rockaway, drawn by my faithful mule, Adrienne, and started South.

It was a frightful journey over mud roads that in places were covered with snow. When we got as far as Columbus you gave notice you were about to appear and a good Christian widow, Mrs. Rebecca Winston, took us into her home to let you be born on Christmas night.

A black Mammy waited on me until you came at midnight, then she left me, saying she was 'plum wore out.' I begged her to stay until morning but she wouldn't do it. She said, 'I'se left you some kinlin wood. When de fire starts to go out you kin put kinlin on it an' git it a goin' agin.

I had to get up several times during the night to keep the fire burning. I am now at Mrs. Winston's and when you are a big man you must thank her for her kindness to me and to you. Gen. Sherman called your father a 'Rebel' and he is a rebel, like Washington was a rebel when he fought for the independence of his country. When you are a big man you must be a rebel, too, if the Yankees are still invading the South, killing our soldiers and burning our homes.

Your loving Mother,

CHAPTER XI

I pass the picket lines. In the wake of the retreating Confederate army. Scenes of heroism, misery and starvation. I make Minor a Confederate uniform which I still have, after nearly sixty years. A chilly reception.

When I awoke in the morning the sun was shining through my window. I looked at my two sleeping children and my first thought was to thank God that they had come safely through the dangers we had passed. But second thoughts, not nearly so pleasant, quickly crowded upon me. Whom could I get to drive me to Holly Springs? And if I could get no driver, would I be strong enough to drive so far? And how could my poor Adrienne continue the journey unless food were given her? I felt like one who is tied hand and foot. Think as hard as I could and still I saw no way out of my dilemma.

As I lay there puzzling almost hopelessly over my problem my kind old hostess came in softly and closed the door behind her.

"I see you are awake," she whispered. "I must tell you something. About two o'clock this morning I heard a tapping on my window and a man's voice called out to me to let him in. 'Who are you? What do you want?' I demanded. I feared it was a Yankee soldier. The man did not answer either of my questions. On the contrary he asked me a question which frightened me."

"What did he ask you?" I queried, sitting up in my bed and looking at my hostess intently; I began to fear something untoward had happened--or was about to happen.

"He asked me if Mrs. Meriwether was sleeping in my house," returned the old lady. "I told him you were here, but that you were asleep and dreadfully tired and could not be disturbed "I don't want you to disturb her," said the man at my window. "We'll see her in the morning. Where can you put us?" I told him I had no place to put him. "Oh, well, it makes no difference," said the man, "we can sleep out here on the porch." I said I had no pillows, no blankets, that they had better go on to the next farm house, but he said, No, they would sleep on my porch. And they are out there now."

As you may imagine, my dear children, this communication from my hostess threw me into a fever of excitement. Notwithstanding her conviction that the men were Confederates I feared they might be Yankees sent to take me back to Memphis and shut me up in the Irving Block away from my children. I feared Sherman's men had learned about my pistol and about the other things I had smuggled through the lines, but my hostess smiled at my fears.

"Honey!" she said, "I can tell a Yankee's voice the minute I hear it. The man who woke me up and talked to me through my window warn't no Yankee. He's a Southerner and a gentleman. Of that I am sure--a gentleman, no rough man but highly educated. Believe me, Honey, I can tell a Southern gentleman from the way he talks. I don't have to see him."

This reassured me, but I decided to take a peep at the men myself; so I got out of bed and tipped softly to the window and pulled the curtain aside. Had I seen two angels out there on the porch I would not have been more delighted than I was when I saw those men. For I knew them both; one was our dear friend, William A. Blythe, after whom my second son was named and whom he loved next to his own "Sweet Soger Papa." Little Rivers called Mr. Blythe "Bligy." The other man was a Mr. Kinney whom we well knew. Both men were sound asleep; when they awoke they explained their coming. Mr. Blythe had received my letter and set out at once to overtake me; finding nothing but a charred ruin at the farm where I had written him I intended stopping my first night out from Memphis, he had pushed on to find us. "And now," he concluded, "you must not worry anymore. Kinney and I will see you to Holly Springs and get you located until you hear from Minor. Just trust to us."

I did trust them. I felt as if a millstone had been lifted from around my neck. Our kind old hostess gave us a breakfast of corn hoe-cakes and roasted sweet potatoes (I suppose she would have given the same thing had we stayed with her a month), and then off we started for Holly Springs, Miss. In Mr. Blythe's wagon were two big grey woolen shawls; in my letter I had told him they had forbidden me to take with me any woolen shawls or blankets and in the goodness of his heart Mr. Blythe bought two big shawls and he wore one over his shoulders while Mr. Kinney wore the other--in those days men used shawls instead of overcoats. And this was not all that our good friend smuggled to me. Under a big bundle of hay and fodder in the bed of his wagon was a new grey coat which Mr. Blythe said could be turned by any good tailor into a military coat for my husband. Minor's coat had long since become rusty, not to say ragged, and this new coat would be greatly appreciated.

Mr. Kinney drove the wagon and Mr. Blythe drove my Rockaway and in due time we reached Holly Springs where our Army was in winter quarters. Minor was there and our two boys were wild with joy when they saw their Big Sweet Soger Papa. And I think Minor was pretty glad to see them, and to see me. Mr. Blythe and Mr. Kinney remained a day or two in Holly Springs, then they returned to Memphis.

When I took the grey coat to a tailor he turned it over and looked at it first this way, then that, a smile upon his lips, as if he pitied my ignorance for imagining a civilian's coat could be made fit for a Major. He said to me:

"You see this rolling collar. A military collar has to be straight, not rolling. And the breast of a military coat has to button straight up to the chin. You can never make this coat button up to the chin."

I took that coat back to my room and had a cry over it. Everybody knows women often cry over trifles, but this coat was no trifle--at that moment it was of very great value. And presently I saw how foolish it was to cry about it when by work and study; I could perhaps make the coat useful to my husband. I took my scissors an ripped off the rolling collar and rolling breast lapels of that grey coat then I studied it critically. I clipped and cut and basted and stitched and at last turned out a respectable military coat. Only a tailor would now know it was a "botch"; Minor did not know it; on the contrary he thought it splendid and declared it fitted him well--as indeed it did I took four silver quarter dollars which I luckily had in my purse and had a jeweller make them into four silver stars. The insignia of a Major were two stars on one side of the breast of his coat and two stars on the other side.

I am writing these *Recollections* in 1916, fifty four years after Minor first donned that grey coat in Holly Springs in 1862; he wore that coat all through the war, and yet as I write these lines I can look up and see that coat. And I vow it seems almost as good and new as it did the day I fitted it for my dear husband more than half a century ago. I do not know how Minor was able to take such good care of the coat during the years he wore it in the War; he wore it all of 1863, 1864 and 1865. Often he slept in it on the ground. He wore it through battles. And when at the close of the war he wore that coat back to Memphis I resolved to keep it for the rest of my life. I had a glass covered case made by a carpenter and in that case Minor's coat reposes today as good, or almost as good, as when I worked on it and made it fit him fifty four years ago. The glass case is on the wall in my St. Louis home, surrounded by Confederate flags and portraits of Confederate soldiers and statesmen. On one occasion a few years ago, when the Daughters of the Confederacy gave a big ball in St. Louis I permitted my son Lee to wear this old grey coat, it fitted Lee as well as if it had been made for him instead of his father. After the ball I put the coat back in its glass case and there it must stay as long as I live. And I believe it will stay there long after I am dead, for my son Lee reveres his father's memory and will keep this relic of his father's part in the War in the sixties.

I had hardly got located in Holly Springs when our Army was ordered to move further South. The enemy was advancing with an overwhelming force and it was deemed necessary for us to retreat. Our soldiers did not appear to be downcast over the retreat. They had great faith in "Old Pap" as they called their commander, Gen. Sterling Price of Missouri. The Army marched south as far as Abbeville, Miss., and there pitched its tents. I found lodgings in the home of a Mrs. Leonidas Smith. Our soldiers were tented all around the Smith home and seemed as happy and contented as if they were pursuing the Yankees instead of retreating before them. But I could see that Minor was downcast; he tried to appear cheerful but I could see he was worried. He knew, what the private soldiers did not know, that the odds against the South were growing greater every day.

The soldiers made pets of our little boys; they fashioned sticks in the shape of guns and bade the boys go shoot the Yankees. And the little rascals would then rush about pointing their sticks at imaginary Yankees and shouting "Bang! Bang! Bang!" Then they would come running into the house and tell me they had killed a hundred, sometimes a thousand Yankees. This was fun for the soldiers and for the boys. But when the soldiers put my little boys on their horses and put the bridles in their baby fingers I thought it a dangerous game. So I called the boys to me, told them their legs were too short, that they could not hold tight on a horse's back, and gave them strict orders not to mount a horse again. Having given them this order very solemnly and very strictly, what was my surprise on the very next morning when I heard my younger boy say to his brother Avery:

"Come! Let's make de sogers ride us on de horses."

"No," replied Avery, "Mamma told us to wait till our legs grow longer."

"Oh come 'long!" insisted Rivers, scorn in his voice. "We don't have to listen to Mamma. She's nuffin but a woman. She can't shoot Yankees!"

This same impudent little chap came to me that same day and showed me some silver quarters and dimes in his chubby fists. "Where did you get that money?" I asked.

"A soger gave it to me."

I told him he should not accept presents of money from a soldier, that he must take presents from no man except his own father.

"Only servants and negroes take money from strangers," I said. "Now, go straight back to that soldier and return him his money."

Rivers did as I commanded. Next day as Gen. Price was calling on me and sitting on the Smith porch, Rivers went boldly up to the General and said:

"Gen'l, is you got any money?"

"Yes, a little," replied Gen. Price. "Why do you ask?"

"I jes wanted to tell you not to give me any. My mudder won't let me take it, so you needn't give me any."

Gen. Price laughed immoderately at this; he had not offered the child any money and thought it very funny to be warned in this way. Though that little boy no longer lives, he grew up to be a good man; he married and left two beautiful daughters, both now married. They may be amused when they read these anecdotes about their father.

I must now speak of an important event that occurred that memorable winter when, in my Rockaway drawn by my old mule, Adrienne, I followed the fortunes of the Southern Army and kept retreating further and further into Dixie Land as the Northern Armies advanced upon us. I mean an event that was important to me and to my family -- course it was of no importance to anyone else. I was expecting a child and Minor was anxious to get me comfortably settled in some place not likely to be invaded by the Yankees. One day while we were discussing this subject an old farmer, overhearing us, said to Minor:

"If you wish you can let your folks come to us. The Yankees never bother to come out to my little farm. We ain't rich people my farm is off the main road. I can't give you any fancy things, but I can give you plenty of bread and milk and eggs, and I reckon that won't be so bad in times like these."

"I should say not," replied Minor, delighted at the suggestion, and forthwith came to an agreement with the old farmer as to the compensation to be paid for our board and lodging. The very next morning under the guidance of this kind old farmer we set forth for his farm which was twenty miles southeast from Abbeville. Minor's body servant, Henry, drove my Rockaway, the two children by his side; Minor sat back with me and the old farmer rode on horseback, often coming along by our side and chatting cheerfully about the War and the South's prospects of winning.

The farmer seemed cheerful and happy until we neared his farm, then his face took on a sorrowful expression. He had told us his one and only son was in the Army and we supposed he was brooding over the thought that any day might bring news of his son's death in battle. On reaching the farm he said sadly, "Walk on in,"--and then *he* walked on OUT, leaving us to introduce ourselves to his wife. Minor looked at me and I looked at him, but we had no time to discuss the old farmer's curious behaviour. While he was walking *away* from the house we walked toward the house and were met at the door by a woman of forbidding presence; she did not ask us in. She merely stood at the door glowering at us and silently waiting for us to speak.

"Is Mrs. Williams at home?" Minor asked politely; the farmer said his name was Williams.

"I am Mrs. Williams. What do you wish with her?" demanded the forbidding looking woman, still glowering at us.

"I wish to see her," Minor replied, still as polite as a Chesterfield.

"Open your eyes and see her," returned the woman grimly.

"Oh, I can see you plainly enough," returned Minor suavely. "I mean I wish to speak with you, and I cannot do that very well standing outside your door. Permit us to enter your house. Your good husband has agreed to board my wife and two little boys for a month or two.

"He never told me about it," said the woman gruffly, neither asking us in nor standing aside so that we might enter. But Minor was not a man to be easily "bluffed." Having come so far and the hour being so late, he was determined not to be imposed on.

"That is too bad," he said smiling; Minor had a way of smiling when he was most seriously in earnest. "Your husband probably overlooked telling you. But be that as it may, we are delighted to accept your hospitality."

With that, taking little Rivers in his arms and telling me to follow with Avery, he pushed the glowering woman aside and strode into the house and presently we were in as cheerless a room as ever I saw. In one corner was a black horse hair sofa; nearby were several horse hair chairs and in the center of the room was a little round table. The fire place was empty and looked as if it never had contained a fire. Glancing around this dismal room, Minor whispered:

"We can endure it for one night. Tomorrow we will go back to Abbeville. Stay here with the children while I go see about Adrienne and Henry."

Minor left us; the little boys were tired and sleepy. I spread our good big shawls on the floor and the little darlings soon fell fast asleep while I sat there in the gloom of that dismal room wondering what manner of man Mr. Williams was and how he had ever had courage to marry such a wife. What a contrast between this glowering, inhospitable woman and the amiable old lady, who took care of me my first night out of Memphis and who was so upset at the cruel way the Yankees had treated me!

When Minor returned and found me sitting in that dark, dismal room he was disgusted and angry.

"A wife like that deserves a horse whip!" he said. "But the husband she's got hasn't the nerve to call his nose his own. Do you know, Lizzie, I found the fellow out there sitting on a log crying. I had meant to give him a tongue lashing for his conduct but when I saw him looking so abject and so unhappy I did not have the heart to berate him."

"What did you say to him?" I asked.

"I told him not to worry over our disappointment, that I could see he needed sympathy more than we did, and that he had our unqualified sympathy. 'We'll go away in the morning,' I said, 'so tell your wife to rest easy.' My sympathy made the old fellow sniffle and blow his nose and he stammered that he wished his wife would be kind to the poor lady who was driven by the Yankees out of her home. Now you couldn't stay angry with a fellow like that, could you?"

I agreed that Mr. Williams was more to be pitied than blamed. We were still discussing our curious hosts when in came a young woman with a lighted candle and she said pleasantly she was sorry supper so late. "Father has been out attending to some business," she said. "It has made everything late, but supper is ready now. Won't you walk out, please?"

This invitation, after Mrs. Williams' reception was so unexpected that Minor and I stared at each other, scarce believing our senses. The young woman, however, was very real; moreover, she was gracious and pleasant. Accordingly we accompanied her to the supper table where was spread a genuine feast--good bread, sliced ham, fresh buttermilk and potato coffee. Real coffee in those days, and in part of the world, cost forty dollars a pound and was hard to get at that price. Potato coffee, made by slicing a sweet potato very thin and parching it brown and crisp, then boiling it in hot water as coffee is boiled, was not unpalatable; that night, hungry as we were, we thought it delicious. And never did ham seem so good! Until the very moment that young woman appeared with the lighted candle we expected nothing at all--and then of a sudden we were asked to sit down to a feast! It all seemed so unreal I had to pinch myself to realize I was not dreaming. Mrs. Williams did not grace the table with her presence, but her spouse sat down opposite us and made an effort to chat with us and with his daughter as if nothing unusual had happened.

Next morning we all arose early and Minor went out to the barn and had Henry hitch up Adrienne so as to be ready to start back to Abbeville. Henry told us that he too had had a good supper. While I was on the porch with my two children I could look through the window into the dining room. The woman who had glowered at us was in the room; when she caught my eye she nodded to me almost pleasantly. She was slowly pouring milk from a pitcher into flour in a tray while a negro woman stirred the milk in the flour with a big iron spoon. I watched these proceedings with curiosity, wondering what they were making. The young woman of the house was in the room arranging the breakfast table. Presently she came out to me and said smiling:

"I reckon you never saw anybody make biscuits as Mama does?"

"No," I said, "that is not the way I make biscuits."

"Well, it is a mighty good way to make them," observed the woman "Mama always has the dough mixed with a spoon. She never allows anyone to put their hands in it."

"I should think it would be hard to mix with a spoon."

"Not once you are used to it," replied the girl. "Aunt Dolly -- negro woman there--gets her biscuits worked and baked very quickly."

I secretly thought the spoon way would never turn out good biscuits; I thought those biscuits would be clammy and tough. But in this suspicion I was wholly wrong. I have never eaten better biscuits than those we had that morning. And the best thing about that breakfast was the lady of the house--the glowering woman, but no longer did she glower. She seemed positively cordial and was good enough to wrap up a dozen of those good biscuits for us to eat on the road. And the farmer gave us slices of cold ham and bread and butter and a bottle of milk for the children. No reference was made to the manner of our reception the evening before, and to this day I am unable to understand why that old farmer invited us in the first place, nor why--having invited us, when we arrived at his farm he left us to go in to his house alone; nor why his wife, having treated us that evening so coldly, so almost brutally, should the next morning be so cordial! It was all very puzzling and we did not care to see more of such people consequently we were glad to be on our way again.

CHAPTER XII

Still retreating South with our army. The Peppercorn family. Starvation stares us in the face. I flee from Columbus to avoid desperate street fighting between Yankee and Confederate cavalry.

After our return to Abbeville the same question perplexed Minor: Where could he find a quiet place for me and my two children to remain until the advent of our third child? To us this question seemed of real importance, but Gen. Price made light of it.

"Major Meriwether," he said, "why don't you get a tent and let your third boy be born in a soldier's tent? Our Lord and Saviour was born in a stable. Tents are as good as a stable. Stop your worrying."

"You forget, General, that this is December. Jesus was born in December, too, but I think Palestine's climate was more genial than ours. At any rate, I prefer my wife to be in a house if I can find one for her."

Mr. James Bowles, a wealthy gentleman who lived two miles from Abbeville and who heard Gen. Price's tent suggestion, spoke up and said:

"Major, send your wife and children to my house. We have lots of room. I am on my way to join Forest's cavalry and Mrs. Bowles will be glad to have Mrs. Meriwether with her."

"Mrs. Bowles may not care for company," said Minor, mindful of our recent experience with farmer Williams.

Mr. Bowles insisted. "Don't you suppose I know what Mrs. Bowles likes? I've lived with her long enough to know. Don't stand on ceremony, Major. In times like these we men of the South are all brothers. That is the way I feel about it and we shall feel honored to your have wife accept our hospitality."

Thus urged, Minor yielded and this time the husband was no more hospitable than his wife, Mrs. Bowles received me as kindly as if I had been her own sister. She was not only lovely to look at, but her manners were lovely. Although not yet thirty, she was the mother of five children, the youngest, a babe in arms. I was given a large, pretty room with servants to wait on me and plenty of good, wholesome food so when Minor left us to return to the Army it was with the feeling that when our third child came it would be well cared for and that I would receive proper attention. It saddened me to see my dear husband go; I could but dread the cruel fate that *War* might bring him. But I tried to put such thoughts aside and set to work as cheerfully as I could on little garments for the expected stranger. In this effort to forget I was only partially successful. War is a monster not easily forgotten. And in this instance the Monster seemed determined to stay close at my heels.

I had been at the Bowles' hardly a week when one morning my dear husband came galloping up with the dreadful news that the enemy in large force was advancing to attack Gen. Price in both front and flank, and that Price had ordered a retreat further South. Although Minor would not admit that our retreat might be the forerunner of final defeat yet I could see in his eyes a deep and painful anxiety. He told me to get ready and retreat with the Bowles; he himself could not leave the army but Henry would drive my Rockaway and Mr. Bowles, who had rushed back to remove his family, would let one of his negro boys carry our things in a wagon. It was a sorrowful parting when Minor bade us goodbye that cold, dreary December day in 1862. Little Rivers and Avery clung to their father's knees crying: "Oh, Big, sweet Soger Papa, don't leave us!" But their big, sweet Soger Papa was compelled to tear himself from their fingers and rush to his horse and gallop back to the army. And I knew, Oh I knew that his heart as well as mine was tortured by the fear that our little family might never meet again!

All that night a cold rain drizzled down. The morning was scarcely less gloomy than the night. There was not a ray of sunshine. The rain continued to fall in a cold, penetrating mist. Henry and the Rockaway and Adrienne were at the Bowles gate awaiting us. My little boys, aroused from their sleep, grumbled mightily at their vagrant life and stood shivering in the cold while I got our things together.

"Mama," said Rivers, the younger boy, looking at me with big, sad eyes, "when will we get a house w-e can h-a-v-e?"

The "Have" was long drawn out; he had not forgotten our home under the big trees near Memphis and could not understand why we roved about so much. Even poor Adrienne, who stood shivering in the cold December rain, turned her head and looked at me as if she feared I had lost my senses and was wandering over the face of the earth simply because I was crazy. For seven years Adrienne had lived with us in peace and comfort; she had ever had a good, comfortable stable to sleep in and plenty of food to eat. But now she slept out in the cold even when it rained, and often had not even an ear of corn nor a wisp of hay to eat! Doubtless this seemed all wrong, all crazy to Adrienne. And in truth, had the poor old mule had such thoughts, would she have been far wrong? What can be more wrong, what can be more crazy than war?

Henry tried to interest Rivers and Avery with tales of the War, tales of his adventures at the battle of Shiloh, but they were too cold to be interested in anything he said and kept asking that unanswerable question:

"Mama, when will we get a house we can h-a-v-e?"

A big cavalcade of negroes and wagons and horses and carriages stood around the Bowles gate ready to start off the minute Mr. Bowles gave the order. Had the occasion been less tragic I would have been amused at the curious picture that cavalcade presented. First there was Mr. Bowles' carriage, a large family coach drawn by two fine bay horses; in the coach were Mrs. Bowles with her baby in her lap and two of her children sitting on a pile of cloaks and shawls and baskets and bundles that was heaped up inside the carriage. In a second carriage were the rest of the Bowles children amid a pile of wraps, cloaks and blankets and guarded by a big black Mammy. Then came a wagon drawn by two mules; in the wagon were a dozen negro women with babies in their arms and older children on their laps and around their knees. A second wagon was loaded with household effects, mattresses, chairs, pillows, etc. In a third wagon were food stuffs, flour, corn, sugar, molasses, etc. And overseeing the whole motley affair was Mr. Bowles, on a large fine horse. One of the out-riders was a buxom young black damsel who rode astride a mule, a rope for a bridle and a piece of sack cloth for a saddle. The mule was stubborn and wanted to go one way while the buxom damsel wanted to go another way; the mule did its best to go to the left while the damsel kept kicking the mule with both of her black heels (she wore no shoes) in the effort to make the mule go to the right. It soon appeared the damsel was trying to ride by the side of my Rockaway and Henry, to his great disgust observed that the damsel smirked and smiled at him.

"I do believe, Miss Betty," he said, "dat fool black gal don't know I've got a wife of my own. But if I didn't have a wife no such gal as dat could ebber kotch me!"

I have not yet spoken of Henry's wife. Her name was Rose. She was a nice featured young woman; her nose was not flat and her lips were not coarse and thick as with some negroes. When Henry accompanied his master to the Army his wife was with my sister, Mrs. Lamb in Charleston, Miss. Rose and Henry had one child named Beauregard as the Southern General's name was rather long, everybody called the baby "Booby," but he was by no means a booby. He grew up to be a bright, well behaved young negro. Further on in these *Recollections* I shall have more to tell you about Henry and Rose and their boy Booby.

Some five miles before reaching Oxford, Miss., we fell in with Gen. Green's division of the Army. His soldiers were sitting around on the cold, wet ground at the foot of a steep hill, eating their dinner of cornbread and a thin, oh such a thin slice of cold *raw* bacon--they had no time to cook the bacon. When we stopped to let Adrienne rest a dozen or more soldiers crowded around the Rockaway and began talking to my boys.

"These kids make us think of home, way back in Missouri," one big, bearded fellow said. And I fancied I saw a tear in his eyes as he added: "I have two little kids in my home. I hope God will be good to them and to me and let me see them again!"

Oh how such sights and such words made me hate the Monster War!

The soldiers did not seem depressed because our Army was retreating. I heard one of them say: "The d----d Yankees thought they'd catch old Pop Price a napping. They can't get up early enough in the morning to do that."

The wet ground, poor food, thin, ragged clothes, the almost shoeless feet did not seem to discourage those men. They had come from Missouri to fight with Gen. Price and in spite of all retreats their confidence in Price and in the success of the South seemed unbounded. The costumes of that army were picturesque. No two men seemed garbed alike. The shirts of some were made of women's shawls, some of window curtains. I saw trousers that were made out of old carpets. Few of the men had real blankets. One soldier, observing that I was eyeing his poor pretense of a blanket, said:

"Never you mind, lady! The next scrap we have with the Yanks we'll capture some blankets. The Yanks have all kinds of good clothes. We always get a nice supply of real shoes and coats after we have a scrap with the Yanks."

We saw the artillery wagons being slowly drawn up the steep muddy hill. Such whooping and cracking of whips over the poor horses' heads I had never heard before. The rail fence of a cotton field ran along side that muddy hill. I got out of the Rockaway and walked up the hill so as to lighten the load for Adrienne. Henry let down a panel of the rail fence and drove through the cotton field so as to pass by the artillery. At the top of the hill I stopped to rest and survey the scene. The whole motley army was now climbing the hill as I had done--not on the road, but through the cotton field alongside the rail fence. The sun had come out and the slant of its rays gleamed on the soldiers' bayonets, on their ragged garments, on their resolute faces and, more beautiful to me than all else, on the happy faces of my own two little boys.

The artillery was now at the top of the hill; the whooping and cracking of whips over poor horses' heads had ceased, and I got back into my Rockaway and resumed my journey. We reached Oxford without any untoward incident; the Bowles family secured rooms in a small hotel but the hotel had no room for me and I found refuge for the night in the home of a Mrs. Trigg. That lady said she could lodge me but that she had no food in her house, so we all had to go supperless to bed. All during the night I heard sharp skirmishing going on. Not until midnight did our cavalry march into Oxford, the enemy beaten back to a point several miles north of the town. Our brave soldiers had no shelter that cold December night; they slept in the open air on the rain soaked ground. In the skirmish that night one of Minor's dearest friends, Lieut. Joseph Wicks of Memphis, was killed--as the report of the day said, "With his face to the foe, he fell, looking up to Heaven from his death bed of glory!"

When I went out next morning to see if I could not find some food for my children, tears came to my eyes when I saw our brave soldiers sleeping on that cold, wet ground, half clad and no blankets to warm them! They had tried to kindle fires to warm their feet, but the wet wood would not burn and the soldiers, too tired to spend much time trying to make wet wood burn, had fallen asleep on the cold ground. One would imagine such hardships would dampen the ardor of even the bravest soldier, would discourage even the most fiery patriot, but if those men in Oxford that night were discouraged they allowed no one to suspect it. They got up from their sleep brisk and cheerful, ate a poor breakfast of cold corn bread and a thin slice of raw fat hog meat and went forth to battle as bravely as the best clothed and fed army in history ever did! I found Henry had gotten up sometime before I did and was already preparing a breakfast for me and the children.

"Where did you get the things to cook?" I asked. He grinned and answered:

"Laws, Miss Betty, don't you know I ain't gwine let Marse Minor's chilluns go hungry? Before we left Mr. Bowles' house I chucked a lot of good vittles in de wagon whar our things are--a lot of sweet pertaters, three chickens and bread and biscuits!"

Henry's forethought was the means of our having an excellent breakfast and prepared us for the dismal journey of the second day's march. During the first few miles we heard our cavalry under Col. W. R. Jackson skirmishing with the enemy's cavalry. Every few minutes there was a sharp report of rifles, followed by the boom of cannon, but the sound became fainter rather than louder and we felt that the tide of battle was not going to engulf us that day.

The roads were frightful--deep ruts and mud that was like glue; had it been composed of glue I do not believe it could have pulled us back and clogged our wheels any harder than the mud of those Mississippi roads did that December day fifty four years ago. Twelve miles was all we were able to travel that day.

As hard as were those days when I, who was about to bring another child into the world, was compelled to care for two little children and follow in the wake of a retreating Army, they were not so hard to endure as the nights. As the sun rose each morning I was glad that the night was over. Somehow I had conceived the notion that babies are born only at night, consequently on stopping each night my first question to the lady of the house where we were to stop was: "Is there a doctor nearby?"

Usually the reply was discouraging--no doctor nearer than five or ten miles; sometimes they said none was nearer than twenty miles. And the thought of what might happen were my third child to appear under such circumstances was a thought that caused me many sleepless nights.

The fourth day of our journey was bitter cold; we came over a mountainous county, Calhoun, and I walked up the worst hills so as to give poor Adrienne a better chance. She could hardly pull the Rockaway up some of those steep, muddy hills, and I was hardly able in my condition, to climb such roads. At the top of every hill I was forced to stop for a long time to recover my strength and my breath.

The fourth night we stayed with a Mrs. L. Davis who had just lost her husband, killed in battle. Her house was a log cabin. All of our party had to sleep in one room, Mrs. Bowles and her children on some blankets, I and my children on our shawls on the floor. It was very cold. All night the wind whistled through the cracks between the logs of that house and all night I was racked with fear lest my third child should make its appearance at that untimely place and hour; I had read that queens have to submit to the presence of witnesses at child birth, but I was not a queen and to me the very thought of so many people being about was dreadful. When morning came and all was safe so far, I thanked God for his mercy to me!

On the fifth day the rain poured so hard we decided not to travel; we had not heard any cracking of rifles or booming of cannon the day before and felt that the Yankees were not so close as to make it dangerous for us to wait a day. The next day was not so bad and we travelled some twenty five miles, stopping at night at a double log cabin, that is, a room on each side of a wide hall running through the center of the house. As we drove up to this house a tall, large, but not fat, woman came to the door and eyed us. I asked if we might stay there for the night? Before the big woman could reply three more tall, big boned women came to the door to look us over. I repeated my question, whereupon the first big boned woman replied cheerily:

"You uns kin sleep here but we uns aint got no feed for you uns and nary a bit of fodder for your mule."

I had not heard "You uns" and "We uns" since my bridal days at the house of the King of Crow Creek in the Cumberland mountains. Thankful to get shelter, we all went into the house. In a wide fire place was a huge log of wood at the back and piled on it, and in front on it, were several small logs. All were burning cheerfully. A big open wood fire is at anytime and any place cheering; on that night after our long day's journey through the bitter cold of a December day over frightful roads--Well, it made that room look so homey, so comfy, I have not forgotten the picture after more than fifty years! My half frozen little boys played about that fire as if they were charmed. On the floor was neither carpet nor rug, but it was clean as a whistle. Two beds were in the room; they were covered with gay colored quilts of red and yellow calico. Two broad shelves ran along one side of the room and on those shelves I noted neat little piles of clothing, towels, quilts and other household articles.

The elder of the two women who had escorted us into the room placed a chair for me ten feet away from the big blazing fire; then she and her sister sat down side by side at the same distance from the burning logs and fixed their eyes upon me. In turn I gazed at them; I watched my two boys, fearing they might in their romping about get too close to the fire, but I found time to watch the big boned ladies, too. They fascinated me; and presently when two more of them came in, making four in all, I could scarce believe my eyes. All four were tall, big boned and exactly alike--the same complexion. The same tawny hair. And the eyes of all four were looking at me as if they had never before seen such a woman as I. For a moment all four sat perfectly still, then one of the four drew from a pocket in her skirt a twist of tobacco, bit off a piece and set to work chewing it vigorously; then each of the other big boned women drew from their pockets twists of tobacco and began chewing as if it were a sort of work, a duty they were compelled to perform. After chewing a while all four began to spit across the floor into the fire. It was a full ten feet, but never once did they miss their shot--the sight to me was as astonishing as it was disgusting.

After regaling themselves in this way until the tobacco juice was exhausted they took the tobacco out of their mouths, wiped their lips and one of them began to chat in the friendliest way.

"My name is Peppercorn," she said. "What mout your'n be?" I told her my name. "I'm a widow woman," she resumed. "My man got killed in a fight seventeen years ago. These gals is my darters. Suky is my oldest darter. The next is Sally and the other is Melverina Elverina. She's a twin. Her twin is named Alexander the Great. We call him Lexy for short." "Where is Alexander the Great?" I asked, not a little interested in this family history.

"In the army," returned Mrs. Peppercorn. "Lexy was jes crazy to jine the army, so when he got to be fifteen years old I let him jine. He's fought in battles but he ain't never got hit yet. And now Melverina's crazy to jine the army, too.

I gazed at Melverina and thought she would make a good soldier. Why not? She was as tall and strong as a man.

"And I'm agoing," interjected Melverina. "I'm older than Lexy was when he jined, and I can shoot jes as well as he ever did. I'm going to jine the fust chance I git."

"Will your mother consent?" I asked.

"Lexy never asked nobody's consent. He jes up and went. And I reckon I'll jine the same way."

I asked Mrs. Peppercorn how it happened that she gave her first two daughters such common place names as Suky and Sally, and then gave her third daughter the flowery name of Melverina Elverina?

"Wall," returned Mrs. Peppercorn, "I've been asked that question before. It was this way. My man's people come from way down South Callina. They had some mighty big ideas, they was rich and had a big rice field and so my man named our first gal Suky after his mother. The next gal he named Sally after his sister. Then jes before the twins was born my man said as how, ef it was a gal baby, he would name her Polly Peppercorn. And I was willing, because Polly Peppercorn sounds soft and smooth like."

"You are quite right," I observed. "Polly Peppercorn is very euphonious."

"Very what?" asked my hostess.

"I mean it sounds very musical."

96

"Yes. That is what my man and I thought," resumed Mrs. Peppercorn. "Well, afore the twins was born my man got killed in a fight. And soon after that along come a painter man, paintin' trees and cows and lan' scapes and sich, and this painter man was a great hand to read poetry. And when the twins was born he said ses he, 'Them babies is too purty to have sich names as Sally and Suky. Them names is good enough for niggers but not for sich babies as them twins.' 'Well,' ses I, 'Can you give me any purtier names?' 'I certainly can,' ses that painter man, and he gave me some names he got outen a book, and that's how Melverina and Lexy got their fine names."

It may seem childish in me, but it is true that I was interested in this Peppercorn family and was anxious to see Alexander the Great. The rain had now ceased and the moon was shining brightly. I hoped we would have a good day for travelling on the morrow. Mrs. Peppercorn, when she saw that the rain had ceased, turned to her daughter Suky and told her to go out and cut some wood. "Sleepin' on the floor this way," said Mrs. Peppercorn, "these chilluns will catch cold if we don't keep up a good fire."

Without a word Suky arose, took an axe from a corner of the room and went out to the wood pile; and presently I heard the sound of an axe chopping wood as if a strong man was swinging it. When Suky re-entered the room she bore in her arms enough wood to keep the fire blazing all night. Next morning I heard that axe again and looking out of my window I saw Suky wielding it as she had done the night before--so steadily and lustily that very quickly was a big pile of the wood cut ready to burn. Scarcely had she brought in that wood than I saw coming across the yard a stalwart young man who so strongly resembled the Peppercorn family that I at once surmised he was Alexander the Great, come home on a furlough. This youth when he came into the house said to me:

"Do you know me?"

"I think you must be Alexander the Great," I said.

"Well, Well! That's fine!" said the youth with a grin. "Why, I'm Melverina. If you can't see I'm a woman I reckon them army men won't see it neither. I'm going to jine right away."

"Has your mother consented?"

"Yes, at fust she was afeared them army men mout guess I was a woman en sass me, but I know ef any man trys to sass me I kin take care of myself."

She looked capable of it and I had no doubt she could do a man's part in the army. I was so much interested in this curious family that I was really loth to leave it; I would gladly have remained with the Peppercorns a day or two longer, but there was no doctor within ten miles and I thought it wise, considering my condition, to get as quickly as possible to some good sized town. Accordingly, immediately after breakfast we bade the Peppercorns goodbye and recommenced our pilgrimage. It no longer rained but it was bitter cold and I was glad when near night fall we drove into the little town of Buena Vista and found comfortable quarters in a hotel. The Bowles family parted from us in

Buena Vista, they going thence to stay with relatives, while early the next morning I continued south toward Columbus. And oh! How glad I was when at last we arrived in that quaint and hospitable southern town! Minor had told me to make Columbus, if possible, before our third child was born; he said I would there receive better care than in the smaller places.

While driving slowly through the streets of Columbus in search of a hotel, whom should I see but our old friend Major Champneys! He told me of a nice boarding house where were some Memphis ladies and suggested I might find this private house more agreeable than a public hotel. So I drove to that boarding house and found there a kind landlady who gave me on reasonable terms a very comfortable room. And I was glad to find there two of my old friends, Mr. and Mrs. Timothy Trezevant, and a Memphis lady named Mrs. Logwood. I wrote a letter to Minor that night and early next morning Henry took my letter and set forth to join his master in the Army. I really thought I was at last settled, and began again to work on those little garments so necessary when a little one is expected. Then came a cruel change. One morning before day I was roused from my sleep by a knocking at my door.

"Who is it?" I cried.

"It is I, Mrs. Trezevant. Open the door. I must speak to you quickly."

A chill of fear went through me. Was there bad news from our army? Had Minor been killed? I opened the door and saw Mrs. Trezevant standing there shaking with nervous excitement. "Hurry!" she whispered. "All the women in town have just received warning to get out of town at once. The Yankee cavalry in large force is advancing on Columbus. It will be here, fighting, shooting in the streets, any minute. Forest's cavalry is here. It will fight to drive them back. There'll be fighting on every street, from house to house. Get your children and fly. We are all packed, ready to take the first train. It leaves in thirty minutes."

And off she ran. I fairly jumped into my clothes and ran to the stable where Adrienne was kept. The stable man was already making ready to fly; I begged him to harness my mule to the Rockaway and he stopped long enough to comply with my request. He advised me to drive to Pickensville, a village twenty three miles from Columbus.

"Pickensville," he said, "Is out of the regular way of travel. I don't think the Yankees will be going that way. And I should say, Ma'am," he added, eyeing me and noting my condition, "I should say you should be getting to some quiet place as soon as you can."

The situation, though little short of tragic, was not without its humorous aspect, too. Get to some quiet place? That was what I had been trying very hard to do. But no matter how quiet a place might be at the moment of my arrival, within a very short time quietness seemed the one thing that was banished and not to be had at any price. Here was Columbus, as quiet, sleepy, humdrum a town as one could find in all Dixie when I drove into it two nights before. And now at break of day I had to hustle away, or else run the chance of having my children and myself blown to pieces by rifles and cannon!

"Well," said the stable man when I spoke of this, "I reckon Pickensville will stay quiet. Anyway, you better get out of Columbus as quick as you can. I'll lend you a wagon and a nigger to drive it. Put your trunk and bundles in my wagon; you drive your Rockaway, and drive fast."

I did as this good stable man advised and all went well for some eight or ten miles; then the mule pulling the wagon began to act badly; he refused to go forward and tried his best to turn around and return to Columbus. In vain the negro boy who was driving him beat him over the head and cried "Whoa! Whoa!" That mule would not budge! I began to fear we would never reach Pickensville. But presently an idea dawned on that negro boy.

"I'se got his feed under de seat," he said. Maybe dat's what ails dis fool mule."

That was the trouble; as soon as the mule had his dinner he proceeded without further balking, and in due time we were on the streets of Pickensville. There was but one hotel in the town, there I was given a nice room and plenty of hot water to scrub my boys. Heaven knows they needed a scrubbing. On such a journey as we had taken it was not always possible to get hot water and soap

I was disappointed in Pickensville. It had been described to me as a quiet, pretty little town where I could get a comfortable room. All this was true; it was a pretty town, and my room was comfortable. But the food set before me at that Pickensville hotel quite dismayed me. They set before me and before my two little children not one thing save cornbread and fried hog meat swimming in grease. This sort of food seemed to me bad enough for adults, but I thought it enough to kill babies. I asked the landlord for a little milk for my children; he said not a pint of milk was to be had in the town--all the cattle, including cows, had been driven away for the use of the army. Then I asked for some fruit, stewed apples or prunes--anything that was not quite so heavy, so indigestible as greasy fried hog meat. The landlord said he had nothing else and could get nothing else.

When I left the hotel and asked at some private houses for food fit for little children I had no better luck. One sad-faced woman told me her husband and son were in the army, the son with a leg shot off, a cripple for life. He was coming home that day and she had tried in vain to find something fit for him to eat. Pickensville had nothing to eat except cornbread and greasy hog meat. So many told me the same story I was forced to believe it, and so I resolved to observe my children closely and see what effect such a diet had upon them. Four days passed and I saw indications of stomach troubles, of acute indigestion --and I asked myself if it might not be better to risk Yankee bullets than face the sickness, perhaps death, that a diet of cornbread and greasy hog meat would probably bring to little children? It did not take me long to decide this question. I went out to the stable where my poor Adrienne was munching away on her meager allowance of feed and asked the stable man to get my Rockaway ready, and also the wagon and the negro boy who had driven it over from Columbus. And within an hour we had left Pickensville and were on our way back to Columbus, arriving there that night. The stable man in Columbus was glad to see me; he told me Forest's cavalry had driven the Yankees back before they got to Columbus, so there had been no fighting in the streets and from house to house, and my trip to Pickensville had been all for nothing.

This good stable man told me if I did not care to board at the hotel, that he knew of a kind old lady who would let me stay in her house - a Mrs. Winston whose home was out on the Military Road a short distance out of town; the house was on a hill surrounded by trees -- a picturesque view. I at once drove there and Mrs. Winston, who appeared to be a kindly old lady, frankly told me she needed Confederate money to pay her taxes; that was her sole reason for telling the Stable man that she would take a few boarders.

It was the night of December 21st 1862 that our faithful old mule pulled my Rockaway out the Military Road and up the hill to Mrs. Winston's place; I could not see the place that night, but even without seeing it I felt that here at last I had found the right place to sojourn until my third child arrived. A broad porch ran around the front of the house; the rooms were spacious, in fact too spacious--it was hard to keep them warm. But Mrs. Winston was kindly, everything was clean and I knew from the supper we had that first night that we would get in that home plain, wholesome food.

Next day, after getting our few belongings placed, the first thing I did was to prepare a few little gifts so that Santa Claus would be ready to do his duty to my two boys. In spite of all my wanderings I had managed to get and to keep a dozen marbles, two tin horns, two picture books and a tiny tin sword. Mrs. Winston gave me a pint of sorghum molasses with which I made a few sticks of candy.

And so when three days later Christmas Morning came and little Avery and Rivers got up at day dawn to see what Santa Claus had brought them--in spite of the Monster War, in spite of Sherman's banishing me from my home and sending me adrift in winter to straggle after a retreating army and survive or perish as Fate decreed--in spite of all these obstacles their little stockings were not wholly empty. True, they did not contain much, but they contained something: and my boys were not spoiled. Those few little gifts pleased them as much as more costly gifts would have done. Especially did the tin horns enrapture them. All day long they ran over the yard blowing those cheap horn. They never tired of the toot, tooting sound of those horns. Luckily Mrs. Winston was not nervous and permitted them to make all the noise they desired.

I, so far from being annoyed by the blowing of those horns, thought it as sweet as any music; for it made me know my little ones were happy. When night came I put them to bed and was settling myself down to read when I was made aware of the fact that at last my time had come.

CHAPTER XIII

My third son born Christmas night 1862. No doctor within 20 miles. What women of the South had to endure during the War. Our army has to retreat again. I follow in its wake with my three children. No cow's milk in all the land, but Baby Lee is nourished by the milk of his Black Mammy, my health giving way under stress of excitement and scanty food.

On Christmas night 1862 after my children, tired from their day's playing with their few little Christmas gifts were in bed and asleep, I wrote a letter to their dear father telling him how happily we were situated at Mrs. Winston's and how our boys could at last have as much bread and milk as they needed. After writing this letter I sat down in my big rocking chair to finish reading Macauley's comment on Moore's *Life of Byron;* I thought Macauley hardly just to Byron; I laid his book down on my lap and sat thinking of the great poet and how he had been so cruelly reviled and exiled from the land of which his genius had shed immortal glory. Outside the rain was coming down in torrents.

And it was at this time and this place that my third child gave notice that it meant at last to make its appearance on the stage of this turbulent world. No Doctor being in the neighborhood, Mrs. Winston called in an old negro woman who lived on the place. Mrs. Winston said that Aunt Tabby had had considerable experience and that there was no need to be afraid. And the event proved this to be true. Aunt Tabby lifted my two sleeping boys out of my bed and laid them a pallet on the floor where they slept on, unaware of the event about to take place.

Aunt Tabby was coal black, strong and self possessed; I think she knew as much as the average country doctor. At any rate, that night at eleven o'clock she laid by my side the new arrival and said to me:

"Now, Honey, you go ter sleep and rest yo'self. I'm plum wore out myself an' I must go home an' rest myself."

In vain I pleaded with Aunt Tabby to remain with me until morning. She said: "Don't you worry, Chile. You doan need me no mo' I've dun fixed everything handy. Here's de kindlin' wood to make de fire burn and here's a kettle ef yo' needs some hot water. I neber stays wid a lady after I'se got her baby born. Der aint no need ter.'

So off she went after I paid her the enormous fee of five dollars for her services--a country doctor would have charged twenty five dollars and would have done no better, if so well. After Aunt Tabby was gone I surveyed the new born baby and he seemed to me the loveliest thing I had ever seen. His head was not bald as are most new babies; it was covered all over with nice, short brown hair. His face was pink not red like some babies. I could not see the color of his eyes but I knew they were all that eyes ought to be, for he blinked and shut them tight when I held a candle before them. He had wide nostrils and a rather flat nose, but I was quite certain its bridge would rise in time and make his nose of Grecian beauty and symmetry. He had the sweetest little feet and, although only three hours old, he could kick them about and wiggle his toes as well as any child of six months old.

As I realized what a lovely little thing this child was I wondered how any woman could ever say she preferred to be a man. No man can form the faintest idea of the rapture a mother feels when the long looked for little one is placed by her side and she finds that it is all right from its head to its heels. While waiting for the little one's arrival I think every woman must have a fear, unspoken but ever in her mind, that her child may be malformed, as are so many other mother's children.

That Christmas night, the first night of my third son's life, I had to get up three times to kindle the fire and warm the water--it was bitter cold and I feared my new baby would suffer if I did not keep the room warm. Early next morning I was awakened by my oldest boy Avery crying:

"Mama, Mama, why did you take us out of your bed and put us on the floor?"

"Because last night Santa Claus brought you a little baby brother," I said. I laid him down by my side and I put you on the floor because I was afraid you two big boys might hurt him."

"Oh, let me see him!" cried little Avery jumping up and running to my bedside.

I turned down the cover and showed the pink face of the new baby. My big boy--from now on, though still quite small, Avery and Rivers seemed to me big in comparison with the new arrival--gazed with wonder and amaze at his baby brother, then he ran back to the pallet on the floor and awaked Rivers.

"Come quick!" he cried, as if he feared the baby might disappear and a moment's delay would make it too late to see him. "Come, Rivers, and see the baby Santa Claus brought us."

Little Rivers sprang to his feet and ran to my bed side and he and Avery stood for a full minute staring at the baby without uttering a word. Then they both began asking questions together.

Did Santa Claus bring him down the chimney? What kept the baby from getting black in the chimney? Did Santa Claus tote him in his pocket? Did the new baby have feet? A tongue? Could he talk? I had no rest until I gave my boys ocular proof of the new baby's possessions. I told them he had a tongue but that he was too little to stick it out for them to see.

When satisfied on all these points they wanted to nurse the baby, to rock him in my rocking chair. I informed them that new babies never liked to be rocked, that all they liked to do was to sleep and eat. So at last my two big boys went off, washed their faces, put their clothes on and went for their breakfast. While waiting for my breakfast to be brought to me I wrote a letter to Minor, knowing how glad he would be to hear he had a third son and that I was feeling so well and strong. While writing this letter I heard an odd gurgling noise by my side and, looking around, I saw the face of the baby almost purple as if choking to death; beside him was Rivers with a piece of sorghum candy in his hand.

"He's et one piece," said Rivers triumphantly, "an I'm givin' him another! "

You may imagine, my dear children, how quickly I thrust my finger down the baby's throat and pulled out the piece of candy which Rivers had given him. It was almost as long and as large as my little finger and would have killed the baby had I not dislodged it so quickly. I told Rivers candy was dangerous for babies, that it would choke them to death; he promised me never to give his baby brother any more, nevertheless from that time on I kept a sharp watch to see that my baby was not put in danger again.

In my letter to Minor I asked how he would like to name our third son Lee, after our great General in Virginia. That same night Minor wrote me a letter; our letters crossed. In Minor's letter to me he said "Should our third child be a boy, how would you like to name him after General Lee whose genius is doing so much to defend our Southland from Yankee invasion?" From the moment I read Minor's letter our baby was named Lee Meriwether and I, his mother, testify now after nearly fifty-four years that he has ever been a good son and proved himself worthy of the great name he bears. He is the only son I have left; both his older brothers died some years ago. They grew to manhood; one, Rivers, married and left two lovely daughters. But in the prime of their manhood they were taken from me and but for that arrival in Columbus on Christmas night 1862 I would now in my old age be childless and alone. It seemed cruel to me to lose my dear sons Avery and Rivers while they were in the pride and prime of splendid young manhood; when cruel death snatched them from me I thought Fate most unkind to me. But I am thankful my son Lee has been spared to me; nothing can be more desolate than old age with no children to comfort and care for you. My son Lee is a good boy; he is a brainy man; it is my hope that I may not outlive him as I have outlived my other sons.

As an instance that General Lee's namesake had even when young a high sense of honor, worthy of Gen. Lee himself, I will tell you what he said just after the war when he was about five years old. My rich old Uncle from Chicago, Mr. McNeil, was visiting us in Memphis when little Lee came into the parlor where Minor was talking to our guest, I said:

"Lee, go in and shake hands with Mr. McNeil."

The child advanced into the room and gazed intently at my uncle but instead of speaking to him and shaking hands with him Lee put both hands behind his back.

"Why don't you shake hands with Mr. McNeil?" asked his father.

"I won't shake hands with a man who steals," replied the boy sturdily.

"What do you mean?" exclaimed Minor, thunderstruck at the child's words. "Why do you think Mr. McNeil steals?"

"Because you told me so!" was Lee's astounding answer. Minor was dismayed; he did not know Mr. McNeil intimately; he realized how natural it would be for my uncle to believe that we had said unpleasant things about him and that our boy had heard us say them.

"What do you mean?" demanded Minor. "Why do you say I told you such a thing?"

"Because you did," insisted the boy stoutly.

It was summer, nevertheless it seemed cool enough in that room to make snow balls; my uncle sat silent, but we had little doubt as to the nature of his thoughts. His face looked stern and grave. Minor knew Lee must be made to explain then and there if my uncle was ever to be convinced of our guiltlessness in the matter. He took the child upon his knees and questioned him kindly but insistently and finally Lee made the mystery clear to us.

"Why father," he said, "don't you know you told me he steals your morning paper? You said the Mackerels take your paper from the front door".

Our morning newspaper had been missing on a number of mornings and Minor had told Lee that the "little street mackerels" were responsible--they would steal our paper in order to sell it. "Mackerels" was the name given by the police to bad boys who played such dishonest tricks and Lee confused the name "McNeil" with the word "Mackerel. When the matter was thus cleared up Minor said: "Now go to Mr. McNeil and beg his pardon and shake hands with him like a little gentleman; You called him a bad name and you must ask him to forgive you."

Lee did as he was told and of course my uncle freely forgave him. But I do not believe he ever would have forgiven Minor and me had not Lee's attitude been explained so quickly, and in his presence so that he knew it was impossible for the child to be "coached" into what he should say.

We remained at Mrs. Winston's until baby Lee was five months old; then Henry came to Columbus to drive me to Tuscaloosa, Ala., where my sister, Mrs. Lamb, and her family were staying; with Mrs. Lamb were Rose, Henry's wife, and their son "Booby." By this time baby Lee was so fat and fidgity that my arms ached when I carried him about. I put a pillow in an old champagne basket and laid Lee in it, then set the basket in the foot of the Rockaway and started off for Tuscaloosa. My two big boys were as happy as birds, the weather was divine (it was spring) the sun shone bright and no more did Rivers ask me that unanswerable question: "Mama, when will we git a house we can h-a-v-e?" Henry talked and joked with them all day. Baby Lee's back broke out with the heat and became as red as red flannel. Everytime we came to a creek Henry took the baby and plunged him in the water to cool him and teach him to swim. Henry stoutly maintained that my baby struck out his fat arms and legs in an effort to swim and that he *would* swim if only I let him give him enough lessens.

We arrived at Tuscaloosa without mishap and as we drove through its streets I thought it a lovely town. The streets were wide and there were rows of fine trees on each side of the street and also down the center; it was like driving through a nice, shady forest.

But even in that retired and lovely spot the Monster War had done its evil work. We could find no hotel, no boarding house to shelter us. Everywhere we were met with the excuse that they had no food and that the negroes were too demoralized to do any work. Every day negroes were leaving in batches in search of the Yankee army, which always welcomed them, gave them rations and required no work of them. No wonder that under such circumstances the towns in the South were denuded of their negroes. It was not that the negroes *wanted* to leave their former white masters, it was because they were hungry! Negroes cannot stand hunger as well as white men; our Southern soldiers cheerfully subsisted on the meagerest sort of rations, corn bread and a chunk of fat bacon--and finally they did not have even that. In the last year of the War our soldiers often went for weeks with no food except chunks of corn bread, and sometimes with only a handful of parched corn. When things came to that pass the white Masters would urge their negroes to run off to the Yankee army--it left more food for the white men and women.

Although we could find no place to board in Tuscaloosa the citizens there were kind to me; they did not leave us out on the street; they put me in a little rickety, "tumble-down" house which seemed as if the wind might blow it away any day. They told me that in all Tuscaloosa not one piece of furniture was to be had for love or money, and not a pan, not a skillet, not a single household article! But they said the citizens would contribute such things as they could spare. And they did. One lady gave me a cotton mattress. Another gave me a pillow, another a table; five ladies gave a chair apiece, and one gave me an iron pot. As to plates, cups and saucers, such things had been smashed up long ago, but a mile out of town was a jug factory and there I had made some brown earthenware cups and plates. The first time my "big" little boys put one of these course jug-ware cups to their lips they complained that it scratched them; that jug-ware was rough enough to hurt any lips. I pacified my boys by telling them that their "soger" papa was glad to get a jug cup, that the soldiers used nothing else and that if they were good enough for the soldiers they must be good enough for us.

The people of Tuscaloosa treated my sister, Mrs. Lamb, just as they treated me--gave her a little house to live in and loaned her household articles just as they loaned them to me. With a borrowed saw and hammer Henry made a bed-stead out of the planks of a fence. While cleaning up our little house, Rose made a discovery that dismayed me: the cracks in our walls were infested with bed bugs! Of all things I loathed bed bugs! How were we to escape the disgusting things? They would torment my boys and baby to death. I felt worried, but Rose took a more cheerful view.

"Don't worry, Miss Betty," she said. "I knows how to manage bed bugs. Just you wait and see!"

She went to a neighbor's and got a pot of home made soap; then she took a knife and plastered over every crack with soft soap. Rose said not only would the soap kill the bugs if they touched it, but it would pen them up and starve them to death. Her plan proved splendidly successful; not one bug dropped from the ceiling, not one escaped from the walls. My three little ones slept soundly and so did I.

A few days after we got settled in Tuscaloosa a kind neighbor took compassion on baby Lee's tender lips and presented him with a white china cup. For a while I was able to buy a quart of milk each day; I gave the biggest share to baby Lee (his mother's milk was fast failing). I could not eat enough corn meal hoe cakes and pea soup to keep up my milk. The Confederate Government gave to each soldier's wife or widow one bushel of corn on the cob every day; this was shelled and sent to the mill to be ground into corn meal; in addition to this we had field peas which we boiled and made into soup. After a while my daily quart of milk was reduced to a pint and finally I could not buy any milk at all, which worried me; my baby could hardly live on corn cakes and pea soup. Again did Rose speak up to cheer me.

"Just wait, Miss Betty," she said. "My baby is coming soon. When he comes your baby can have half of my milk. I'll have enough for two."

This promise was faithfully kept. Rose's baby was a pretty brown skinned little girl and it was a sight to see that dusky mother nursing her own baby at one breast while my white baby tugged at the other! Rose seemed to love my baby fully as much as she loved her own. And my Lee came to love his Black Mammy as if she were his second mother. That brown skinned daughter of Rose's is still living in Memphis, I saw her the last time I visited my old home city. She is an expert pastry and cake cook and does a profitable business, providing the refreshments at important social affairs. She called to see me and baked a cake for me and asked about my Lee who shared with her her mother's milk in Tuscaloosa in the summer of 1863. This daughter of Rose married a worthy colored man and is now named Alice Meriwether Owens. Her mother, our faithful Rose, died in the cholera epidemic of 1867. So little did I then know of that dreadful disease, I allowed Lee (then only four and a half years old) to go to see his Black Mammy during her illness and after her death; Lee tells me that Rose was the first dead person he ever saw--he loved Rose and grieved for a long time after he saw her that day lying cold and still in death!

But to return to Tuscaloosa. Shortly after we arrived there an epidemic of whooping cough broke out and my three boys had it, also Rose's baby, Alice, which came near strangling everytime it coughed. Rose would run to me saying her baby was about to choke to death; then I would thrust my finger down the child's throat and remove the phlegm. I could not induce Rose to put her finger down her baby's throat and save its life; she declared her finger was too big.

In the very height of this whooping cough epidemic Minor and Henry rode up to our little house on a three days furlough. Rose was at our front gate with Baby Lee in her arms. This was the first time Minor and Henry had come to see their new babies, consequently Rose naturally expected them to make a great ado over them; Rose thought of course Minor would stop at the gate and take his new baby (five months old) in his arms and "make over" it. Instead of which, as Rose indignantly reported to me, Minor gave the baby only a careless glance and said, "I hope he'll grow up to be better looking. Then he rushed into the house to see our other boys and their mother! I have often heard men say that all babies look alike to them--which only shows how blind a man can be! Every mother knows that *her* baby is totally unlike any other baby in the world. On this baby subject women have a clearer vision than men and I told Minor he needed glasses if he could not see that baby Lee was perfectly beautiful.

Minor's furlough allowed him to stay only three days and they were three rapturous days for our two big boys and for their father. But poor Henry had trouble every night of those three days, for his little Alice kept him busy all night nursing her and trying to save her life. It was Henry who walked the floor with Alice and who would run to me begging me to save her from choking to death; now that Henry was there Rose calmly went to sleep, leaving her husband to care for her baby.

Minor was not riding his old horse; he had a fine charger that he had captured on the battle field; this horse had a flesh wound in his haunch. Henry had led the horse off the battle field and dressed the wound and it was almost healed when I saw it. The horse seemed to have almost human intelligence; he seemed very grateful for the kind treatment he received and would follow Minor about the yard and rub his nose on Minor's shoulder as if wanting to caress him. At the same time Arab (that was the horse's name) had a fierce temper. I was always afraid to go near his mouth. Once I saw a gentle cow enter the lot where Arab was grazing; the stallion resented the intrusion by seizing the intruder by the nap of her neck and literally swinging her around and then dropping her on her feet. The cow was not much hurt, but she was badly frightened and as soon as Arab let her down on her feet she ran away as fast as her legs could take her. Before the three days furlough expired Minor became better acquainted with his third boy and admitted that he was a fine child; I could see, however, that in his secret heart he still believed baby Lee was not good looking, and I resolved to buy Minor a pair of strong glasses the first chance I had. Just before leaving, while Henry on his horse and Arab were waiting for him at the gate, Minor took little Rivers on his knees while Avery stood close by, his arms around his father's neck, then with a serious face and tearful eyes Minor said:

"I want my little boys to listen carefully to what I am about to say. Promise me you will, and that you will remember every word."

"We promise, Big Soger Papa," answered Rivers and Avery together.

"Well boys, I'm going off to the war. I may be killed by the Yankees. If I am, I want you to promise not to let your mother marry again. A step father would mistreat my little darlings."

"What would a step father do to us?" inquired Avery gravely.

"He would certainly be less kind and loving to you than your own father; he might beat you. He would never let you get in bed with your mother and hug and kiss her. He would push you out of the room and make you bring in wood and make fires."

I was intently watching this little scene. Minor had asked me to promise not to marry again, should he be killed in battle; I had refused to promise. I told him I did not *think* I would ever care to marry again, but I would not bind myself by a promise.

As he finished cataloging the cruel things which a step father would do, little Rivers spoke up fiercely.

"Mama shall marry again! I want her to marry!"

Minor was astonished. "Why do you say that?" he demanded. "Why do you want your sweet Mama to marry again?"

"Because I want to devil that old step father to death!"

This answer made Minor laugh, and I made his humor still better when he kissed me goodbye by whispering in his ear that I loved him better than I could possibly love any other man in all the world and that I knew I would never care to marry again.

And now while I am writing these *Recollections* more than half a century after that little scene in Tuscaloosa I wish to say that in all of the nearly sixty years we lived together my dear husband was as good and true to me as he was when I was a bride with youth and had, as many people said, beauty to commend me. I was glad the good God brought him through those years of war and spared him to me until we both were more than four score years old.

CHAPTER XIV

War prices in 1863. My husband not using tobacco, I trade his army tobacco allowance for corn and bacon. I steal corn from Dr. Drisch after he refused to sell me any. This brings me a friend as well as food.

Shortly after we got settled in Tuscaloosa it became apparent that my little Rockaway needed an overhauling; the wheelwright who examined it said it would soon fall to pieces if not repaired. "How much will it cost?" I asked. The man said for fifty dollars he would make it as strong as ever. My purse was nearly empty and Minor told me it was often months and months before his modest Colonel's salary was paid him; he, knowing the condition of our Government, never asked for his pay; when it was sent to him, well and good. When pay day came but no pay--well, that was not so good, but Minor gritted his teeth and determined to get his little family through the War somehow, just how he did not know; but he never gave up hope and, considering the frightful situation we as well as our country were in, I think it marvelous how my brave husband was able to be so hopeful and cheerful.

When the wheelwright told me it would cost fifty dollars to fix my rickety old Rockaway I feared it was not destined to be fixed. And then I bethought me of the ancient times before the days of money when people filled their wants by bartering away the things they did not want, or at any rate what they did not absolutely need, for the things they were obliged to have. Gen. Sherman had not given me time to buy what I most needed; he had commanded me not to stand on the order of my going, but to go at once! And so instead of being filled with the useful articles which I would have procured had I been allowed even a single day in Memphis to do shopping, my trunk contained a lot of fine things which were of little use to a poor refugee flying from pillar to post before the advancing Yankee army. One of the things in my trunk was a sky blue silk gown which was as fresh and pretty as when delivered to me by my dress maker in Memphis. The wheelwright had a young daughter; to her went I with that sky blue gown and it proved the wheelwright's undoing--at least in so far as his fifty dollars was concerned. For his daughter was enchanted with my sky blue gown; she simply had to have it! And so Mr. Wheelwright agreed to fix my Rockaway and take the sky blue gown in payment.

The officers of the Confederate army were allowed by the Government a certain quantity of tobacco every month. My husband did not use tobacco in any shape or form, so every month he sent me his tobacco allowance and I traded it to the farmers about Tuscaloosa for eggs, butter, milk and the like. Those farmers were as eager to get Minor's tobacco as I was to get their vegetables.

One morning our army Commissary gave out the joyful news that he would that day give to each soldier's wife and widow five pounds of smoked bacon. We had not had a taste of meat of any sort for three months and after living so long on corn bread and pea soup that bacon certainly did taste good. I laid my five pounds on our kitchen table before Rose's admiring eyes; she gazed at it so long that I began to fear she saw defects in it; worms or bugs.

"What is the matter with it?" I asked. "Is it bad?"

"Bad?" repeated Rose, showing her white teeth. "Laws, Miss Betty, it's jes too good to eat. I'se studyin' how to make dis meat las' till we gits back ter Memphis."

Then Rose took out of a drawer our table knife (we had only one knife) and said:

"I'se gwine cut two thin slices from dis nice fat end an' I'll fry dem two slices in de skillet 'en give our chilluns de gravy to sop deir bread in. Den I'll cut dem slices inter little square pieces 'en give yo' two big boys an' my boy-- a piece. Dat'll leave a piece for you an' one for me. Oh, Miss Betty; won't dat be a gran' dinner?" I said it would be a very grand dinner compared to what we had been having, and Rose continued: "Den termorrow we won't gib our chilluns no bacon gravy for deir dinner. Tomorrow we'll make 'em eat tobacco eggs (eggs paid for with Minor's tobacco). In dis way, Miss Betty, we kin make dis bacon las' mos' till we git back ter Memphis."

After our "Grand" dinner I got my sister's little boy Sidney to drive me and all the four of our boys (my three and Rose's one) to see our Army Commissary, and I said to him:

"I've got these four boys to feed; can't you give me another piece of meat? It seems to me, with such a lot of children as this, I ought to get two portions."

The officer was kind and sympathetic and said he certainly would give me another portion if he had it, but unfortunately there was not another pound of bacon in his store house; he said that just as soon as he got more bacon he would send me some. Then we started back to our little house. As Adrienne was slowly ambling along Tuscaloosa's main street we heard a strong voice shout:

"Say, Boys, there's Meriwether's mule!"

The next minute half a dozen young men rode up and surrounded my Rockaway. They were from Memphis where they had often seen Adrienne taking me about the city, and they were glad to see me and I was glad to see them. They belonged to Forest's cavalry and after chatting with me a few minutes one of them asked if I could tell them where they could get a bite to eat.

"We're 'most starving, truly we are," said one of those young cavalrymen; he was hardly more than a boy, only eighteen, and he really did look gaunt and thin. What was I to say? There was no restaurant in Tuscaloosa; there was no shop or grocery where meat could be bought. But there were five pounds of bacon in my little house.

When I went into my kitchen, after leaving those six cavalrymen out on the porch, and told Rose to cook that bacon and such of the "Tobacco" eggs as we had left, the poor woman almost fainted. "Cook dat lubly bacon?" she cried.

"Yes," I said. "Fry it, fry it with the eggs and make some hoe cakes."

"For de lub of Heaben, Miss Betty, ef we cooks all dat ar bacon what we gwine lib on?"

"Haven't we lived all this time on corn bread and pea soup?" I demanded.

"Yes, Miss Betty, but--"

"No 'Buts,' Rose," I interrupted. "We have lived on corn bread and pea soup and we can continue to live on it--though the Commissary promised me today another five pounds of bacon. It will be here soon, but even if it doesn't come we can't refuse those brave soldiers a mouthful of food."

Once at the work, Rose became cheerful; her disposition was naturally happy. Through her smiles her white teeth gleamed; she buzzed about that kitchen, fanned the fire to a blaze, broke the eggs into the skillet and very soon those six calvarymen were having the best meal they had eaten since the war began. It did Rose's heart as well as mine good to see those brave fellows eat that bacon; they needed it more than we did. If any of those six men are yet alive, even though they be crippled and bald--or as grey haired as I now am--if I could see them I would feel like throwing my old arms about them and kissing them as if they were my own sons. The oldest of the six was under twenty, therefore some fifteen or eighteen years younger than I--but even so, it is probable not one of the six is now alive in this year of 1916. Although if living they would be only some seventy odd years old, even seventy is beyond the average of human life and so it is that I can no longer count on seeing the friends of my youth and middle age.

As time passed it became more and more difficult to get food for my children. Nobody wanted Confederate money and I had traded off all the fine things I had brought from Memphis. My sister, Mrs. Lamb, had a tin can containing about eighty dollars in gold and forty dollars in silver. She had brought this can all the way from Memphis and at each place where she made any prolonged stay she would bury that tin can so as to keep it from being taken by the Yankees, in case they made a sudden raid on the place where she was staying. To this day I see before me the picture of my sister, on arriving at a new stopping place, going out into the yard and telling one of the negroes to dig a post hole. "I want to put a post here," my sister would say. Then, when the hole was dug she would say: "Oh, I don't want it here; I would rather put my post over there." Another hole would be dug in another part of the yard and there my sister would stick a post; but in the middle of the night she would get up, go out into the yard and bury her precious tin can in the first hole. And there it would stay until the advancing Yankee army compelled her to "pull up stakes" and move further south in Dixie Land. In this way Mrs. Lamb had managed to keep that can of money since the beginning of the war; I thought if the worst came to the worst I could borrow some of the contents of that can.

"I'll let you have it, sister," said Mrs. Lamb, "that is, when you simply must have it. But don't ask me until there is no other way. Spence (Spence was her husband) told me to keep this money as a very last resort."

Although many times it seemed as if the time had come when I must go to my sister for some of that money, it did not quite come--which later on we both regretted. For when the war ended and Mrs. Lamb was back in Memphis one of the first things she did was to get into a spring wagon, that can under the seat, and set forth for the bank with the purpose of buying greenbacks with her gold and silver. A gold or silver dollar was then worth about two greenback dollars. All the way to the bank my sister was turning over in her mind the things she would buy with all that paper money. Alas! On arriving at the bank and looking under the wagon seat that tin can was not there. It had vanished, vanished utterly! How it vanished, when, whither it had flown--Mrs. Lamb did not know. Nor does she know to this day; only recently, in March 1916, when visited by my son in Memphis she told him the mystery of that tin can still puzzles her. Even after all these years, more than half a century, it vexes my sister to think how she safely carried that old tin can through four years of war only to lose it between her home and the bank in Memphis in 1865!

I wanted my three boys to grow up to be tall, strong men and I feared a long continued diet of corn hoe-cakes and pea soup, with no milk, eggs, fruit or the like, might dwarf my boys. So far, however, they seemed to thrive; they were large for their age and were sturdy and well. They lived in the open air night as well as day, for gales of wind blew through our rickety little frame house. My boys never came into the house to escape rain; they went bare footed and bare legged, since they had no shoes and they had outgrown their clothes so that the ends of their trousers did not reach below their knees.

On one side of our house were several other little frame shanties occupied by poor refugees; on the other side of us was a forest of pine trees under whose branches Adrienne nibbled at such scant blades of grass as she could find. Not far away was a corn field. I watched the growth of the corn in that field determined when the ears were ready to be boiled or roasted that I would see the owner and buy from him enough corn to appease the appetites of my little boys. I was told the owner was a rich old man who lived half a mile away; I could see his home from our porch. It was a large, white mansion approached by a long avenue lined on both sides with tall trees. Dr. Drisch was the name of this rich old man; he had but one child, a daughter who was insane and was kept on the third floor of the house, attended by negro nurses.

When at last that corn was ripe enough to eat, my sister's young son, Sidney Lamb, drove me in my Rockaway up that shaded avenue to the Drisch mansion. My two "big" little boys were with me. When we reached the end of the long, tree shaded avenue Sidney remained in the Rockaway to keep Adrienne from wandering about, while my two boys and I opened the gate and went up to the door of the big imposing white mansion. I rang the bell. No one answered. I rang again, still all was silent. I began to fear that the insane daughter had escaped and that all the household was out hunting for her. However, I rang once more, this time more clamorously than ever, and presently I heard footsteps within and the door opened slowly some six or eight inches and the eyes of a negro girl peered out at me in a scared sort of way.

"Is Dr. Drisch at home?" I asked.

"No--no--mum," stammered the girl, looking as frightened as if I had thrust a pistol in her face. Her hand still clutched the door knob and she still held the door open a bare six or eight inches.

"Open that door and let me in," I commanded. "I won't hurt you. Open the door!"

As I spoke I pushed the door open and entered a wide, spacious hall. My little boys followed close at my heels. The negro girl stared at us as if we were ogres. Had I thrust three pistols in her face and threatened to fire them all she would not have turned more ashen. I said to the trembling negress: "Show us into a room where we can sit down and wait for Dr. Drisch." The girl only stared at me. "Go to Mrs. Drisch," I said sternly. "Tell her a lady wishes to see her at once."

The negress still stared at us as she sidled along close to the wall toward the door in the rear. Realizing that she had no intention of showing me into a sitting room, I entered the first door to my right and, seeing a sofa in that room, I placed my boys on it and bade them make no noise.

"Is Yankees in this house?" asked little Rivers, evidently thinking that there was no evil, no disagreeable thing which did not owe its origin to Yankees. I told him to keep quiet, that I did not know who was in the house. For half an hour we all sat in dumb silence. The floor was uncarpeted; not even a rug was on it. But there was much dust, and even some dead leaves, from which I judged no broom had been present for a long time. The furniture, too, was covered with dust. A more dismal, depressing room I had never seen. Even my usually alert and noisy boys felt the depression and sat on that sofa as mute as mice.

In the course of half an hour the lady of the Mansion stole in softly, noiselessly, and looked at me in the same scared way as the negro girl had looked; and, like the negro girl, this lady also sidled along the wall of the room instead of walking straight across the floor. All the time she was approaching me she stared at me and at my boys as if we were sort of queer animals. On finally reaching a chair she slowly and gently let herself down into it, all the time staring at me in that scared sort of way. I waited for her to say something but she spoke no word. Then I got up, walked over the dust covered floor and stood before that strange lady of the Mansion.

"Madame," I said, "I am the wife of a Confederate officer. These little boys you see here are mine. They need food. I wish to buy some of the corn I see growing in your fields." The lady of the Mansion only continued to stare at me. Not a word did she reply. Was *she* insane, as well as her daughter? But, sane or insane, I was determined to have an answer. I repeated my wish to get some of her corn, and at last the lady spoke.

"Dr.--Dr.--Drisch is the Master," she stammered.

"Is Dr. Drisch at home?"

"I--I--don't know," stammered the lady.

At that moment, happening to glance out of the window I saw two men on horse back riding up the avenue to the house. One of the men was white, the other was black. "Is that Dr. Drisch?" I asked. The lady of the Mansion nodded her scared head, whereupon I went to the sofa, got my boys and hurried out of the house just in time to face the master of the house as he dismounted from his horse. I stated the purpose of my call; he eyed me critically, then said harshly:

"No, Madam, I will not allow my corn to be pulled from my field. That corn is to feed my negroes this winter. If I allow corn to be pulled now it won't be a week before my negroes will strip the field."

With this Dr. Drisch turned away and started to enter his house as if the whole matter was settled. But I did not feel that way. I followed him to the door and said:

"Wait a moment. The father of these boys is in the army; he cannot now provide food for his family; do you not feel it is your duty to keep a soldier's children from starving?"

"I have answered your question," returned Dr. Drisch harshly. "I have nothing more to say. My corn must not be pulled now."

He started again for his door, but again I halted him. "Before you go, Dr. Drisch," I said, "I give you fair warning that I mean to go into your corn field and pull enough corn to feed my children. Good morning, sir."

And I turned on my heel and started for my Rockaway. As I turned I heard the man say: "You'd better not go into my corn field!" But I did not give him the satisfaction of knowing that I heard him, nor did I mean to pay any heed to his command. "Did he give you any corn, Aunt Betty?" asked my nephew, Sidney Lamb, as we drove away, I told him of my reception by Dr. Drisch. "The stingy old miser!" was Sidney's comment. "I wouldn't have his old corn anyway."

"But I shall have it," I replied. And on emerging from the shady tree-lined avenue I ordered Sidney to drive up close to the fence, then jump over into the field and pull a lot of corn.

"Oh, Aunt Betty, that would be stealing!" said my nephew. "I can't steal." Sidney was a very straightforward, conscientious lad. I was not so conscientious.

"Very well," I said, "I will do the stealing."

Thereupon I climbed over that rail fence, pulled several dozen ears of corn, threw them over the fence, then climbed back into the road and put the corn on the floor of my Rockaway, and was about to drive off when I saw a negro galloping down the Avenue toward us; I waited to see what he wanted. When he got to us he stammered out that his Master had sent him to say we'd better not pull his corn, that he would come right after us if we didn't stop. This made me smile. "What will he do when he comes after us?" I asked.

"I doan know, Miss," said the negro. "Nobody doan know what Marse Drisch gwine do. I only know you mustn't pull his corn, kase he doan allow it."

"Well, it can't be helped today," I answered. "Tell him I had it pulled before you got to me. And here, Sambo," I continued, taking two Confederate paper dollars out of my pocket. "Give your master this money. I don't want to steal his corn. This will more than pay for the few ears I have taken."

The negro took the money and I drove on back home. I gave my sister half of my corn and she and her boys had a feast, too. In a couple of days, however, the corn was all gone and we were getting hungry again and I decided to visit the amiable Dr. Drisch's field again. But just as we were about to set forth on this second foray a wagon drove up to our house and an old grey haired man spoke to me.

"Are you a Refugee?" he asked. I told him I was a refugee, that Gen. Sherman had banished me from my home in Memphis and that I had taken refuge among the good people of Tuscaloosa.

"Well," said the friendly little grey haired man, "I am glad to know you. My name is Whitfield. My son is in the army. Is your husband in the army?"

"Yes, he is a Colonel of Engineers. I hope your son will come out of the War safe and sound, as I pray my husband will."

"That is my daily prayer," replied the old man sadly, then he added gravely: "But God's will be done; if it be God's will that my son shall give his life for his country I will bear it."

"Is your son's mother living?" I asked.

"No. And Jim is my only boy." There was a tear in the old man's eye. More than ever did I hate the Monster War! The Monster which was desolating our land and filling so many hearts with anguish. There was silence for a while, then the old man spoke up cheerfully: "Yesterday morning as I was driving by Dr. Drisch's fence I saw inside his field four or five negroes and each one had a gun on his shoulder. It ain't common for negroes to tote guns, so I asked what was up? 'What are you niggers doing with those guns?' They told me their Master had sent them there to keep refugee women from stealing his corn. I was astounded; I could not believe I had heard aright. 'You mean your master put you in that field to shoot *white* women?' I asked. 'Dat's what Marse Drisch tole us ter do ef dat ar refugee woman come to steal corn again,' answered one of the negroes. I told the rascal if he or any other nigger dared shoot a white woman he'd be hung to a tree and filled full of bullets besides."

I laughed at the old man's seriousness; his disgust was so deep, his anger was so genuine that he screwed his face up until it looked very comical to me. "Mr. Whitfield," I said, "I was the refugee woman who stole Dr. Drisch's corn. But after stealing it I paid him for it. I sent him two Confederate dollars. Was not that enough?"

"Enough?" cried the old man. "Drisch is a contemptible, miserly fool. Your husband is in the army helping to drive the Yankees back from his corn field and he refused you a miserable little thing like a sack of corn? My God, I didn't know a man could be so mean! When the Yankees come I hope they will take everything Drisch owns!" Then the old man cried: "Sam!" The negro sitting in the back of his wagon awoke from his doze, sprang out of the wagon and said, "Yes sir, Master, Yes sir! " "Sam," said the old man, "give the lady that basket"!

At this command the wooly headed negro lifted a big basket out of the bottom of the wagon and set it on my porch. In the basket were bunches of beets, turnips, parsnips, onions, potatoes and even some grapes. As I stared dumbly at these good things the old man said to me: "These vegetables and things are for you and your children."

I said: "Mr. Whitfield, you are kind to bring these things to me, but I have not enough money to pay for half of them, no, not for a quarter of them. My husband has not been paid his salary for four months. I am therefore very short of money."

"Short of money?" burst out the old man. "What's that to me? Do you think the world big enough to hold two Dr. Drischs? If your pockets were full of gold you couldn't pay me a cent for these things. It is an honor and a pleasure to me to be allowed to serve the wife of a man who is fighting the Yankees. I've got a little farm three miles from here where these vegetables grow. When I come to town Monday I'll bring you another supply."

Dr. Drisch's meanness never brought a tear to my eye but this unexpected goodness from a total stranger did; I put my arm on that good old man's shoulder and the unbidden tears from my eyes rolled out and down on the back of his old rusty, threadbare coat. And the dear old man's eyes also became a little misty and moist; he drew out an ancient red bandanna handkerchief, blew his nose, wiped his eyes, said, "Goodbye and God bless you," and drove off.

The more we saw of Mr. Whitfield the more we liked him; indeed, we came to love that dear, good old man--he was so kind, so generous to the wives and widows of our soldiers. The Confederacy's cause was a religion with him; for his country he was ready to give his all. He was too old to join the army, but he had sent his son, and we soon learned that his whole life was devoted to doing what lay in his power to help those who were in want because of the Yankee invasion of the South. It is more than fifty years since that summer day when Mr. Whitfield drove up to my shanty in Tuscaloosa and made me cry by his goodness, a goodness quite unexpected after the way Dr. Drisch had treated me; Mr. Whitfield has been dead many, many years. And now that I am in my ninety third year and in the course of Nature must soon cross the river, too, I say to myself:

"If Heaven's gates are ever opened for me I know Mr. Whitfield will be there to welcome me. For surely no man ever deserved God's favor more than the dear old man I knew in Tuscaloosa during the summer of 1863."

House in Columbus, Mississippi, in which Lee Meriwether
was born on Christmas Day, 1862.

CHAPTER XV

I receive $500 for a short story. But soon spend the five hundred. Flour costs $600 a barrel, sugar $30 a pound and a turkey $175. President Jefferson Davis' brother reads my story and comes to see me. Offers to marry me should Minor be killed in battle. Mr. Davis was eighty-four years old. I declined his offer. I trade a $450 pair of satin slippers for fifteen pounds of sugar.

One day in Tuscaloosa when my finances were at their lowest ebb I read in a Southern paper called the *Mississippian* an announcement that five hundred ($500.00) dollars would be paid by the publisher for the best story submitted by a certain date. At the time I saw the announcement the time limit had almost expired, but when I thought of my three children--how almost naked they were, their very flesh showing through holes in their ragged clothing, their growing bodies needing food I was unable to buy them--when I thought of these things I determined to go after that prize and to go after it strong. I began at once to write a story which I entitled *"The Refugee"*; it was founded largely on my own experiences beginning with the day Gen. Sherman drove me out of Memphis, and perhaps this fact, and the deep feeling which such personal experiences enabled me to put into my work, gave the story some merit. At any rate, it won the prize and that five hundred dollars seemed to me like a million. The first thing I bought was some cotton cloth with which to make my boys underwear and night gowns; they had outgrown all their underwear and as for night gowns, such homely garments they had not known since leaving Memphis.

Then I bought a few pounds of flour; as expensive as flour was I decided to let my children know for once the taste of biscuits and white bread. They had come to think hoe-cakes and corn bread were the only breads in the world. In those frightful days of war wheat was so scarce in the South that when white flour was to be had at all it was used only in the hospitals for sick and wounded soldiers. At the time I wrote that prize story flour in Tuscaloosa cost six hundred dollars a barrel and so, as you may know, my dear children, I bought only a very few pounds--just how many I do not now remember; but I do remember that it lasted us only two days and then I was sorry I had bought it, for my two big boys (Baby Lee was too young to say anything) liked the biscuits I made them and clamored for more and could not understand why they had to go back to hoe-cakes and corn bread when there were in the world such good things as white biscuits!

Sugar at that time cost thirty dollars a pound; I bought one pound. A ham cost three hundred dollars; coffee and tea cost so much I did not even think of spending any of my prize money on them. The price of a turkey was one hundred and seventy-five dollars, so I did not buy even a leg or a wing of a turkey. I did buy six pounds of what was called "Middling Meat," meaning that portion of the hog between the ham and the shoulder of the animal; that part is now called "Breakfast Bacon." I mention these petty details because they will without further words make you understand that even with five hundred dollars to spend we indulged in no banquets and bought no fine clothes. But things in this world are relative: compared with the luxuries which in 1916 are at the command even of poor people the modest meals my children and I enjoyed for a week or ten days in the summer of 1863 seem mean indeed. What laborer's wife today would not think herself badly treated if she had only a pound of sugar and six pounds of bacon once a year? But in 1863 even the barest necessities of life were so scarce that during that "Sugar and Bacon" week we felt as if we were indulging in one long feast!

Although my story, measured in purchasing power, brought me a very trifling sum, it brought me a very pleasant visitor. Shortly after the *Mississippian* published my story two mules drawing a carriage stopped at our gate and an old gentleman got out of the carriage and came up on our porch where I was sitting. "You are Mrs. Meriwether?" said the old gentleman with a courtly bow, his hat in his hand. I told him I was. "I imagined as much," continued the old gentleman. "I read *"The Refugee."* It is an excellent story. It is a vivid and a true picture of our times. It ought to live. It will live. The Historian of the future can reconstruct the South of these troubled times by studying your story."

As you may imagine, my children, this eulogy of my story from a strange old gentleman surprised as well as pleased me. I thanked my visitor for his compliments and asked him his name.

"Joe Davis. I, too, am a refugee," said the courtly old gentleman and, taking a seat on the porch, he told me of his experiences. Like most young persons I imagined old persons must necessarily be tiresome; but my visitor proved anything but tiresome. In his long life--he was eighty four years old--he had seen much of the world and he knew how to relate his adventures in an entertaining way. He was a brother of our Confederate President, Jefferson Davis, but, being some thirty years his elder, looked upon him more as a son than a brother. "Jeff is a good boy," he told me. "Nobody knows him better than I. I raised him and if only the world knew him as well as I do it would say nothing but good of him." It sounded odd to hear our President spoken of in this familiar way as a "good boy," but Mr. Joe Davis was thinking of the little lad he had reared, not of the man who, in Gladstone's words, had created a Nation and was now, as that Nation's head, marshalling vast armies to protect the Nation he had made.

During the remainder of our stay in Tuscaloosa not a week passed that Mr. Joe Davis did not call and sit on our porch and talk with me about almost everything under the sun, from the myths of the ancient Greeks to the latest ailment of my

Baby Lee. Mr. Davis owned a large plantation in Mississippi; Yankee cavalry had descended one day on his plantation and, learning that he was the Confederate President's brother, they carried his sick wife out of the house, laid her on the grass under a tree, then set fire to the house and burned it to the ground. Next they burned his barns, cotton gins and fences, then those brave Yankee cavalrymen rode away. Mrs. Davis, old and ill, died that night in one of the negro cabins--killed by the excitement and rough handling to which she had been subjected. The day after his wife's burial Mr. Davis started south with a few of his negroes and at the time of his call at my little home he was living on a farm two miles out of Tuscaloosa.

My novel *"The Refugee"* proved such a success that the proprietors of the *Mississippian* urged me to write another "War" story; I did so, and concerning that second novel I found the following letter in my book of "Old Letters":

Mississippian Office,
Selma, Ala., Dec. 28, 1864.
Mrs. Eliz. A. Meriwether:

Your favor of the 25th is at hand containing proposition relative to *"The Yankee Spy."* We are very anxious to secure the copyright to this book, as it is a sequel to *"The Refugee."* We are willing to give you $800.00 for the copyright; we hope you will be willing to sell the copyright, when we will print at an early date in the Sunday paper. And after we succeed in supplying ourselves with paper, will issue both *"The Refugee"* and the sequel in book form.

If you feel justified in acceding to this proposition we further agree to print one thousand copies of your drama at cost.

We are very respectfully,

COOPER & KENDALL

Alas! Within a hundred days from the receipt of that letter Lee had surrendered at Appomattox and the Southern Confederacy existed no more save in History!!! The *Mississippian,* went up in smoke and I presume my story went up with it. At any rate I never saw it again and--it is probably quite needless to add--neither did I ever see the $800.00. which was hardly a matter for regret, since Confederate money (in which payment for my novel would have been made) became within a few months of Cooper & Kendall's offer worth only a few cents a pound. There were no typewriters or carbon sheets in those days; only one copy of my novel did I write and so when that copy became lost the story was gone forever.

As the winter of 1863-1864 approached the question how properly to clothe my children caused me great anxiety. My boys were in rags and tatters. The sleeves of their jackets came only to their elbows; their legs were naked from the knees down to the tips of their toes. They had outgrown everything. Their shoes had long since been thrown away. The little woolen hats they had on their heads when we left Memphis had been soaked so often by rains and stretched while wet on their heads that they seemed to grow in size as my boys' heads grew, consequently I did not worry about new hats. But new jackets and breeches seemed absolutely necessary. Then, too, Baby Lee was nearly naked. The six little calico slips he possessed the day he was born had been washed so often and he had crawled in them so long over rough, carpetless floors that they were hardly worth keeping even had they been suficiently large--which they no longer were. Lee was now able to stand on his feet and pull himself about the floor while holding to a chair--the calico slips he wore six months before were entirely too small for him. Some new slips simply had to be made for him!

I found a woman who carded, spun and wove a cloth made of cotton with a little wool mixed in. She called it "Linsy-Woolsy" cloth and charged twenty-five dollars a yard for it. At least two yards were needed to make my baby a dress and bitterly did I then regret buying that bacon and sugar. Every dollar of my five hundred dollar prize was gone and it began to look as if my baby would have to go literally naked through the winter when, just in the nick of time, I received from Minor two large twists of tobacco. Both the Linsy woman and her old father were very fond of tobacco and they readily agreed to trade me two yards of "Linsy-Woolsy" for my two twists of tobacco. Thus it was that Baby Lee began the winter of 1863-64 with a short dress to walk in; and soon he was toddling over the house and yard on his own feet, happy as a bird. He was too young to realize the frightfulness of the times in which he then lived. When he reads these pages (he has promised to edit my *Recollections* and so perforce must read them) he will no doubt be interested in learning these details of his childhood in Tuscaloosa. Lee now has a fine mansion of his own with a garage and two automobiles and, though not a rich man, seems to have the comforts and even luxuries of life. I trust he will be wise and prudent and keep what he has. He did not mind the poverty of his early life, for then he knew nothing else; it would be different now. Now that he knows what it is to have the good, even the expensive, things of life, to come and go and travel when he likes, it would go hard with him were he to be reduced to anything like the poverty of his boyhood.

As Christmas of 1863 approached Rose and I were desirous of getting something sweet for Santa Claus to bring our children. We had no sugar; I was unable to pay thirty dollars a pound for it, and I had traded off all the fine things I brought from Memphis except a pair of white satin slippers which I had worn only once, consequently which were as good as new. Rose heard of a lady who had a barrel of brown sugar; this lady had a daughter. Here at any rate was a working basis. To that lady I took my white satin slippers, I dilated upon their beauty; they fitted the daughter to perfection. A white slipper had been the making of Cinderella. These beautiful slippers might possibly attract the eye of another Prince Charming, and they would certainly be very becoming to her daughter and make all the other girls in town wild with envy! The daughter "fell" for this talk and finally the mother asked on what terms I would trade.

"On Peace Terms," said I.

"What are Peace Terms?" queried the lady.

"This is what I mean by Peace Terms," I said. "In Peace times my slippers cost three dollars; in Peace time your sugar cost six and a half cents a pound. You count your sugar at peace prices, I'll count my slippers also at peace prices. That will make my slippers worth a little more than forty five pounds of sugar."

The lady of the sugar barrel thought this proposal one-sided; her sugar was new, my slippers had been worn.

"Yes, but only once," I said. "You can see for yourself that they are as good as new."

"Mebbe, but they ain't worth forty five pounds of sugar," answered the lady.

"I'll take forty pounds," I answered. But she refused to give even thirty pounds, so I took my slippers back home. Now, it happened that next day some of Forest's cavalrymen came to Tuscaloosa and the citizens arranged to give them a dance. On the afternoon of the dance the sugar lady's daughter came to see me and said her mother would give me fifteen pounds of the brown sugar for my slippers. I thought they were worth at least thirty pounds, but Christmas was so close at hand and there seemed no other way to avoid disappointing my three boys (I knew how dearly they loved sweets), accordingly I agreed to accept fifteen pounds of sugar for the slippers and told her I would send for the sugar in the morning.

"But I want to wear the slippers tonight," said the girl.

"That is all right," I replied. "I will trust you. Take the slippers now. Rose will get my sugar tomorrow."

Alas! Next day Rose returned from the sugar lady with the message that she had not authorized her daughter to buy my slippers; Rose held the slippers in her hand, but oh how sadly changed they were! The girl had worn them at the dance; she had stretched them; she had gotten them soiled and dirty.

"Rose," I said, "take the slippers to Mrs. B. and show her what her girl has done to them and say she must give me my fifteen pounds of sugar. No matter what answer she makes, you leave the slippers at her house. Under no circumstances bring them back to me!"

Rose obeyed; in half an hour she returned and told me the sugar lady said I could blacken the slippers with ink and that then they would be as good as ever. And barely had Rose delivered this message when in came the sugar lady's servant and laid my poor, ruined slippers on the table, then without a word walked away. That afternoon Rose took the dirty slippers to the sugar lady, set them on the table before her and asked her please to give her the fifteen pounds of sugar she owed me. The sugar lady returned the slippers by her servant within half an hour. Next morning Rose took them back to the sugar lady and repeated her demand for the fifteen pounds of sugar. Rose said she enjoyed the game and declared she would keep it up until the end of the War and we went back to Memphis. Finally, however, the Sugar Lady surrendered and about five days after the battle began, when Rose returned from her forty fifth visit, it was without the slippers and with the sugar; and we both went to work making sweet things for the childrens' Christmas.

My dear children, I would have forgotten this incident had I not been reminded of it long after the war by my old friend Col. Matt Galloway. He was at my home in Memphis and all of a sudden began to laugh, not gently, but loudly, uproariously! "What on earth is the matter?" I asked. I feared my friend was not quite well. The weather was unusually hot.

"Oh, I am perfectly well," he said. "The heat has not gone to my head. I just happened to think of what some one said to me last week in Tuscaloosa."

"What was said to you?" I asked. "I know Tuscaloosa. I was there during the war."

"I know you were, but I didn't know you were a terrible woman and did terrible things there."

"I deny being a terrible woman, I deny doing terrible things," I said. "What are you driving at, Col. Galloway?"

Then he explained. He had just come from Tuscaloosa and while there he had met the sugar lady.

"On hearing that I was from Memphis," continued my friend, "she asked me if I knew 'that terrible Mrs. Meriwether'? I told her I knew a Mrs. Meriwether, but that she had not seemed 'terrible' to me. 'Well,' said the Tuscaloosa lady, 'she is terrible, the most terrible quarrelsome woman I ever met. She forced, actually forced, me to give her fifteen pounds of brown sugar for a pair of her dirty old slippers with a hole in them--and sugar worth thirty dollars a pound-- four hundred and fifty dollars for a pair of dirty old slippers! Don't you think a woman who would do that is a thief as well as quarrelsome and terrible'? I said it did look pretty bad to *force* a lady to give four hundred and fifty dollars worth of sugar for a pair of dirty slippers, but that I could not believe my Mrs. Meriwether would do such a thing."

"Oh, but I did!" I exclaimed. Then I told Col. Galloway exactly how it happened, and he laughed again.

"Under those circumstances I don't blame you at all," he said. "Still, you must admit you got a good price for second hand slippers--four hundred and fifty dollars worth of sugar!" And Col. Galloway laughed until the tears came to his eyes. I thought if the episode seemed so funny to him that it was worth remembering, so when he finished his call that day in Memphis I went at once to my desk and wrote notes about the "Sugar Lady." I had entirely forgotten the episode until, on looking through my old papers preparatory to writing these *Recollections,* I came across the notes which I wrote the day Col. Galloway called to see me years ago in Memphis. That is why I say the insertion of this episode in these pages is due to a friend's calling to see me years after the episode occurred.

With the help of those fifteen pounds of sugar, Christmas of 1863 passed fairly well for my three boys; they had never been surfeited with toys and cakes and candies as so many boys today are surfeited on Christmas day, consequently a few pounds of home-made candy seemed to my children a rare treat and they talked of it long after every stick of the candy and every piece of the cake was gone. My financial condition grew desperate in the spring of 1864; I hoped for a while that the rents from my Memphis property would be restored to me, but this hope was dashed to earth by a letter that came to me from my friend Mr. Blythe. He wrote me that while in Washington he had interviewed President Lincoln and urged him to revoke Gen. Sherman's order confiscating my property. Mr. Blythe told the President that I was a woman, not a soldier; that I was not fighting the Union armies. Military law might justify the taking of an enemy's property, but what justification was there for taking a woman's property? Lincoln told Mr. Blythe his argument might be sound, conceding the facts to be as stated, but that it was not his province to countermand military orders. That was a matter for the Secretary of War to handle, and he referred Mr. Blythe to Mr. Stanton. Mr. Blythe saw the Secretary of War and stated my case, but Mr. Stanton curtly refused to interfere.

"Gen. Sherman did right," he said frowningly, "it would have been wrong not to confiscate the property of a traitor's wife. To give that property back to the wife is equivalent to giving it back to the traitor himself. Traitors must suffer for their crimes."

Such was the substance of my friend's letter; it was the last time I ever heard from him. He died soon after his trip to Washington--a true friend, a loyal, knightly gentleman! Peace to thy ashes, William Blythe! I, thy young manhood friend, have never forgotten thee! If there be another Life and another world, soon shall I greet thee!

CHAPTER XVI

Frightful hardships in Tuscaloosa. I resolve to steal into Memphis in quest of money and supplies for my suffering babies. How I tricked Old Wick into giving me my gold.

After Mr. Blythe's death it seemed to me someone should go to Memphis to look after our interests there and to pay my taxes; and, Gen. Sherman to the contrary not withstanding, it further seemed to me that I would have to be that one. If I entered the city quietly and remained secluded while there it was likely I would not be molested. But before taking so serious an action I decided to consult my husband.

In Demopolis, a town some forty miles from Tuscaloosa, was quartered the division of our army where Minor then was and thither I drove in my old Rockaway, drawn by the faithful Adrienne. Minor approved my plan and, thinking that the army would remain at Demopolis until I could go to Memphis and return, he wished me to bring my two "big" boys to stay with him and leave Baby Lee with my sister, Mrs. Lamb, and with Rose until I returned to Tuscaloosa. This plan was carried out and words cannot describe the rapture of little Avery and Rivers when they found that they were to he left with their "Big, sweet Sojer papa!" And I think Minor's delight was as great as theirs. He had been in the army some three years and during that time had seen but little of his family--and no more domestic, affectionate father ever lived than my dear husband. Yes, I can truthfully say he was enraptured at the thought of having his two little sons with him at army headquarters in Demopolis.

The railway would take me as far as Grenada, Miss. From that town on to Memphis the rails had been burned and warped into scrap iron by the Yankees so that part of the journey would have to be made "overland"--whether by wagon, horseback or afoot I could not tell until I got to Grenada. On the train from Demopolis to Grenada the cars were crowded with sick and wounded Confederate soldiers who were on their way to home and relatives. Tears filled my eyes when I saw those brave men so thin and worn, dressed in rags. their feet almost bare, yet never one word of complaint coming from their lips! Some of those wounded men were educated, some were what the pampered slaves of rich Southerners scornfully called "Po' white trash!" Trash? These men, poor and half educated though they were, were God's Noblemen! For they, too, had fought heroically in defense of their country. Without a murmur they had borne hunger, fatigue, the ice of winter, the burning heat of summer. And for three long years they had almost daily risked their lives on their country's altar. Is it any wonder that my eyes filled with tears, that my heart was wrung with anguish at sight of those noble men ill, emaciated, suffering from wounds received while battling for our beloved Southland? How I longed to do something for them, to help them! But there was nothing, nothing that I could do save speak to them words of gratitude and sympathy. I told them the time would come when the people of the South would record their deeds on tablets of bronze and on monuments of marble; I said that History would honor them and that posterity, whether we won or lost the war, would ever honor the soldiers of the South as patriots and heroes! Those wounded, crippled, battered men only smiled and pressed my hand; they were as modest as they were brave. But my words were not mere compliments. The world today does honor the men who fought for the South in that dreadful war of the Sixties, honors them as few soldiers have ever been honored or ever deserved to be honored.

I parted from these Confederate veterans at Grenada and started north in a skiff over land which had been submerged by the back waters of the Mississippi. The Yankees had destroyed the levees and thus rendered that whole section of country subject to inundation every time the river rose. Arrived at the northern end of the overflowed section, I was lucky enough to find there a man with a wagon who agreed to drive me as far north as Hernando, some thirty miles from Memphis. Despite my entreaties to take me on beyond Hernando the owner of this wagon refused; he said he dared not go all the way to Memphis because the Yankees had a habit of arresting men who came up from the South; with or without suspicion men who came up from the South were apt to be imprisoned as spies. And men charged with being spies seldom left prison except for the purpose of being stood up against a wall and shot. No, said the wagon owner, he would *not* take me to Memphis for all the gold in Christendom! And so it was with a heavy heart that I bade my driver goodbye on arriving at Hernando and sought my room in the little hotel to rest up for the ordeal before me on the morrow. For I knew thirty miles was a long distance for me to walk. And yet it seemed walking was my only chance.

But next morning when I came down to breakfast in that little Hernando hotel a man arose from the table where he was eating, came over to me and exclaimed: "Well, well, if this isn't a pleasant surprise! Where on earth did you come from? And how did you get here? Is the Colonel here?"

This gentleman was Mr. Sam Walker, an old friend of my husband's. I explained my situation, whereupon he said jovially: "Well, I am in luck! I have a spring wagon here in Hernando and I am going to Memphis just as soon as I finish my breakfast. Can you wait half an hour? "

Half an hour? I would have waited half a month rather than set forth on that thirty mile walk! When I told Mr. Walker this he laughed. "Then everything is settled," he said. "Come to my table and have breakfast with me."

I did so and while we breakfasted, and later while in the wagon on the way to Memphis, Mr. Walker described the situation in Memphis and advised me how to avoid offending the military rulers of the city. He said all the large buildings, private as well as public, had been converted into hospitals and were crowded with Yankee wounded soldiers. Yankees were everywhere in the city, on the streets, in the hotels, in the shops, and I must be careful of what I did and said.

"Ask no questions about the war," cautioned Mr. Walker. "Make no comment on any battles. The city is full of spies who would be glad to trump up a charge against you. The Irving Block is crowded to suffocation with prisoners charged with one thing or another, with corresponding with rebels, with talking treason, with showing dislike for Yankees--"

"For showing dislike of Yankees?" I interrupted. "Do you mean they lock people up for disliking Yankees?"

"I said for *showing* dislike," laughed Mr. Walker. "Dislike them all you please, Mrs. Meriwether. I know you can't help disliking them, but if you value your freedom you will take care not to *show* your dislike."

The thought of being locked up in the Irving Block and thus unable to get back to my three little children so affrighted me that I assured Mr. Walker my lips should be tightly sealed. I would even bottle up my thoughts lest some of the Yankees might be mind readers and, reading the scorn I felt for our Northern invaders, betray me to our military masters and cause me to be thrown into the dreaded Irving Block!!

The road to Memphis was desolate and dreary; the farm houses on either side of the road were either in ashes or abandoned by their owners. We saw no animals on the way, not a horse or cow or sheep--silence reigned everywhere! Six miles out from Memphis we saw two cavalrymen in blue, on their horses, one on each side of the road. The two horses were standing still and their riders, too, were motionless; they spoke no word until we had approached within a dozen yards. Then one of them called out: "Seen any Rebs on the way up?" Mr. Walker calmly replied: "We have not seen a single white man this side of Hernando."

From the voice and accent of that cavalryman I knew him to be a German. Mr. Walker told me Memphis was full of German and negro soldiers; negroes and Germans seemed to accept each other on a basis of perfect equality. No other white soldier, not even the men from New England, accepted the negroes as their social equals. But the Germans did. It was a common sight during the War to see Germans fraternizing in a sociable way with their black brothers.

We entered Memphis in the afternoon and Mr. Walker drove me to the home of my friends, the Laniers; it was from their house that I had set forth more than a year before when ordered by Gen. Sherman to leave the city and I knew they would welcome me back and take care of me during the few days I should have to remain. I was not mistaken--the Laniers gave me an affectionate welcome and until late that night we talked over the thousand things that had happened since I had been under their roof in December 1862. Next morning Mrs. Lanier drove me in her carriage to the Union & Planter's Bank in which I had left my box of gold. Arrived at the Bank, Mr. Fred Smith, the Cashier, handed me the box but not the key. "I think," said he, "that since Mr. Blythe's death the key has been lost. At any rate it is not here in the Bank."

Accordingly Mrs. Lanier then drove me to a locksmith who without much trouble succeeded in opening the box; then we returned to the Lanier home and there examined the box's contents. I had left thirteen hundred dollars in gold in the box; when we examined that box on our return to the Lanier home it contained only eight hundred dollars in gold. A memorandum in my dear friend Mr. Blythe's handwriting accounted for the missing five hundred dollars--he had paid my taxes and he had also sent one hundred dollars to my brother Tom who was a prisoner on Johnson's Island; the balance of the vanished five hundred dollars was covered by two notes, one note of two hundred dollars executed by a Mr. K., a northern man but long a prominent resident of Memphis, and another note of sixty dollars executed by another prominent Memphian, Mr. James Wickersham. Both were demand notes, the makers promising to pay Mrs. Minor Meriwether on demand *in gold!*

On that same afternoon Mr. Lanier accompanied me to Mr. K.'s office (I do not give his name--he married a Southern woman and some of their children are still living in Memphis) to collect my two hundred dollar note. On the way Mr. Lanier told me how Mr. K. had become rich since the beginning of the war, not from his law practice, but from buying what the Yankees called "Abandoned" land, i.e., land owned by Confederate soldiers. They had "abandoned" their land to join the army and fight the South's invaders and this "abandoned" land was appropriated by the Federal Government and sold for a song to such speculators as Mr. K. Mr. K. also bought up at tax sales the property of Confederate wives and widows who had to leave Memphis, as I had done, but who--less fortunate than I--had not had a loyal friend like Mr. Blythe to attend to the payment of their taxes. Before the war Memphians imagined that Mr. K., though originally from New England, had come to feel and sympathize as a Southerner. Not until Memphis was captured by the Yankees did Mr. K. begin to talk glibly of rebels, of traitors and treason. I said to Mr. Lanier: "If Mr. K. is that sort of man I fear he will not pay me my gold."

My friend replied that although Memphians disliked Mr. K., regarding him as a turn coat, they did not believe that he was dishonest in money matters. I think the event showed Mr. K. to be both a turn coat and dishonest. When I entered his office he greeted me politely, but when I told him the object of my call he declared he had not understood from Mr. Blythe that I would wish my money until the war was over.

"But I want it now. I need it now," I said.

Mr. K. looked very solemn and repeated that he had not expected to be called on to pay his note until after the war. "Your note contains no clause about waiting until the end of the war," I urged. "It is a demand note, a promise to pay on my demand. Well, Mr. K., I demand payment now."

"That is too bad, too bad that a misunderstanding like this should arise," murmured Mr. K. gravely.

"What misunderstanding?" I queried innocently. "I see no misunderstanding. It all seems perfectly clear to me. You promised to return my gold on demand; I now make the demand and you must keep your promise and return my gold."

"But I can't," returned Mr. K. "Gold is very scarce. I can give you green backs. I will give you four hundred dollars in green backs, but I can not give you gold."

I called Mr. K.'s attention to the fact that his note promised to pay in gold, and I said that I preferred gold because green backs were not current beyond the Federal lines.

"Oh, you are going down South?" asked Mr. K., eyeing me sharply. I nodded my head. "Then," continued he, "it will be far better for you to take green backs. Gold is contraband. You can't cross the lines with gold."

"What do the people in Tuscaloosa know about greenbacks?" I demanded, perhaps a little angrily; was it not time to become angry? Here was a man of wealth refusing to pay me a paltry two hundred dollars of my own money! I told Mr. K. I wanted gold and that I meant to have gold or nothing. "If you wish to dishonor your own note, and do not mind having the world know it, all right," I said. "That is your affair. But I shan't take your old paper money when you promised to pay in gold." And then Mr. K. asked me to wait a day; he would see what he could do and would I please come back on Thursday? I said I would, then Mr. Lanier drove me to Mr. Wickersham's office. "And if he pays you a single dollar," said Mr. Lanier, "I fear I'll drop dead of heart failure. Old Wick has the reputation of borrowing from anybody unwise enough to trust him, and never paying a cent of what he borrows!"

This was disheartening; but I had known old Wick before the war and feared Mr. Lanier's prophecy was only too likely to come true. Mr. James Wickersham was thought by the Memphis girls of the Fifties to be the ugliest man in the South. His nose was large, not flat; he was raw boned, gawky, slovenly. And he had a way of trying to steal his long, bony arm around a girl's waist that made the girls detest him. If a girl was sitting on a sofa and Old Wick approached, the girl would get up and take a chair so that he could not come close to her.

This was the man who had my sixty dollars in gold. I dreaded having to approach him; I feared he might put out that long, bony arm of his and try to touch me, but my children were in need of both food and clothing and so I nerved myself to go to Old Wick and even to accept his proffered hand and say I was glad to see him. He replied that he was glad to see me, but there was no gladness in his face a moment later after he had learned the object of my visit. For a moment he looked at me in silence, as if speechless with astonishment, then he asked--irrelevantly as I thought:

"Do you know that Mr. Blythe is dead?"

"Yes," I answered. "He was a very dear friend of mine and of my husband's. It was a shock to both of us when we heard of his death."

"It was a sad loss to our city," said Mr. Wickersham, and as he spoke I thought he was a meaner and lower type of hypocrite than Pecksniff. He paused and rubbed his big bony hand across his nose. I wondered why this ugly hypocrite had chosen to introduce the name of that courtly gentleman and dear friend of mine, William Blythe. Presently, when he told me why, I wondered still more. "You know, of course," he added, "that I cannot pay you your gold until Mr. Blythe's estate is settled?"

What did the settling of Mr. Blythe's estate have to do with an honest man's paying an honest debt? Nothing, absolutely nothing. I so told Mr. Wickersham; I further told him I expected him, as an honorable man, to keep his written promise, which was to pay me sixty dollars in gold on my demand.

"Ah, but you see, Mrs. Meriwether, I never thought you would call for your gold until after the war. Mr. Blythe understood that when he made the loan for you."

The note says nothing about waiting until after the war," I said. "I shall stand on your written promise to pay, Mr. Wickersham, not on what you say you think Mr. Blythe understood."

"Oh no, not what I think," replied Mr. Wickersham. I am talking of what I *know*. That is just what Mr. Blythe understood. And so you will have to wait, you really will."

"Wait how long?"

"Until either the war ends or Mr. Blythe's estate is settled up. It was understood I was not to pay until then."

I did not believe this; I was morally certain my friend never loaned my money on such terms, but I was helpless. There was no civil law to which I could appeal; I knew that our military rulers would sooner pitch my gold into the Mississippi River than aid me to get it--so I left Old Wick feeling that my case was well nigh hopeless.

During the above interview I had observed that Mr. Lanier spoke no word of remonstrance; he made no argument in my favor although he knew mine was a just and needy cause. In a day or so I learned why Mr. Lanier had kept quiet. Like Mr. Sam Walker, he felt the necessity of cautious silence. He feared that Old Wick might spitefully accuse him before some military martinet of aiding a rebel women in her attempt to get gold to carry beyond the Federal lines. It was a serious offense to carry gold through the lines and such a charge, had Old Wick made it would have caused my friend Mr. Lanier the most deadly danger.

When we went back to Mr. K.'s office the next day he was sitting by a table on which were two small packages. Mr. K.'s right hand rested lovingly on these packages and when we entered it seemed as if his eyes were reluctant to leave those packages even long enough to look up and greet Mr. Lanier and me.

"Mrs. Meriwether," he said without rising from his chair or lifting his hand from the two packages, "here are two hundred dollars in gold," tapping one of the packages; "and here," tapping the other package, "are four hundred dollars in greenbacks. Which will you have? Remember, four hundred is twice as much as two hundred."

"I remember that," I answered. "Still, Mr. K., I shall take the two hundred gold. Green backs are of little use in the South beyond the Federal lines."

Thereupon Mr. K.'s hand that lay on the gold package gently pulled the package forward until it fell into the half open drawer of the table. I knew not what to say; I was puzzled to guess what he meant, but he did not leave me to puzzle long.

"Since you will not protect yourself I will protect you," he said. "I well know that if you attempt to pass the Federal pickets with gold in your possession you will be arrested and imprisoned in the Irving Block. And I would be imprisoned for giving you gold to take South.

Surely, Mrs. Meriwether, you see that in refusing to give you this gold I am acting the part of a true friend?"

"No," I answered thoughtfully, "I only see that you dishonor your note, your written promise to return me my gold on my demand "

"Ah, my dear Mrs. Meriwether, the circumstances have changed since I gave Mr. Blythe that note. Consider a moment what it is I am doing: I am saving you from very probable imprisonment and at the same time I offer you four hundred dollars instead of the two hundred you loaned me. What could be fairer?"

"Some men might think you would be fairer were you to keep the promise you made in writing--repay me in gold on my demand."

Mr. K. looked at me and sighed as he closed the desk drawer containing the package of gold; the other package still lay on top of the desk, in full sight, as if to tempt me.

"Good deeds are not always appreciated at the moment of their doing." he said unctuously, "but the day will come when you will thank me for refusing to let you rush head long into prison."

I looked at him a moment in silence, then without a word I walked out of his office. This interview with Mr. K. took place more than half a century ago but the day has not yet come when I have felt any gratitude toward him for his action, nor did he ever receive the thanks or respect of his fellow Memphians for his course during the war. On the contrary he was generally despised as both a rascal and a renegade. He was known to have defrauded a number of poor wives and widows of Confederate soldiers, but I am glad to say that in my particular case his efforts to defraud did not succeed, for I transferred my claim to Mr. Lanier, who was *not* going South beyond the Federal lines, and after some little pressure Mr. K. gave Mr Lanier the two hundred dollars in gold, together with interest, and took up the note which I had endorsed over to Mr. Lanier. Mr. Lanier, of course, gave me my gold as soon as he left Mr. K.'s office.

The same day that I had this good fortune another piece of luck came my way. As Mr. Lanier drove me down Second Street we passed one of my buildings, a grocery store, and the grocer ran out to greet me. I had not seen him since my banishment from Memphis more than a year before. He seemed delighted to see me, asked me how Col. Meriwether was and if I was going to stay in Memphis. I told him No, that I was not allowed to remain in the city, that my stay would have to be limited to a few days at most. "Then wait here a minute," he said. "I have something of yours and if you are going to leave I had better give it to you now."

And before I had time to ask what thing of mine he could have he had darted across the side walk into his store. In a few minutes he returned and, coming up to where I sat in Mr. Lanier's carriage, he reached out his arm and thrust a small package into my hand. To my amazement the package was a roll of green backs. "What money is this?" I asked. "Why are you giving it to me?"

"It is yours," answered the Grocer, "your rent money."

"My rent money? Has Gen. Sherman stopped collecting my rents?"

"Oh no," returned the Grocer cheerfully. "He sends his collector around regularly. But you see, when he stole your property I did not think it necessary to tell him the real amount of rent I was paying for this store. I told him you let me have the store for seventy five dollars a month. You know, of course, that the rent is hundred and twenty five dollars a month. Well, I have set fifty dollars aside for you each month since you have been gone. Those green backs are in large bills; you will find in that roll nearly a thousand dollars."

How foolish it is to lose faith in human nature because of the rogues and rascals we sometimes see! My two days struggle with Old Wick and Mr. K. had soured me, had begun to make me think a man or woman was a simpleton to trust anybody with anything. And here was a man, a plain grocer, not an educated, cultured lawyer like Mr. K., who was not obligated to pay me a dollar, who even ran the risk of imprisonment if Gen. Sherman's collector learned of his action, and yet who handed over to me nearly a thousand dollars! The contrast between the action of my tenant and Mr. K. and Old Wick overcame me; tears came to my eyes; I could not speak; I simply reached out and grasped that grocer's hand. But words were not needed to make him understand that I appreciated his more than honest action; I felt justified in calling it his chivalrous action.

"How can I ever thank you?" I at last managed to murmur.

"Don't do it, Ma'am, don't do it," returned the Grocer, and I could plainly see that he was distressed and nervous. "I am only giving you your own. Please give the Colonel my good wishes. I am not fighting in the army but"--he paused a moment, glanced quickly around to see that no one was within earshot but Mr. Lanier and me, "but you know, Mrs. Meriwether, where my heart is. Take that money and God bless you and bring you back to Memphis when this cruel war is over.

With that he ran back into his grocery and we drove on, my faith in human nature, as well as my finances, much restored by what that worthy man had done.

CHAPTER XVII

Story of Old Wick continued. I get my clothes and gold and start South in a carpenter's wagon. A dead horse filled with quinine.

There is an old saying that it never rains but it pours; well, it seemed that prosperity having rained upon me, it now meant to pour upon me. The very next day after getting my gold from Mr. K. (through Mr. Lanier), and the roll of green backs from my grocer tenant, Mr. Fred Smith, Cashier of the Union & Planters Bank, brought me a letter that had just come addressed to Minor in the Bank's care. This letter was from a man in Kentucky to whom my husband had sold some land before the war. Four thousand dollars of the purchase price remained unpaid and the buyer now wished to take up his note and so stop interest.

As green backs were of little or no value in Tuscaloosa I thought it best not to accept that four thousand dollars; moreover, green backs were then worth less than fifty cents on the dollar; they could hardly depreciate any more, and might soon become more on a parity with gold. The note for that four thousand dollars was not due, consequently the maker could not require me to surrender it--and so I wrote him my husband was in the army where he could not get at the note and that the business would have to be postponed. But I determined to use that letter from Kentucky on Old Wick. Mr. Lanier drove me to see him again and forcing myself to seem cheerful and glad to see him (it required much effort, he was so ugly and so tricky) I said:

"Mr. Wickersham, I have come to you for a little advice."

"Advice?" repeated Old Wick; and his face looked relieved. Evidently he had thought I had come to dun him for my sixty dollars again.

"Yes," I said. "A Kentucky gentleman to whom Col. Meriwether sold a farm wants to take up his note for four thousand dollars. Here is his letter." And I handed him the letter which the Cashier of the Union & Planters Bank had brought me. Old Wick read it carefully, then looked at me inquiringly.

"Well?" he queried. "What do you want me to do about it? This looks very nice for you, very nice indeed."

"But it isn't nice at all, Mr. Wickersham," I replied, "unless I can find something to do with that four thousand dollars. As I told you the other day, greenbacks are not accepted in Tuscaloosa where I am going. Now, if I could put this money out at good interest in Memphis --*that* would be nice indeed. I thought perhaps you could advise me how to place it."

While saying this I furtively but closely watched Old Wick's face; his watery old eyes plainly manifested his Money-Greed mania; this greed was so strong that it affected his nerves. His fingers twitched and kept opening and shutting as if they were reaching out to grab money. Mr. Lanier looked at me as if he feared I had taken leave of my senses, but I disregarded his warning look and added cheerfully:

"I do hope Mr. Wickersham, you can tell me of some safe man who will pay me good interest on my four thousand dollars."

"My dear Mrs. Meriwether," said Old Wick, recovering his power of speech at last, "I do know a safe man. I am willing to borrow it myself, not that I really need it. But I shall not absolutely lose by borrowing it, I can put it to profitable use--at any rate, I am willing to take the risk in order to help an old friend like you."

"Oh, what a load you have taken off my mind!" I exclaimed. "Col. Meriwether, too, will be relieved when he hears that I have loaned it to you instead of to a stranger. You must tell me, though, what interest you will pay. My husband told me not to lend it unless the borrower was willing to pay good interest."

"What do you call good interest?" asked Old Wick warily.

"I think six per cent is the lowest interest on loans, isn't it?" I asked. "Col. Meriwether told me to try to get seven, but he said not to take less than six without first writing to him."

"Seven per cent is out of the question," said Old Wick decisively. "Nobody pays that much interest." (The old hypocrite! As a matter of fact, seven per cent was quite common during those troubled times.) "Five or five and a half per cent is considered good interest in Memphis," continued Old Wick. "But I won't haggle with an old friend over a trifle. Call it six per cent, Mrs. Meriwether."

"Thank you ever so much, Mr. Wickersham," I murmured as if overjoyed at his generosity; Mr. Lanier still looked at me as if he thought I had suddenly gone insane; he pulled my sleeve and whispered "Go slow," but I paid no attention to his warning. "I'll write to Kentucky tonight," I resumed, "and just as soon as the money comes, will you be ready to make out the papers?"

"Yes, come when you like. It will take but a very few minutes to prepare the papers."

I thanked him again and turned to leave his office, but on reaching the door I paused and exclaimed: "Oh, Mr. Wickersham, while I am waiting for this money from Kentucky I want you to do me a little favor. Will you?"

"Certainly. What is it?"

"I have been South a long time and down South you know it is impossible to buy many things a woman and children need. I want to do some shopping while I am here but I can't do it without money. I wish you would let me have that sixty dollars so I can be buying things while waiting to hear from Kentucky."

A troubled look came into Old Wick's eyes; he squirmed, he wriggled as if his soul, or what in him passed for soul, was suffering acute pain. I silently watched him, wondering if my stratagem would succeed and if he would part with the gold he adored. Presently a pleasanter look came into his face and he said almost cheerfully:

"I hadn't ought to do it but for *you* I will. I don't mind doing anything for an old friend. Wait a minute." He opened an iron box that he took out of a drawer in his desk and the next minute the gold was counted out into my hand.

"Thank you," I said. "This will keep me busy in the shops while waiting to hear from Kentucky. Goodbye, Mr. Wickersham, I will let you know just as soon as Mr. Fred Smith tells me the money has come to the Bank."

For ten minutes after we left Old Wick's office Mr. Lanier was too dazed to speak. Finally he managed to ask if I really meant to entrust my four thousand dollars with such a rogue as Old Wick?

"Entrust four thousand dollars with Old Wick?" I exclaimed. "Of course not. I would as leave throw it into the Mississippi river.

"Why then are you going to do it?"

"I am not going to do it. Did you never read the fable of the greedy dog with a nice bone in his mouth? On seeing in the water a reflection of that bone the greedy dog let loose of the real bone in order to grasp the shadow. Well, while Old Wick's mouth is watering for my four thousand dollars I shall be enjoying these sixty dollars in gold." And I jingled the money in my purse and thought the noise it made was very sweet indeed.

Mr. Lanier smiled, then he laughed until the tears came into his eyes. "I didn't know you were so clever," he said. "You certainly took me in as well as Old Wick. I thought you meant to let him have your four thousand and began to fear you had lost your senses. What an easy way to make sixty dollars!"

In a way it had been easy, but I was destined to do a good deal more work for that gold before the episode closed. There was a carpenter named Renfrow who had relatives in Alabama. Renfrow was going in a wagon to visit his relatives and he agreed for a moderate fee to give me a seat in his wagon and drive me all the way to Tuscaloosa. I planned to start South with Mr. Renfrow a few days after my interview with Old Wick and during those few days I received not less than half a dozen notes inquiring when the money from Kentucky would arrive and when I would be ready to make the loan. To each note I returned a polite answer saying that I had not yet heard from Kentucky. Then Old Wick came to see me and when I again told him there was no news from Kentucky his greenish old eyes watered and his bony old fingers twitched and after squirming and twisting a minute he said:

"I hadn't ought to have given you that gold until Mr. Blythe's estate is settled up."

"Oh, Mr. Wickersham," I answered cheerfully, "You oughtn't to bother about Mr. Blythe's estate. That has nothing at all to do with the money you owed me."

"You ain't a lawyer," returned Old Wick. "I am an old lawyer and I know I hadn't ought to have paid you that gold until Mr. Blythe's estate is settled up. You must give it back to me, Mrs. Meriwether. I will keep it safe for you until Mr. Blythe's estate is settled up. I'll pay you good interest and in this way you won't run any risk of being arrested when you pass through the picket lines."

"That does sound like a good plan," I said thoughtfully. "I will think it over, Mr. Wickersham."

"When are you going South?" asked Old Wick.

"I don't know exactly," I answered. "I have still a great many things to do. It will not be for sometime."

This answer seemed to relieve him a little; he went away and the next day I received from him two pages of fools-cap paper closely written with many fine legal phrases and words intended to convince me of the great danger to him as well as to me if I were caught carrying gold South. I wrote in reply thanking him for his kind consideration and urged him to let his mind be at rest as I intended remaining sometime in Memphis and meant to spend every dollar of my gold before leaving the city. I hoped this would end the matter, but the very next morning Old Wick called at the Laniers and insisted on reading to me two more pages which he had written in the hope of convincing me of the wisdom of giving him back my gold. I listened with an air of great patience and when he had finished reading I asked him to leave the paper with me so I could study it and ponder over it.

"No, no, I can't do that," returned Old Wick hastily. "I must make some corrections in it before giving it to you. But be guided by reason, Mrs. Meriwether. It will injure your reputation to have it told about town how you tricked me into giving you this gold."

"Tricked you?" I exclaimed, as if both amazed and indignant. "What do you mean? Why need I 'trick' you into giving me what was my own?"

"Oh, you know, Mrs. Meriwether," replied Old Wick, his bony fingers again twitching and his greenish old eyes gazing at me angrily.

"You know I would not have given you this gold if you hadn't offered to lend me your four thousand dollars. I hadn't ought to have given it to you anyway. I knew it wasn't right to give it to you until Mr. Blythe's estate was settled up."

I felt like laughing in the old rascal's face, but I knew diplomacy was my role, so I pretended to be impressed by his argument. "I'll think it over," I said. "I shall be here with the Laniers for at least a month. In that time maybe the money will come from Kentucky. And anyway, if on reflection it seems right that I should return the gold to you I shall do so and leave my shopping undone."

"Yes, that is by far the best course to pursue," said Mr. Lanier. Then, turning to Old Wick, he added: "We shall keep Mrs. Meriwether with us at least a month. That will give her ample time to straighten this matter out."

How anybody with a grain of sense could have been deceived by such talk I can't imagine, but Old Wick did seem relieved at what he heard and when he went away it was with almost a smile on his ugly old face. Of course my plan was to start South the very next morning before day, and before Old Wick had time to come at me again.

The afternoon before the carpenter Renfrow was to start South with me, Mr. and Mrs. Lanier drove me out to see our home, "Ridgeway"; pickets still camped out in front of our gate and the house was occupied by people to whom Gen. Sherman's Collector had rented it. The Hanovers still lived opposite Ridgeway and just as we were coming away from calling on them an old friend of mine, a Mrs. McAllen, drove up and expressed great delight at seeing me. "Let us sit right here, Betty Meriwether," she said, "and have a visit under the shade of Mr. Hanover's trees. From here we can look across the road and see your old home and the soldiers camped by your front gate."

I was glad to see Mrs. McAllen; her husband was a Captain in the Confederate army and we had much to talk about. But my time was limited, and anyhow I didn't wish to stay out there under Mr. Hanover's trees. But my friend insisted.

"At any rate," she said, "stay here with me until that dray yonder passes by." I looked in the direction she indicated and saw two men approaching on a dray on which lay the carcass of a dead horse. When the dray stopped in front of the Federal pickets Mrs. McAllen clutched my arm and I felt her tremble. I was mystified. I could not understand why she should be so interested in two dray drivers and a dead horse. We saw the officer of the Picket Post approach the dray and we heard him ask the drivers where they intended taking the dead horse.

"Anywhere we can put him," returned one of the men. "Nobody seems to want a dead horse dumped near 'em. Everywhere we've started to dump him somebody's kicked up a row."

"Guess you'll have to take him out into the country," said the officer. And thereupon the two men drove on.

Mrs. McAllen watched the dray disappear down the road, then she turned to me, a look of great relief in her eyes.

"Did you recognize the men on that dray?" she asked. I told her No, that I had never seen them before. "Oh, yes, you have," said Mrs. McAllen. "You know them both. One of them is Captain McAllen and the other is my brother Ben." Mrs. McAllen laughed when she saw my look of astonishment and incredulity. "Sounds crazy, I know it," she continued, "but it is true. Capt. McAllen came into Memphis disguised as an Irishman. That is a red wig you saw on his head. He came partly to see me and partly to get a view of the forts and forces about

Memphis. I have been in mortal terror every minute since he came here. You know they would hang him as a spy if they caught him."

"Yes, I know that," I answered. "Thank God they are now past the lines."

"But they are not out of danger," said Mrs. McAllen. "I won't breathe easily until they are through the Confederate lines. What did you think of that dead horse?"

"Think of it? What do you mean?"

"I mean don't you think that a fine idea? My brother Ben thought of it. That horse is stuffed full of quinine, shoes, socks, gloves and other articles our soldiers need. Ben heard of a dray man with a dead cow who was ordered to drive it beyond the lines out into the country, so he bought a poor old skeleton of a horse and let it die of starvation --cruel to the poor old horse, wasn't it? But our soldiers do need quinine and clothes so badly; Ben said he would kill a dozen horses to help them."

It was a long time before I heard from Mrs. McAllen after I left her that afternoon in her carriage under the Hanover trees; when at last I did receive a letter from her she told me both her husband and her brother succeeded in entering the Confederate lines with their dead horse stuffed with quinine and other things our soldiers so sadly needed. Another letter which I received in Tuscaloosa was from Mrs. Lanier telling me how Old Wick behaved when he called again and found that I was gone. "Gone?" he exclaimed. "Why did you let her go?"

"She got bad news about her children;" answered Mrs. Lanier. "She felt that she had to go to them at once."

"Children be damned!" cried Old Wick. "She had no right to go without seeing me. At least she should have left my sixty dollars. Did she leave it with you?"

"No, she said nothing about any sixty dollars," answered my friend, hardly able, as she wrote me, to keep from smiling; she knew I had no gold belonging to Old Wick; she knew the sixty dollars were *my* dollars. And so Mrs. Lanier listened to the old rascal with serene composure knowing he had neither moral nor legal claim on me for any money.

But now, my dear Children, I must tell you how I left Memphis with Mr. Renfrow, the carpenter, and journeyed with him in his wagon through the Federal lines to Tuscaloosa.

CHAPTER XVIII

The Yankee Censor strikes the book "Miscegenation" from the list of things I may take into Dixie. Northern writers urge intermarriage between whites and blacks in order to SAVE (!) the white race from deterioration. I return safe to my babies in Tuscaloosa. End of the War.

Bright and early on the morning Mr. Renfrow had appointed for our departure I arose and got my things together ready for the journey. I had bought a little trunk and filled it with useful articles, having submitted a list of things to the Military Censor and received his approval. Of course my list contained no contraband articles, but even so, the Censor, who scanned the list most critically, drew lines here and there; in particular he drew a line through the item of quinine; I remember this because there was quite an argument over that item--I urged that my children had chills and fever and needed a little quinine, but the Censor was inexorable. "It is not our Government's duty to furnish medicine to a rebel's sick children." That was the Censor's curt response to my pleadings, and so the small bottle of quinine was stricken from my list.

I had twenty yards of flannel on my list; this also was stricken out, but when I pleaded that winter was coming and that I had three small children who would freeze to death if they had no clothing, the Censor relented a little and inserted over the erased item: "Permit for ten yards of flannel." I had on my list a dozen hanks of woolen yarn; this item appeared to worry the Censor. After scanning it for a full minute he demanded to know why I wanted so much yarn?

"I want to knit my children some stockings," I answered. "Their little legs get very cold in winter."

"Their rebel daddy's legs get cold, too, eh? That's what you really want with that yarn, isn't it?"

I did intend to use some of it for knitting Minor some socks, but of course I did not tell the Military Censor that I had such intentions. "That little pile of yarn is hardly enough for the children's socks," I said, "much less for their father's."

"Hum, I don't know about that," said the Censor reflectively. "Guess I'll cut it down to six hanks anyway."

And, drawing his pen through the word "One Dozen" he wrote in the word "Six," and so it was that woolen socks were knitted only for my husband. For I thought my children could better go barefooted than Minor--they were more accustomed to it; and if the weather got very cold they could stay indoors while a soldier, no matter how cold or muddy or freezing it might be, had to go where he was ordered.

140

No objection was made by the Censor to the articles of feminine apparel which were on my list, but we had quite an argument over one of the several books on the list. The book which excited the Censor's suspicions was entitled: *"Miscegenation."* The author advocated intermarriage between white and black people on the ground that the Southern white race had become effeminate and effete and could be rejuvenated and restored to virility only by the infusion of another race's newer and stronger blood. The negroes of the South, the author said, had fresh, virile blood in their veins which, by intermarriage with the white race, would freshen and invigorate the latter.

"Have you read this book?" the Censor asked, eyeing me sharply.

I told him I had read it.

"Why then do you wish to take it with you?"

"I wish to show it to my friends. They have never heard of this doctrine. It will interest them greatly."

"Well, you can't take this book with you. You do not want it for any good purpose."

And thereupon a heavy black line was drawn through *that* item.

"Miscegenation" was published anonymously; at first its authorship was attributed by the newspapers of the day to Theodore Tilton, then to Henry Ward Beecher. I believe however that finally it was shown to have been written by Anna Dickenson, called by her admirers, "The Modern Joan of Arc" because of the fiery lectures she delivered all over the North and her success in arousing hatred of Slavery and Southern slave holders. The "Modern Joan of Arc" also wrote a book entitled *"What answer?"* which was intended to show that the author's arguments in favor of miscegenation were unanswerable. In *"What Answer?"* Miss Dickenson makes a Negro her hero; he falls in love with and marries a beautiful white girl. And the educated white men of her story are made to fall in love with and marry black negro women.

Now that the passions and prejudice of the War Between the States have subsided it is hard to believe that anybody not an absolute lunatic could have written such books as *"Miscegenation"* and *"What Answer?"* but War is a monster which blinds even men of brains and genius. Wendell Phillips was a very talented man, but in one of his lectures delivered just after Lee's surrender, Phillips made the startling announcement that "Negroes are our Nobility!" And Gov. Stone of Iowa, in a speech at Keokuk on August 3rd 1863, said:

"I hold the Democracy in the utmost contempt. I would rather eat with a negro, drink with a negro and sleep with a negro than with a Copperhead (Democrat)."

141

James Parton, the well known writer, wrote thus in one of his biographies:

"Many a negro stands in the same kind of moral relation to his master as that in which Jesus Christ stood to the Jews . . . he stands above his master at a height which the master can neither see nor understand."

In February 1863 the New York correspondent of the London *Times* wrote his paper a letter describing the then love of the North for the Negro race.

"It has been discovered here (wrote the London *Times* correspondent) that in many important respects the negro is superior to the whites; that if the latter do not forget their pride of race and amalgamate with the 'purer and richer' blood of the blacks, they will die out and wither away in unprolific skinniness. The first to give tongue to the new doctrine were Theodore Tilton and the Rev. Henry Ward Beecher. The latter recently declared that it was good for a white woman to marry a black man and that the passion and emotional nature of the blacks were needed to improve the white race. Mr. Wendell Philips has often hinted the same things."

Long after the war was over, when I was lecturing on Woman's "Rights" in New England in 1880 I was a guest of Mrs. Isabella Beecher Hooker (Henry Ward Beecher's sister) and she told me that she would be perfectly willing for her only son, then a youth of seventeen, to marry a black, wooly headed negress when he was old enough to marry, provided he loved her and she was honest and moral. I said I loved my sons more than I loved my own life, but that I would rather see them dead and in their graves than married to negro women, no matter how moral or honest. Mrs. Hooker raised her hand in horror at this reply; she said I was blinded by Southern prejudice.

But all this is a digression; let me return to my story. After the Military Censor had O.K.'d my list and given me a pass to go through the picket lines,

I went with my list to Lowensteins dry goods store (that store still does business in Memphis, being today, as it was half a century ago, one of the leading stores of the city); and while buying my things a lady came up to see me; I had known her before the war; she had married a Vermont man who was rich, and riches had turned my acquaintance's head. Rushing up to me in Lowenstein's store in the friendliest way, this lady asked me how I was and if my husband was still in the rebel army? I did not like the word "rebel" from her lips. Both her mother and father were Virginians; I felt she should know that the soldiers of the South were no more rebels than the soldiers of Washington. But I said nothing of this to her; she had married a northern man and evidently was now able to see only through her husband's eyes. I replied quietly that my husband was in the Confederate army. Observing the list in my hands, she next asked me what that was? "It is a list of things the Censor lets me take South," I answered. "See what a pitifully little list it is. This is all he would sign for." *"All?"* echoed Mrs. C. "I wonder they let you take anything South, knowing your husband is in the rebel army."

I said pleasantly: "Is your husband in the Yankee army?"

"No, he isn't in any army," said Mrs. C. sharply. "But he is truly loyal. He is no rebel." And with that she left me to continue my shopping.

It may be interesting, my dear children, to tell you right here what happened later on to that amiable lady. After the awful war ended and all the "Rebels" who had not been killed by the Yankees were home again, trying to reconstruct their fallen fortunes, Mrs. C.'s husband owned a newspaper in Memphis called *The Post;* this paper in season and out of season "boosted" Mrs. C. socially and Mr. C. politically. No Southern family would have anything to do with the C.'s; their social activities were confined wholly to a select circle or "Carpetbaggers" who had settled in the city, like a flock of vultures, to feed and fatten on a prostrate people. But the *Post* was forever publishing items about the grand dinners and parties which Mrs. C. attended, and about what a grand representative Mr. C. would make Tennessee in the United States Senate. As time passed, however, the Hon. Mr. C. still remained in Memphis; Tennessee obstinately refused to send him as her Senator in Washington. And finally the Hon. Mr. C. began to drink too much; he lost his fortune; Mrs. C. no longer drove about in a carriage--she had to walk, or use a street car. When Mr. C. died after one of his drunken sprees it was found that his debts exceeded his assets and his widow had to take in sewing for a living. Ordinarily my heart goes out to a woman who, once knowing the sweets of fortune, is reduced to poverty; but I despise a renegade, and I must confess that I did not grieve over Mrs. C.'s misfortunes.

The things which the Censor allowed me to keep on my list were packed in my trunk; the gold which my diplomacy had gained for me from Old Wick was of course not on that list which the Military Censor saw; I had no notion of trying to take that gold through the Picket lines. I knew if I did so, and if I were discovered, that I would be imprisoned in the dreadful Irving Block, so what I did was this: I made a girdle of strong cloth and "quilted" my gold, piece by piece, in that girdle. I thought that if anyone happened to touch the girdle they would think the hard stuff merely my corsage stiffened with whale bone. A friend of Mrs. Lanier's, a certain Mrs. J., a good Southern woman, lived five miles beyond the Picket lines and, being a quiet, prudent woman, she had never given the Yankees any cause for offense and so had been favored with a pass which allowed her to go freely between her home and the city. This good woman agreed to wear my girdle to her home, where I could stop and get it after my examination at the Picket lines and after I was safely on my way to Tuscaloosa. Well, I was seated on my little trunk at Mr. Lanier's by day break that morning half a century ago when Mr. Renfrow drove up with his wagon. He also had a trunk, a much larger one than mine, filled with shoes, calicoes for women, socks, etc., which he meant to sell "Down South." Why they let him carry so much more than they permitted me to take with me I do not know, unless it was because I was a "traitor's" wife and therefore merited severer treatment than other mortals. They did, however, pass Mr. Renfrow's trunk without question; mine also was passed, since it contained only articles O.K.'d by the military Censor. A few miles beyond the lines we stopped at Mrs. J.'s farm, where I got my girdle filled with gold, then our pilgrimage into Dixie Land really began.

Mr. Renfrow was kind and polite to me and I found him amusing. When we stopped at a wayside farm for water or dinner or lodging the first thing he did was to introduce himself. Not once did he fail to do this.

"My name is Renfrow. Can you give us a drink of water?"

Or "My name is Renfrow. Can you put us up for the night?"

He never introduced me; he appeared to think it entirely unnecessary to mention my name, but evidently he did not believe he could get even a drink of water unless he told the farmer that his name was Renfrow.

There was no retreating army to follow on this journey, as there had been the time I fled from Memphis upon Gen. Sherman's order, consequently my progress was more rapid and was accompanied by less incident. We arrived at Demopolis in what seemed a really short time, and there waiting to greet me were my dear husband and little Rivers and Avery, all three well and strong and in raptures at seeing me safely back again. As for me--well, Minor understood the joy that flooded my heart at seeing my loved ones well and happy. And to swell my flood of joy Minor showed me a letter which he had that day received, from my sister, Mrs. Lamb, saying that Baby Lee was "as well and happy as could be!" Minor was so glad that I had returned without mishap, when I related how Mr. K. and Old Wick had behaved he said: "The old scoundrels!" and seemed not to give them another thought. He was the more rejoiced at my return on that particular day because the army was about to leave Demopolis and he had been worried greatly what to do with our little boys. They of course could not go along with the army, and it seemed equally impossible to leave them in Demopolis with strangers. My timely arrival solved the problem and Minor felt a load taken from his shoulders when he saw me drive up in Mr. Renfrow's wagon, for he knew then that whatever happened to him, I was there to care for his two darling boys.

After one happy day together our little family had again to endure the pang of separation; Minor held his two boys on his knees and kissed them again and again and enjoined upon them the necessity of their growing up into big, brave, good men so they could take care of their mother in case their father died in battle. Everytime one of these separations occurred the thought would come to us that perhaps this time the farewells were for eternity; when a soldier goes forth to battle there is no assurance that he will return, and this thought always made the partings from my husband during those dreadful war days peculiarly sad and harrowing. Little Rivers and Avery gravely promised their father that they would take care of me if anything happened to their "Sweet, Big Sojer Papa," then Minor embraced me and bade me farewell! My eyes followed him as he rode away and became lost amid the thousands of soldiers who followed him, then I sadly climbed into Mr. Renfrow's wagon, my children were seated beside me and we began the long drive to Tuscaloosa.

However much a woman may love her husband, she loves her baby as much, if not more; the pain of parting from Minor in Demopolis was offset at least in part by my joy in seeing Baby Lee again. My sister had employed a negro girl to look after my baby during my trip to Memphis. This girl became very fond of her charge, and proud of him, too--proud of all of my baby except his nose. Some of that nurse girl's negro friends told her Baby Lee's nose was a "Rale nigger nose flat jes like a nigger's," and in an effort to make it a "White Folk's" nose the nurse began to pinch little Lee's nose and pull it and try to make it stand up. When I first saw my baby I noticed that his nose seemed sore and inflamed but I did not suspect the cause until the day after my return to Tuscaloosa. Then, while I was out on my porch chatting with old Mr. Joe Davis, who had heard of my return and come to welcome me back in Tuscaloosa, I saw the nurse girl take Lee's nose between her black fingers and pinch the two nostrils together so hard that the baby screamed with pain.

"What on earth are you doing?" I cried, springing to my feet and rushing to the girl and taking my baby from her.

"Laws, Miss Betty, I ain't doin' nuthin' 'cept makin' yo' baby pretty!" replied the girl, grinning.

"Making my baby pretty?" I repeated. "You are hurting him. And you are ruining his nose."

"No, Miss Betty, I ain't ruin his nose, I'se makin' it pretty. It's a nigger nose now, flat an' ugly jes' like a nigger. But I'se gwine pinch it up so it'll stan' up like a White Folk's nose."

"You will do nothing of the sort," I said severely. "If I ever catch you doing that again I shall have your Master whip you."

Old Mr. Joe Davis sat looking on at this scene smiling and seeming to enjoy it hugely. "You are quite right," he said to me after I had restored the baby to the girl and again cautioned her not to pinch its nose again. "I have seen a hundred such noses. They are fine noses for babies; wide nostrils take in lots of air and lots of air makes fine lungs. Did you never notice that consumptives have thin, pinched nostrils? With those wide open nostrils your baby will never have consumption. He will grow up to be a fine looking man."

Mr. Davis' prediction has thus far proved true; Baby Lee grew up to be a strong, healthy man. I consider him a handsome man, but what if it be merely a mother's blindness which makes me think him good looking? Good looks count for little in a man. What counts are good morals, good health and brains. All these my son Lee has and so I am content even though his nose is neither Grecian nor Roman.

One day there came to us in Tuscaloosa news of a big battle and not for sometime after that did I hear from my husband. Fearing that he had been either killed or taken a prisoner, my heart was very heavy and sometimes while on my front porch brooding over the frightful times in which my life was cast I would give way to fits of crying.

I was in one of these despondent moods one afternoon when old Mr Joe Davis called; he was distressed at my distress and begged me to tell him what was the matter. When I told him, the good old man patted me kindly on my shoulders and said:

"Don't cry, my dear child, don't cry. If your husband is killed in this war I will marry you and help you rear your children."

Was not this good of him? I thought so, but I also thought the situation had a comical aspect. Was it not comical for an old man of eighty four seriously to propose to marry a woman not yet forty, and to help her rear three noisy, turbulent boys? I thought an eighty four year old husband, instead of being a help to me, would be but another burden placed upon my shoulders. This aspect of the case evidently did not present itself to Mr. Davis; he was perfectly serious and no doubt believed to his dying day that the return of my customary cheerful manner was due to my knowing a protector would be at hand in the event of my husband's death in battle. In truth I became cheerful again simply because my nature was to be cheerful and because my common sense told me no good could come from repining over the inevitable. Moreover, good old Joe Davis in spite of his eighty four years was a man well calculated to dispel the blues. He had seen much of the world and knew how to talk of what he had seen in a way that was exceedingly entertaining. After catching me crying on my porch and after dispelling my sorrows, as he thought by his promise to be my protector, he interested me for an hour or two with anecdotes of the celebrated men he had known in England. He told me intimate details of the life of Bulwer, how the novelist' wife hated him, hated him so bitterly that she would write him letters addressed to "Lord Lytton *Liar* Bulwer!" And once, Mr. Davis told me, when it was announced that Bulwer was to make a speech in a certain English county, Lady Bulwer got into her carriage, drove to the place of the speaking, ran up the platform steps and in the presence of the audience began to pour out the most venomous abuse of her unhappy husband, accusing him of almost every crime in the calendar! Mr. Davis said poor Bulwer stopped in the middle of his speech, gave his wife one glance, then turned and left the platform. His wife pointed her finger at him as he was going away and screamed: "Coward! Coward! Coward!" Had such an episode occurred in the United States among people as widely known as the English novelist and his

146

wife the newspapers of New York and other big cities would have told about it on their first pages under big headlines; as an interesting side light on the methods of English journalism, and the respect which English editors feel for men of talent, if not genius, Mr. Davis said that not one London newspaper so much as mentioned the disgraceful way in which Lady Bulwer broke up the meeting her husband was addressing.

Of the last year of the war it is unnecessary to say much; like the years which had preceded it, that sad year of 1864, and the first half of 1865, were filled with sadness and hardships and anxiety. Month by month, almost day by day the fortunes of the Confederacy fell to a lower and lower ebb. Our brave soldiers fought heroically but the very stars in the Heavens were against us. What devoted sacrifice, what steadfast courage, what wonderful military genius could do to save our independence was done. But we were surrounded by millions of soldiers. The North had the world to draw on; we were hemmed in. The oceans of the world were to us as if they were oceans of fire--or as if they did not exist. Nothing could we sell to the Nations of the world, nothing could we buy from them--but our enemy was free to obtain supplies from every country on the globe. And so the end was inevitable.

But inevitable as was that end, when at last it came, strange as it may seem, the blow was as unexpected as it was stunning! Gen. Lee had so long kept Gen. Grant's hosts at bay; Richmond, so long beleaguered by almost countless legions equipped with an unlimited supply of the most terrible engines of war the world at that time had ever known, had so long hurled those legions back, the South had shown so dauntless a spirit that its sons and daughters had come to think victory would finally perch on our banners in spite of the frightful odds against us. Thus it was that, inevitable as the issue was from the very beginning, when the news of Lee's surrender reached Tuscaloosa the citizens stood about on the streets almost stunned; they discussed the news in whispers; could the report be true? No. For four years, with all the world to draw on, the North had not been able to traverse the few miles that stretched between Washington and Richmond; the Confederate army, led by its incomparable Captain, a Captain worthy to rank with Caesar and Napoleon, had withstood all the armies the North had been able to hurl against the South. Was not Lee still there? Were his soldiers not as brave, as heroic as ever? No, the report of a surrender at Appomattox was merely another vile Yankee invention!

But in their hearts our people knew the report was true and tears filled the eyes of men even as they stood in groups on the streets and declared they knew Lee had not surrendered, that the great Virginian would never surrender. I suppose these scenes which I witnessed in Tuscaloosa were only such scenes as occurred all over the South in the later half of April 1865. Of course a very few days sufficed to convince even the most skeptical that Gen. Lee had surrendered and that the war really was ended. Minor wrote me that it might be a month or two before he would be free to leave the army, even if he were then free--no one then knew just what the Yankees would do to the conquered Southern soldiers; and so he advised me to return at once to Memphis and there await developments. I left Rose and her two children, "Booby" (Beauregard) and Alice, who was born in Tuscaloosa and shared her black mother's milk with my Baby Lee, in Tuscaloosa; I told Rose to wait there until my husband and Henry came for her. Then I set forth in my old Rockaway on that long lonely journey to Memphis. Dear old Mr. Whitfield gave me a bushel of potatoes which Rose baked and put in the bottom of my Rockaway before I started; I also laid in a supply of corn bread, and on that long journey cold potatoes and cold corn bread were about all we had to eat. I tried at many farm houses to buy eggs and milk but not once did the farmers have any to sell. The whole country seemed to have been stripped bare of food for both men and beasts. My poor Adrienne got so weak and thin, I was in constant fear lest she should die of starvation before we got to Memphis. What would have happened had this occurred? To this day I shudder at the thought. With three children on my hands, all three small and one a baby in arms, it would have been a serious matter to be left on the road side with a dead mule, no chance to get a live one, and the country about me destitute of food and shelter.

Happily this calamity was spared us; Adrienne managed to exist on such scant grazing and fodder as fortune afforded and a few days before we reached Memphis the food supply of the country began to improve. To this day I remember with what ecstasy my boys--and I too, if the truth must be confessed-- sniffed the first bacon we had seen for nearly a year. We were approaching a little cabin in front of which sat a comfortable looking fat old negro "Mammy"; in the little yard around the cabin were a dozen or so chickens and from within the cabin came the fragrant scent of frying bacon. Could it be that the world still possessed such things as chickens and eggs and bacon? The last year in Tuscaloosa had almost convinced us that such delicious viands existed only in story books, or in the imagination. But here they were in an old negro woman's cabin and the desire to possess some of them overwhelmed me. I determined to have some of those eggs and bacon if I had to give my faithful mule for them. Luckily, the old negro Mammy did not know how desperate was my desire, or she was not overly grasping. At any rate, when I broached the subject of getting something to eat she was more than amiable and reasonable.

"Git you an' yo' chilluns sumfin' to eat?' she said. "I sho' can." And the comfortable old Mammy got up and waddled into her cabin. Liza Jane," we heard her say, "git a dozen eggs an' boil 'em hard, mind you, hard, case de lady wants ter take 'em wid her. An' put some mo' bacon in de skillet an' cook a batch ob hoe cakes. Dem poor chilluns looks monsus hungry. Git a move on you, Liza, an' doan loaf aroun' in dis heah cabin ef you doan' wanter get sumfin' you doan like."

Having delivered herself thus, the comfortable fat old Mammy waddled out again and resumed her seat before the front door. "Liza Jane's a good gal," she observed. "She'll have yo' things cooked purty soon.'

My two "Big" little boys climbed out of the Rockaway and played about the yard; I remained in the carriage, Baby Lee in my arms chatting with the old Mammy until Eliza Jane came out, which she did in about a quarter of an hour, carrying a basket filled with the results of her culinary labors, eggs, bacon and plenty of hot hoe cakes --not much of a feast according to the standards of peace times. But I assure you, my children, Lucullus himself never had a banquet which was more exquisite than that basket of hard boiled eggs, fried bacon and hoe cakes seemed to me and my children that April day in 1865. You can imagine how it impressed me when you see how even the details of that roadside meal have remained fresh in my memory after more than half a century--next month, April 1916, it will be fifty one years since my three boys and I stopped in front of that old negro Mammys cabin. When I asked her how much I owed her, she said five dollars, but she refused to take greenbacks; she said she didn't know "Nuthin' about Yankee money," so I gave her a ten dollar Confederate bill, and I may add that this was the last time I ever bought anything with Confederate money. As we neared Memphis Confederate money became more and more worthless until at last it had no value at all.

My dear Children, if you have read these *"Recollections"* thus far you will recall an odd family with whom I spent a night on my flight from Memphis after Gen. Sherman's order of banishment--the Peppercorns. Their place lay only a short distance off the road I was travelling on my return to Memphis in 1865 and I resolved to stop and see them. I was curious to know if Melverina Elverina had joined the army, and if Alexander the Great (Lexy for short) had escaped Yankee bullets and come back from the war alive. When Adrienne stopped in front of the Peppercorn place I called "Hello! Hello!" And, just as had happened two years before, the big boned Mother Peppercorn came out and stood in the passage way between the two rooms and stared at me. I cried out: "Can you 'uns let we'uns stay all night with you'uns?"

"Laws a mussy!" exclaimed Mother Peppercorn, "is that you'uns?"

She ran out to my carriage, picked me up as if I were a child and set me on the ground; then she took my children out of the Rockaway one by one and set them on the ground, then she stared at Baby Lee, now a sturdy chap two years old. "Well, Well!" exclaimed Mother Peppercorn, "so you'uns have gone and had another boy baby? I reckoned it would be a gal baby. You'uns already had two boy babies, why didn't you'uns make this one a gal baby?"

I told Mrs. Peppercorn I was very well satisfied with Baby Lee as he was and that anyway the determination of the sex of my children was a matter beyond my control.

"Well, with two boy babies this one ought to have been a gal," persisted Mrs. Peppercorn. "I ain't denying, though, that he's a fine baby. Come on into the house."

And she led the way into the same room where we sat that night before the wood fire, and where I had watched her and her huge daughters chew tobacco and squirt the juice onto the blazing logs. There was no fire there now; the weather was mild, and had been mild since we left Tuscaloosa.

"Where are your daughters?" I asked, after we were seated. Mrs. Peppercorn said that Suky and Sally were at a neighbor's, weaving. "And Melverina?" I said, "did she join the army?"

"Oh yes, she jined," answered Mrs. Peppercorn. "But she never seen no real hard service. She only fought onct in a battle."

There was almost a note of scorn in Mrs. Peppercorn's voice, as if her feeling was, not of wonder that a girl should have fought at all, but of chagrin that she had fought so little. "Why did she quit so soon?" I queried.

"Well, it was all on account of Alexander the Great. He got shot in the leg and was sent to a hospital, and his twin sister quit the army and went to nurse Lexy. The last I heered from 'em Lexy's leg was purty nigh well and he was going back to the army and Melverina was going with him. Of course, 'twon't be no use now, now that Gineral Lee's gone and surrendered. Oh, how I hate them Yankees!"

The feeling of hate is an ugly feeling, it mars and scars the human soul; but I fear in those dark days just after the close of the war, hate was a feeling that came into many a Southern woman's breast. The Southern men were too busy trying to retrieve their fallen fortunes, but the women--they had more time to brood over the wrongs that had been done them, they had not had the excitement of battle to sustain them, they suffered even more than their husbands and sons and brothers. For these reasons, or perhaps just because women are less forgiving than men, it took the women of the South a long time before they were able to feel kindly toward their conquerors. To this day I cannot truthfully say I love a Yankee, but my dear husband who fought four years in the Confederate army, seemed to feel no bitterness in his heart, not even in the years immediately following Lee's surrender. Were he living now, more than fifty years after Appomattox, he would probably be as kindly and as just in his estimate of a northern, as of a southern, soldier. I cannot feel that way--at any rate, I cannot feel kindly toward Gen. Sherman. He was a monster and I want the whole world to know it.

CHAPTER XIX

Return home of the Refugees after Lee's surrender. Negroes told they may occupy the lands of their former masters. My home surrounded with negro "Squatters." How I got rid of them.

In the bottom of the Rockaway was feed for Adrienne. Mrs. Peppercorn helped me unharness and feed the faithful old mule, then she milked her one lone cow and so my children had corn bread and milk for their supper. Suky and Sally, the two big, raw boned sisters, returned home shortly after the children finished their feast of corn bread and milk, and they seemed genuinely glad to see me; during times of trouble and war no matter how wide apart men may be mentally and socially, if they have at heart the same common cause the feeling between them is almost that of brothers. In the morning those big Peppercorn women insisted on feeding and harnessing Adrienne and on giving me and my children as bountiful a breakfast as their modest larder afforded. And despite their poverty, not one dime would they accept in payment for their hospitality. I never again saw this interesting family, but I heard from them sometime after the war ended.

Mrs. Peppercorn could not write but her daughter Suky wrote for her mother and gave me the news. Sally was married to a one armed soldier who was helping Lexy (Alexander the Great) run a little farm; they had two cows and were raising a lot of sweet potatoes and also a fine bunch of hogs. Melverina Elverina had a fine sweetheart that she had met while she was in the "horsepittal" (that is the way Suky spelled "Hospital") nursing Lexy; this sweetheart was still being "doctored" for a bullet wound in his hip; as soon as he was able to leave the "Horsepittal" he and Melverina were to be married. Suky said she "warn't never going to be married," that she meant to live always with "Ma," who had the rheumatism in the knees so bad she "couldn't hardly stand up."

I was so pleased with this labored epistle of Suky's that I sent her a box filled with things which are useful to a farmer's family--a bolt of calico, handkerchiefs, neck ties for Alexander the Great and his one armed brother-in-law, a dress for Suky and a bolt of white muslin stuff with which to make Melverina a bridal dress when her lover was able to leave the "horsepittal" and marry her. In the remoter coves of the Cumberland mountains there may still be big, raw boned women who chew tobacco, say "You'uns" and "We'uns" and not only are physically able to take a man's part but actually take it, even shouldering a gun and going to war like men do, when necessity demanded such heroic action. But such women are hardly to be found elsewhere even if any still exist in the mountains-I have dwelt with some detail on my two nights visit with the Peppercorns because they represent a day and a type that have vanished forever; the little picture I have attempted to draw may help you, my dear grand children, to see with your minds that curious type which your eyes may never behold.

As we drew near Memphis the country around seemed more and more desolate and dreary; the farm houses on the road side had been either deserted or burned to the ground. No inhabitants of the country did we see, nor human beings of any kind excepting occasionally we saw troops of Union soldiers marching northward. Some of those troops were black. They spoke no word to me, I spoke no word to them; their black faces and blue uniforms affrighted me. When at last we reached the front gate of "Ridgeway," our home on Kerr Avenue I rejoiced that our weary pilgrimage was ended, but there was still many things about my situation calculated to depress me. Looking from my gate toward the river I could see Fort Pickering where were encamped more than two thousand negro soldiers and three thousand white yankee soldiers. All these, I knew, hated me and mine; I was alone with three little children; my husband was, I knew not where-perhaps a captive on his way to some Northern dungeon. In those days, just after the war, we did not know what the Yankees meant to do to the crushed and conquered Confederate soldiers. Many alarming rumors went about-Jeff Davis was to be hanged, his generals were to be shot and the private soldiers of his armies were to be imprisoned! These rumors worried me. And I was worried, too, at the thought of what might happen were some of those black soldiers to leave Fort Pickering at night and wander in my direction. Men but lately released from slavery, men but a degree removed from savagery sometimes do terrible things when suddenly entrusted with power. Those negroes were armed; they would get leaves of absence; they could walk from Fort Pickering to Ridgeway in half an hour; no friends or neighbors were near me. Can you wonder, my children, that I was uneasy?

I got out of my Rockaway, opened the front gate and led Adrienne into the yard; then I stood still surveying the scene. I wish I had power to paint it. Such a scene, typical of thousands of others happening at that time, should be painted by a great artist and entitled "The Refugee's Return." After four years of bloody war, after wanderings and trials and tribulations that might fairly be said to rival those of Ulysses in Homer's *Odyssey,* there was I at my home again and like Ulysses, I was "marred by many ills," but there was no Athena with a magic wand to endow *me* with "supernatural beauty and vigor." Ulysses had, too, if I remember aright, patient Penelope waiting to greet him; but no member of my family was at Ridgeway to greet me. And so my plight may fairly be said to have been even more pitiful than Homer's hero.

But a pleasant surprise was in store for me. After finishing my survey of the scene, after noting that the big forest trees were still standing and that the fences and the house were in good condition, not at all "tumble down" as was the case with most southern homes to which the refugees of that day returned, I guessed the reason why--my home was occupied, occupied by someone put there by Gen. Sherman! I had no real hope that this tenant, whoever he was, would recognize my rights to the premises, still I would see him, I would demand possession. It would do no harm, the worst he could do to me would be to order me off the place. If he did order me off, what was I to do? Where could I shelter my three little children? These questions filled me with fear. But, concealing that fear as best I could, putting on as brave a face as I could, I climbed back into the Rockaway and drove up to the house. And there I received the pleasantest surprise of my life--a surprise all the greater because so unexpected, so in contrast with the conduct of the last occupants of that house, the Hickeys.

Bidding my boys sit still in the Rockaway, I went up the steps to the front door and rang the bell. The man who answered was a pleasant looking Irishman. He looked at me inquiringly; my heart beat so fast, the uncertainty of my reception so worried me, my tongue was tied; I stood like a simpleton, absolutely speechless, saying not a word to explain who I was or what I wanted. The man looked from me to the Rockaway and then to my children. One glimpse of Adrienne and the battered, mud stained old Rockaway which for three years had been rolling about the war worn roads of the Confederacy, sufficed to tell our tale. There was no mistaking the fact that we were pilgrims, refugees returning from the War. A look of comprehension came into the Irishman's eyes.

"You must be Mrs. Meriwether?" he said. I nodded my head; my tongue was still tied. "Mrs. *Colonel* Meriwether?" queried the Irishman. Again I nodded my head, like a simpleton, without saying a single word. Then the surprise came. "Well, well, I sure am glad to see you," said the pleasant faced Irishman, his face all beams and smiles. "I am glad to welcome you to your home, Mrs. Meriwether. Come right in. I'll bring the children in and Sam will look after your mule. When will the Colonel he here?"

Then at last my power of speech returned. I took that honest man's hand and shook it warmly as I thanked him for his kindness and told him that my husband was coming "soon"; just how soon depended on when his army was disbanded.

"Oh, that will be in a very short time," responded Mr. O'Donell (such was the Irishman's name) cheerfully, "and we'll be mighty glad to see him. The Yanks have whipped us, whipped us good and hard but the South will never forget the brave soldiers that fought for her. This is Mrs. O'Donell," turning to a smiling, healthy looking young woman who came out into the hall to see what detained her husband. I greeted Mrs. O'Donell and shook hands with her, and we liked each other from the start.

"I am sure you must be hungry," said Mrs. O'Donell. "Just excuse me for half an hour so I can get you and your children a little supper. Mr. O'Donell will look after you until supper is ready."

"I sure will do that," responded Mr. O'Donell heartily. And in a very few minutes Adrienne and the Rockaway had been taken around to the stable, while my children and I were seated comfortably in my old room, the room where I had passed so many happy hours before the outbreak of that terrible war. A little later we sat down to a fine supper, and then Mrs. O'Donell said to me:

"We have only one room furnished with a bed but I will make a pallet on the floor and hope you can manage with that for tonight. Tomorrow we'll do better. Mr. O'Donell will certainly be able to get a bed somewhere."

I told her we did not mind sleeping on a pallet, that we had often slept on floors; Mr. O'Donell said that just as soon as he could find a little house he would move his family out of my way.

"You mustn't do that," I said. "I will be glad to have you stay here until my husband comes. If you will drive me to town tomorrow I will buy a few housekeeping things so as to make my room comfortable. Then, if Mrs. O'Donell won't mind my cooking on her stove, I can get along very nicely."

The O'Donells readily consented to this arrangement and when I lay down that night on a pallet on the floor by the side of my three children I was very happy; for after fully expecting to arrive in Memphis a homeless wanderer it seemed positively heavenly to be there sleeping under my own roof and near such good, friendly people as the O'Donells! I rejoiced in the possession of a few green back bills and also of a little gold which I carried in a girdle around my body. This gold, however, I did not intend to spend; I meant to keep it and hand it to Minor. My purchases would have to cease when my small store of greenbacks became exhausted.

Next morning on the way into town I saw things which both distressed and alarmed me--blue uniformed negro soldiers swaggering, and some staggering, on the streets; some of these soldiers were playing the gallant to ugly, gaudily dressed negro women. During my walks from one shop to another I sometimes had to get off the sidewalk into the street in order to make way for these negro soldiers-they walked four and five abreast and made not the slightest effort to let white women pass. Had I not voluntarily gotten out into the street they would have elbowed me off the sidewalk. As it was, when I stepped off the curb to let them pass they gave me insolent looks and laughed and sometimes one of them would say: "We's all ekal now. Git out o' our way, white woman!"

Any stranger, seeing those negroes, would have supposed the Blacks not the Whites, were masters in the South. Of course the white women stayed indoors except when urgent necessity obliged them to go out; the few white women whom I saw that first morning of my return to Memphis were garbed in faded, rusty old black calico gowns. I knew they were the sisters or mothers or daughters of our slain Confederate soldiers; on their faces was a settled sadness.

When they stepped off the sidewalk into the muddy street to make way for black soldiers those proud Southern women did not show by any word or act that they felt any sense of humiliation; their faces showed no sign of anger, no tinge of resentment. It was as if they had stepped aside to get out of the way of a drove of dirty dogs.

As I saw those things that first morning in Memphis, and as I myself experienced them, the thought came to me that, if negroes were to dominate life in the South, it would be better for us to emigrate to some country where white people were respected. Mr. O'Donell told me that every policeman in Memphis was an Irishman, but that they dared not interfere with negro soldiers. It often happened, he said, that negro soldiers would get drunk and bully and knock down a white man, or insult a white woman; but if a policeman dared to arrest a negro for such misbehaviour all the soldiers at Fort Pickering, white soldiers as well as black ones, would rally around their brother soldier who was arrested and demand his instant release. And such was the hatred for the South of the Army officers, or such their indifference, that the soldiers were permitted to have their way and bully the civil authorities into releasing black offenders no matter how flagrant their offense!

I bought two mattresses, three pillows, some sheets, towels and two cheap bedsteads, also a few cups, saucers, knives, etc.; then Mr. O'Donell drove me home and as we passed through the big front gate Mr. O'Donell pointed to a small pile of lumber under one of the trees and told me it had been put there by some negroes. When I asked why they put lumber in my yard he said the negroes intended to build a house there.

"They said this land was 'Bandoned,' said Mr. O'Donell, "and you know, Mrs. Meriwether, the Yankee Government has allowed the negroes to settle on any land that was 'abandoned'--that is, on land deserted by its owners and its taxes left unpaid. I told those negroes that this land was not abandoned, that I was the owner's caretaker and that the taxes were all paid. They listened to what I said and scratched their wooly heads, but--not being wholly convinced--they went to Fort Pickering and returned with five negro soldiers to whom I repeated my story. 'De house ain't 'bandoned' was their decision after listening to what I had to say, 'but de land am. You kin stay in de yard,' turning to the negroes who wanted your place, 'An' you kin build yo' own house an' lib in it an' you'll be inside de law so long's you doan tech the big house what ain't 'bandoned!' Such was the decision of those five soldiers, from which I knew of no way to appeal. So there are several negro families on your place now, in the sheds and barn. And I suppose when this lumber is built into a house that some more negro families will move in."

As you may imagine, my children, this news distressed me greatly; it was lovely to be in my own home again, but a home surrounded by insolent, half savage negroes! The very thought was dreadful! I resolved then and there to do my best to persuade Minor to emigrate from the South, if this rule of the negro was to be permanent. That very same afternoon I saw three negro men come through the front gate with axes, saws and other tools in their hands and, advancing to meet them, I asked what they wanted.

"We're gwine cut down dem big trees," answered one of the men.

"Why do you wish to do that?"

"Dey's in de way. De house's gwine ter be built here."

"You are not going to build any house here," I replied firmly. "I own this place. You must leave at once."

"Dis is 'bandoned land" said the first of the three negroes, the one with the axe. "We's got a right to build on 'bandoned land."

"Certainly," I said smiling, but with all the assurance in my manner that I could muster, "certainly. Nobody denies negroes have a right to build on abandoned land, but this land is not abandoned. It belongs to me. Mr. O'Donell has been taking care of it for me all the time and I've paid all the taxes. You darkies had better see a lawyer if you don't want to get into trouble. Your lawyer will tell you land isn't abandoned when the owner pays the taxes. He will tell you, too, that if you were to build a house on land that wasn't abandoned, the house would belong to the owner of the land. Go ahead and build a house on my land if you want to, but it will be my house and you will have to pay me rent for it. Ask your lawyer if you don't believe me."

With that I walked off with an unconcerned air, leaving the three negroes scratching their heads and arguing between themselves as to what they should do; finally they picked up their tools and went away. I was only partly relieved, for I feared those negroes would put more trust in the thousands of lawless soldiers in Fort Pickering than in what any lawyer might tell them, and I knew that if the Fort Pickering soldiers told them to go ahead and build on my land the civil law would be powerless to stop them. The following day my heart sank; when I saw those three negroes drive a wagon through my front gate; but my spirits soon rose, for the wagon was empty and I saw that it had been brought for the purpose of hauling the lumber away. Piece by piece the negroes put the lumber on the wagon and as they drove away they told me with a grin that they had found a "Sho 'nuff piece of abandoned land," and land, too, that was better than mine and closer to town! Some of the negroes who had moved into the barn and outhouses on my place were standing around, watching the loading of the lumber on the wagon. To them the big negro with the axe said: "You niggers better git out o' heah an' move onto sho' nuff 'bandoned land. A lawyer dun tole us dis ain't no 'bandoned land. You niggers'll have to git out o' heah!"

You can't imagine, my children, what a load these words lifted from my mind; the very sun seemed brighter, the whole world seemed a better place to live in. I rejoiced that the negroes left our place before my dear husband returned-I knew how disgusted he would have been to find such a motley, dirty crew camped in and around our beautiful Ridgeway. This hegira of the negroes from

Ridgeway I regarded as the biggest single piece of luck I had had for a long time; another piece of good fortune befell me in this way.

On the day that Gen. Sherman's men were at my home, carrying out the order to drive me out of the city, an old friend of ours, a Mrs. Kirkland whose father had been a patient of my father's, was with me, helping me gather together the few things I was allowed to take with me on my pilgrimage into Dixie. Just as I was climbing into my Rockaway Mrs. Kirkland whispered:

"I shall stay here as long as I can and before the Yanks have a chance to take all your things I may be able to slip out some of the furniture and table ware--at any rate, I'll hang around and do what I can."

Before I could even thank my friend for her offer Gen. Sherman's men hurried me off and the episode was quite forgotten by me until I saw Mrs. Kirkland a week or so after my return to Ridgeway. Then she told me of the trick she had played on the Yanks. "You remember how sick old Uncle Lewis was at the time Gen. Sherman drove you away?" she said. I told her yes, I remembered very well. "Well," continued Mrs. Kirkland, "I told the Yanks that Uncle Lewis had the smallpox; he was out in his cabin a hundred feet from the house, but that made no difference. You ought to have seen how quick those Yanks got off your place. They said they would send the ambulance for the nigger, then they left right away. After they were gone and before the ambulance came I got a lot of your things loaded into a wagon and hauled them to my home. They are ready for you as soon as you want them."

I told Mrs. Kirkland to keep them until the O'Donells moved, that for the present I had no place to put them. Among our belongings which were thus saved to us through all the wreck and pillage of War was Minor's favorite easy chair. Furniture men tell me such solid, strong, durable chairs are not made now. That chair was made of solid walnut and upholstered in leather; it is now, nearly seventy years after Minor bought it, in my son's St. Louis home, as handsome and as comfortable as the day it was made. Of course, it has been upholstered many times, but the walnut frame has never been mended and is as strong now as the day it was made. Mrs. Kirkland also saved my set of fine china, from the big oval platter, large enough to hold a twenty pound turkey, down to the small after dinner coffee cups. This set, which was very beautiful and very costly, and which I have given to my grandson Lee Meriwether, Jr., is now in my son's home in St. Louis. Fifty one years ago when Mrs. Kirkland restored that set to me I spread it out on a table and my boys stared at it in amazement. They had so long been accustomed to ugly, rough jug ware, or to tin utensils, that they stood almost in awe of china that was so beautifully decorated. Little Rivers, who in particular hated the rough jug ware of Tuscaloosa, after gazing at the china set for several minutes in absolute silence, at length found his tongue.

"Is all this our very own, Mama?" he asked in a whisper.

"Yes, dear, every piece of it."

With a still more cautious whisper he put another question. "Mama, will the Yankees take it away from us?"

"No, dear, I think not."

"Oh, Mama, I'm so glad. Now we won't have to eat out of old jugs and tin." And off he went, radiantly happy. I was not so happy, for in truth I was not at all certain that the Yankees would not take my china away; I did not know but that they might even drive me out of my home again when my return became known to the authorities. I did not wish my children to worry, however, consequently to them I maintained an air of complete confidence. Half an hour after those questions about the china I saw little Rivers walking about the lawn, now and then stopping to look up at the big trees or at the garden and the barn and the sheds. Then presently he came up on the porch where I was rocking Baby Lee in my arms and, waving his little hand toward the lawn and the stable and the garden, he said:

"Mama, is all that ours?"

"Yes, dear; it is all ours."

"Will the Yankees take it away from us?"

"I think not, dear, I think not."

Again did his little face light up with joy and as he ran off to play I breathed a fervent prayer that the Yankees would let us live in our home and that Minor would be allowed to come back to his little family! Were these two things vouchsafed to me I felt, now that the motley crowd of negroes were gone, that my cup of happiness would indeed be full.

CHAPTER XX

Death of Baby Lee's Black Mammy. Grief of my children. How Henry "tried" out candidates for his hand before marrying again.

It was not many months after my return to Memphis that our conquered, paroled, ragged, shoeless soldiers began to pour into our town, and among them was my own dear husband. In spite of the four years of War, of the exposure to all sorts of weather, of the poor food he had been obliged to eat, he was well and strong, and I could see that he was trying to look cheerful and resigned to the crushing defeat of our beloved South. Minor was always a resolute man and when a thing was inevitable, no matter how bad was that thing, he determined to make the best of it. Oh, how glad I was to see him! And how wild with joy were his little boys at seeing their "Big, sweet Soger Papa" once more!

With Minor came Henry, Rose and their two children, "Booby" and Alice (who now runs a Caterer's business in Memphis). They came in a wagon drawn by two mules which had belonged to our army and which had been surrendered to the Yankees, but the Yankees permitted Minor and his servants to return to Memphis in the wagon on condition that on arriving in the city he would immediately turn the wagon and mules over to the military authorities.

The first thing Rose said to me was: "Now, Miss Betty, we kin get all de sugar we wants." "Yes," I answered, "and we shan't have to give for sugar slippers worth four hundred and fifty dollars!" Rose grinned and showed her gleaming teeth. "An' I won't have to keep pestering no po' white trash lady to get de sugar, will I, Miss Betty?" she queried with another grin. I verily believe she enjoyed her forty five visits to the Sugar Lady. Henry and Rose and their two children remained on our place with us and we began to feel somewhat settled and satisfied, then trouble came as it often does when unexpected. The negro soldiers camped at Fort Pickering wanted to get acquainted with Rose and Henry, but they hated "Yankee Niggers" and, as they told me, "Froze 'em away." This "freezing" made the negro soldiers spiteful; they abused Rose and told her she was "stuck up"; they said she thought herself better than anybody else, whereas in truth she and her husband were both "D--- Secesh Niggers who didn't have no better sense than to be slaves to a Secesh master!"

This sort of abuse, heaped upon Rose and Henry day after day, made them very uncomfortable; we advised them to keep quiet and pass the abuse by silently as if they had not heard it. They could not cope with a regiment of soldiers; if they gave those blue uniformed negroes only half a chance to harm them, that harm certainly would be done them. Our faithful servants followed this advice, but the more patiently they bore their tormentors' abuse the worse that abuse became, until at last we feared the negro soldiers might shoot or bayonet Henry, and perhaps Rose, too. So we decided to send them away from Ridgeway into the city where they would be among Memphis negroes, consequently more safe from those insolent soldiers.

In the rear of one of our Union Street dwellings was a vacant lot which we told Henry he might use; he was a capable carpenter and, with the help of other negroes who understood house building, Rose and Henry and their children were comfortably settled in a little frame cottage before the summer ended. Henry made a good living for his family by doing carpenter work about the city and they continued to occupy that little cottage for a number of years. Early in the summer of 1867 Henry came to me one day and begged me to come at once and see Rose--he feared she was very sick, she "had been took" all of a sudden and was "acting monsus queer." I hurried over to the little cottage in the rear of our Union St. dwelling and found Rose unconscious, a doctor standing by her side. The poor woman was dying; she breathed her last a few minutes after I arrived. Henry told me she had seemed to be perfectly well when she went to bed the night before. My little boys grieved greatly over her death and I was unwise enough to take them with me to see her in her coffin just before they carried her away from the little home where she had been so happy during the two years that followed the four unhappy years of war. I knew it was the cholera of which she had died, but my boys insisted so hard on saying "goodbye to Mammy Rose" that I took them to the cottage just before the funeral. At that time I was woefully ignorant about diseases; in my later life I read many medical books and listened to many doctors lecture. Had I known as much about germs and infectious diseases in 1867 as I know now I would not have permitted my boys to stand over the open coffin of their "Black Mammy."

Although Henry really loved Rose and had made her a kind husband, hardly was she in her grave before he began, as the darkies say, "to look about" and one morning a few months later a comely, well dressed negro woman came to see me and enlist my aid and sympathies in her behalf.

"What can I do for you?" I asked.

"Dey tells me you's got 'fluence wid Henry," said the comely negress, tears welling into her eyes, "an' I thought mebbe you could make him 'have hisself."

"How has he been misbehaving?" I demanded. "Henry has always been a good negro. I never knew him to misbehave."

"He's a good nigger now, Miss Betty," replied the woman, the tears streaming down her cheeks, "but he sho is misbehavin' hisself. Henry wants to git another wife, now's Rose went an' died, an' he won't marry no woman till he tries her fust. He's tried two already an' turned 'em off. Den he took me to try, an' he's had me four weeks an' now he's gwine turn me off an' try another. An', Miss Betty, I dun my best to please him, I was good to his chilluns and I cooked him good vittles, an' yit he ain't gwine to keep me. He dun tole me so dis mawnin'."

160

"You mean you have been living with Henry the same as if you had been married to him?"

"Yes, Miss Betty, dat's de way Henry tries a woman. He says he won't marry de best woman on earth 'less he tries her first and knows she's jes what he wants."

I explained to that comely negress how wrong, how imprudent she had been, but she could not understand my point of view at all. "Laws Miss Betty, you mustn't jedge niggers by white folk's ways. Our ways is different from your ways." That was her answer to my lecture on the immorality of her and Henry's conduct. I told her to send Henry to me and I would see what I could do with him. Henry came next morning, a grin on his face, his hat in his hand, his step shuffling and halting. I tried to convince him of the great wrong he had done and he listened patiently and the grin left his face and he became very serious. But when I finished my talk he made a vigorous argument to prove the justice of his conduct.

"Miss Betty," he said, "I've got my old mother to keep; she's allus been good to me, an' I'se got to be good to her. Den I'se got two little chilluns. Now, a man can't drive his mother an' his chilluns out of his house an' if dey stays dere an' his wife treats 'em mean, what he gwine do? Nacherlly jes beat de head off'n dat fool woman. Now, as I doan want to beat no woman's head off, ain't it better to try her fust an' see if she's de kind of wife I wants? Miss Betty, sho'ly you must see a nigger in my position's got to be monsus 'tickler what kind of a woman he marries."

I told him it was wise to be particular, to study the woman's character well before marrying her, but that it was very wrong to live with her as if he were married to her. This argument, however, Henry seemed wholly incapable of understanding. He made no spoken reply, but he shook his head in vigorous dissent. Then I took another tack.

"While you were trying this last woman did she mistreat your children? Did she make your mother unhappy?"

"No, Miss Betty, not zackly unhappy, but she warn't like Rose, no whar like Rose, Miss Betty, an' so I thought I'd better not marry her."

"But you must marry her, Henry," I urged. "You have been living with her and you admit she was good to your mother and children. You will be doing a great wrong if you cast her away. You don't want to be wicked, do you?"

"No, Miss Betty, I doan want to be wicked, but I doan want to marry dat gal either. But, Miss Betty," he added, seeing how hurt I looked, "I'll think it over, I sho will, an' I'll marry her ef my mother kin git along wid her."

Two months later Henry came to me with a beaming face. "Miss Betty," he said, "I'se brought my wife to see you." I thought he had come to his senses and righted the wrong he had done the poor woman who had begged me to help her. But when I began complimenting him for what I supposed he had done he gave a sheepish grin and said: "Laws, Miss Betty, I couldn't marry dat ar woman, I jes nacherlly couldn't do it. We nebber would hab got along. But I'se got a powerful nice gal now an' I wants you to see her. Lethy, come in here an' see Miss Betty."

Responding to this call, the door opened and in walked a comely mulatto girl and stood shyly before me; she was both younger and better looking than the poor woman who had come to me crying.

"Henry," I said severely, "are you going to mistreat this girl, too?"

"Laws, no, Miss Betty," grinned Henry. "We wuz married last night in de Babtis' church."

"An' he nebber tried *me*" giggled the young wife. "I wouldn't let him try me."

This marriage proved a happy one and we often saw both Henry and his wife up to the day of their deaths a few years later. As I have already told you, Henry's daughter Alice who shared her mother's milk with my baby Lee, is still living in Memphis, a sensible, prosperous woman, married to a Negro named Owens who seems to love her and treats her well.

CHAPTER XXI

Horrors of the "Reconstruction" era. A Congressional Committee reports outrages upon "Mrs." Francis Thompson, who turns out to be a sensual negro man. White women elbowed into the gutters by negro men.

After Lee's surrender the people of the South were anxious to know how their conquerors were going to treat them. Would they be merciful? Or would they be bitter and cruel as they had been during the four years of war? The newspapers stated that President Lincoln had gone to Richmond on April 3, 1865, that the people there received him kindly and that he instructed Gen. Weitzel (who was in command in Richmond) to permit the insurgent ("Rebel") legislators to assemble at once and enact laws for Virginia as they had done before the state seceded from the Union.

This merciful treatment of Virginians by Lincoln evoked from every Southern heart the deepest appreciation; the people of the South hoped and believed that at last the hate and bitterness of the war were to die out on both sides and a true friendship between North and South was to make the country really one again. For one happy week this hope and belief were entertained; then a wintery blast blew over the South and chilled every heart! Secretary of War Stanton blew that blast upon our war torn land! Mr. Stanton vigorously opposed Lincoln's instructions to Gen. Weitzel in Richmond; Stanton sent for the President and Lincoln went over to the War Department and seated himself on a sofa in the Secretary's office and there listened to his Secretary's arguments. Stanton declared that the conquerors, not the conquered, must control Virginia, that to permit the "Rebel" legislators in Richmond to make laws would be to give away the scepter of the Conqueror and transfer the victory of the Federal arms in the field to the very men who for four years had borne arms against the North.

"Mr. President," concluded Stanton, "the people will not sustain you in such a policy. If you permit your order to Gen. Weirzel to be carried out it will nullify our military victories!"

President Lincoln remained silent for some minutes after Stanton finished speaking, then without a word he got up, walked to the Secretary of War's desk, took pen and paper and began writing. "There!" he said after writing for a few moments. "I think that will suit you!"

Stanton took the paper which the President handed him, read it, frowned and said: "No, Mr. President. It does not suit me. It does not go far enough. Gen. Weitzel should be ordered positively to prohibit the Rebel legislators from assembling."

Mr. Lincoln read the paper he had written, hesitated a moment, then with a shrug of his shoulders, crumpled the paper and tossed it in the waste basket, then he seated himself and wrote another order. This time he wrote it in such a way as to meet the Secretary of War's approval; the order was sent to Gen. Weitzel and thus, even before Booth's dreadful deed of ten days later, the South knew that Stanton, not Lincoln's policy was the one that was likely to prevail. Of course, after Lincoln's death on April 15th the temper of the North was roused to white heat and the Secretary of War, freed from the President's gentle restraint, launched his policy of ruthless revenge and hate which, under the name of the "Reconstruction Era," will long remain a blot upon the pages of our history. In a life of Stanton, published in 1905, his biographer says that Stanton took great credit to himself for having made Lincoln rescind his order to Gen. Weitzel. I dare say Stanton also prided himself on the results of his policy, a policy which postponed for a quarter of a century the era of good feeling between North and South which now exists and which would have begun almost immediately after Lee's surrender had Lincoln's policy of reconciliation been allowed to prevail. As a sample of what Stanton's policy of hate brought about let me quote a paragraph from a letter I received from a North Carolina friend in 1868:

"At a banquet given here the other day, among the guests were three ex-Governors, two ex-members of Congress, and ex-Justice of the Supreme Court, besides a number of lawyers, doctors and prominent business men. But the only persons in The Banquet Hall who could either vote or hold public office were *the negroes who waited on the table!*"

It is reasonable to believe that such a travesty on sense and morals would never have taken place had Lincoln lived and enforced *his* policy instead of Stanton's. In one of his famous joint debates with Stephen A. Douglas (on September 18, 1858) Lincoln said:

"I am not, nor ever have been, in favor of making voters or jurors of negroes, nor of qualifying them to hold office, nor to intermarry with white people, and I will say, in addition to this that there is a physical difference between the white and black races which I believe will forever forbid the two races living together on terms of social and political equality."

Lincoln, the Great Emancipator, as appears from these words out of his own mouth, did not believe negroes should or could be on a plane of political equality with the white race. But those who came after Lincoln not only advocated equality for the negro, they demanded that the negro be placed *above* his former white masters! This unwise policy, born of hate and passion, led to untold suffering on the part of the negroes as well as the whites; for of course no people of a white race will permanently live in subjection to negroes. The people of Memphis stood the insolence of the Blacks for a while; for a while delicate white women were elbowed off the sidewalks into the muddy streets by coarse Negro men--then something happened, something which is known in History as the "Memphis Riots." In spite of the soldiers at Fort Pickering, before those soldiers could arrive on the scene, there was a swift uprising against the negroes, many of them were killed, hundreds of them were wounded, all of them were thoroughly cowed and frightened! The North was aghast. Radicals in Congress declared the South was plotting another rebellion, drastic laws were enacted and a Congressional Committee was sent to Memphis to investigate the "horrible" affair. In company with a friend of ours, Miss Mary Body, I attended the sittings of that Congressional Committee and, in the light of subsequent history, some of its findings were remarkable. For example that Committee listened to testimony concerning one Francis Thompson, and reported to Congress in terms of virtuous indignation that "Rebels," while pretending to believe themselves superior to the black race, did not hesitate to vent their passions upon black women, and that owing to this damnable trait of rebels Francis Thompson, an honest, God fearing negro woman had been shamefully seduced and assaulted. Miss Boby and I were present at the sitting of the Committee when Francis Thompson "herself" testified; "she" (you will learn presently, children, why I use quotation marks with the words "Herself" and "She") was coal black, kinky wool on her head, thick, coarse lips, the upper one showing distinct marks of a stiff mustache, closely shaved off. This odious creature swore that seven former Confederate soldiers had entered her home and ravished her, one after the other, and that as a result of this frightful treatment she had been confined for weeks to her bed.

"Did you have medical attendance during the weeks you were confined to your bed?" asked the Hon. Elihu Washburn, a noted radical leader in Congress who was Chairman of the Investigating Committee.

"Yas sah. Dr. Rumbllt dun attend to me," answered the big, black witness.

"How long did the seven Confederate soldiers stay in your house?"

"Nigh 'bout foah hours. It wuz nigh 'bout day light when dey dun went away.

"Did they say anything when they went away?"

"Yas sah! Dey said dey wuz gwine burn up de las' damn nigger in de city!"

When Francis Thompson stepped down from the witness chair she was followed by her companion, a negro girl named Lucy Smith, who testified to the villainous treatment to which she also had been subjected by the seven Confederate soldiers; her story certainly was harrowing and the Hon. Elihu Washburn and his honorable brother Congressmen actually shed tears as they listened--at any rate, they got out their handkerchiefs, wiped their eyes as one does when wiping away tears. and gave audible expression to the indignation which surged within them at this evidence of the depravity of Southern rebels!!!

Miss Body and I felt morally certain that both these negroes had told foul falsehoods; we did not believe that a Confederate soldier could entertain for such repulsive looking creatures any feeling but that of disgust. That Congressional Committee, however, believed every word of the two negroes' testimony and on July 25th 1866, submitted to Congress its report in which the whole world was called on to note how debauched and depraved were the men of the South, the men who had rebelled against the Government of their country. Here is a paragraph from Congressman Washburn's report:

"The crowning acts of atrocity and diabolism committed during the riots was the ravishing of colored women by these fiends in human shape." ("Fiends" meant ex-Confederate soldiers). "These outrages are too shocking to be given at length. It is a singular fact that while the rebel mob was shooting down negroes as if they were dogs, yet when they found unprotected colored women they at once conquered their prejudices and violated unprotected colored women with the most licentious brutality, as *the case of Mrs. Francis Thompson will show!"*

Then Mr. Washburn's report gave "Mrs." Thompson's testimony in full. Well, my dear children, you may imagine how Congressman Washburn and the other Congressmen who signed that report, felt when two years later it was discovered that "Mrs." Francis Thompson was a man! Only the day before "she" was discovered to be a man, in the way that I shall relate in a moment, I saw Francis Thompson in Lowenstein's dry goods store in Memphis. I had not seen her since the day I heard her tell her sad story to the Congressional Committee, but there was no mistaking so conspicuous and so ugly a figure. I recognized "her" at once--the same coarse, sensuous face, the same broad, burly body. On "her" head was a jaunty bonnet, around "her" shoulders was a gaudy shawl. "She" wore an immense hoop skirt over which hung a baby blue muslin skirt ruffled up to the waist. This style of costume made the "woman" look elephantine in size. Naturally I, in common with nearly everybody else in Lowenstein's, stared at "her" and recalled the terrible story which she had told the Washburn Committee and which, read on the floor of Congress, had so startled the people of the whole country. In a spirit of mischief I said to Miss Body, who was with me:
"Isn't that lady's shawl beautiful? I never saw one like it before." "Neither did I," returned Miss Body. "It must be imported. I wonder if it came from Paris?"
Both of us spoke distinctly, with the desire that the Thompson person might hear us. "She" did, and turned her ugly black face to us as she said with a pleased grin:
"You'se right, ladies. My husban' gib me dis shawl in Paris on my weddin' tower."

"Well, my Children, the very next day after that episode in Lowenstein's store an honest, respectable negro woman filed a complaint against "Mrs." Francis Thompson. This respectable negro woman had hired her young daughter to "Mrs." Thompson as "her" house maid, the daughter was about to become a mother and when questioned as to who was her unborn child's father, she answered "Mrs." Francis Thompson! As you may imagine, this story created a sensation! When arrested "Mrs." Thompson vehemently protested that the girl was crazy. "How," "She," demanded, "could a woman be the 'Father' of a baby?" This question might well puzzle scientists to answer; but the Memphis police answered it in short order. For on investigation by a jury of medical men, appointed by the Court, it developed that "Mrs." Thompson was a big, robust negro man! Thereupon the police made "Mrs." Thompson remove the hoop skirt, the muslin dress and other female apparel, and don apparel more suitable for a man. This done, he was put in a room, the barred window of which looked out on the street, and a crowd of negroes, both men and women, gathered in front of that barred window and gibed and grinned and jeered at the ugly brute sitting in his prison. Not one word did the brute speak; he seemed to wilt and shrivel and shrink under the scorn of his own race. He kept his eyes closed, but he was not asleep and evidently heard the questions that were hurled at him. "What'd you want to be a woman for?" asked one of his tormentors. "You mus' be a dam fool!" said another. A third said: "Why you fool dat little gal, nigger? Her mammy ought to have you hanged!"

Dr. Hewett, our family physician who was one of the medical men appointed by the Court to examine "Mrs." Thompson, told me the fellow, ugly brute that he was, was so affected that he could not eat; he became actually ill and it was sometime before he was strong enough to serve his sentence, which included labor in the "Chain Gang." In those days certain prisoners, hobbled with chains, were made to clean the streets and the next time I saw the brute who had so aroused the Hon. Elihu Washburn's sympathies and, through the Congressional report submitted to Congress on July 25th, 1866, the sympathies of the whole North, was when he was working with a number of other brutal looking men, his legs hobbled by a chain, his hands holding the implement with which he was scraping the mud off the Memphis streets!

Shortly after the "Memphis Riots and Massacre" (as they were called in the Hon. Washburn's report) an incident occurred which I shall relate so you may understand social conditions in the South during the "Reconstruction" era. In testifying before the Congressional Committee Gen. Stoneman, the Union officer in command in Memphis, said:

"Neither I nor any other Union Officer occupy any social position in, Memphis; the whites, being all rebels, keep to themselves. They have nothing to do with us socially."

This was true; when we saw a Union officer or a Union officer's wife or sister we simply didn't see them--we just looked straight through them, as if they didn't exist. In view of the doctrine then being taught by Northern leaders, that rebels were all vile and that the negroes were superior to Southern whites, you might suppose the Union officers and their women folk would be supremely indifferent to this aloofness policy of our people, but they were not. On the contrary, they resented it and sometimes even attempted to change it.

One day I was at an afternoon tea given by a friend of ours, the wife of a former Confederate officer when the maid ushered in two ladies who were not known personally to our hostess, but she knew who they were; her cook had told her about these two ladies. One was the wife, the other was the sister, of a Union officer who lived across the street. My friend Mrs. G's cook said some of *her* negro friends had attended social affairs given by the Union officer's wife, consequently when Mrs. G. greeted her unexpected visitors it was with no great degree of cordiality. The Union officer's wife announced that she had recently moved into the neighborhood and that she and her sister-in-law had called merely as a "neighborly act."

"That is very good of you," said Mrs. G. sweetly, "and at any other time I should be glad to talk with you and learn how you like our Memphis negroes-- my cook tells me you have many friends among them whom you have entertained--but as you see, I have rebel ladies here taking tea with me and I know their society would be distasteful to you after enjoying the society of your negro friends. Mary (to the negro maid who still stood at the door, staring at the Union ladies) show these ladies the way out."

The Union officer's wife and sister looked daggers at Mrs. G., but they left without a word, and needless to say they never called again.

One good result of the "Memphis Riot and Massacres," was the improved behaviour of the negroes. White men and women were no longer pushed out into the streets; white women no longer needed to fear to go about the city alone; negro soldiers no longer swaggered about the streets, feeling and acting as if they owned the city. The negroes now had some respect for the police and the dozen or more brutal men and women who occupied the cottage next door to where we were then living, at No. 95 Union Street, moved away to a less respectable quarter when they found that their drunken orgies could no longer be indulged in without prompt arrest and a sentence of thirty days or more on the Chain Gang. The owner of that cottage, glad enough to get rid of his horrible tenants, had it cleansed and purified and papered and repaired, then rented it to decent white people.

CHAPTER XXII

My brother Tom gets a pardon from Andrew Johnson. I, too, go to Washington see President Johnson. He refuses to give me back my property. I see Secretary of War Stanton. His icy treatment of me as the wife of a "Traitor." I see Charles Summer, Carl Schurtz and other celebrities.

Not long after Andrew Johnson became President he issued a proclamation pardoning all Rebels excepting those who owned property worth more than twenty thousand dollars. This left my brother Tom without a pardon, for his real estate was worth much more than twenty thousand dollars. Following the assassination of Lincoln a wave of hatred toward the South swept over the North and Congress was importuned to confiscate all the land of the South, divide it into forty acre tracts and give each negro family one tract. The slogan of the day was "Forty acres and a mule" for every adult negro man! Brother Tom did not like the notion of having his land cut up into forty acre tracts and given to negroes, and for a while that appeared to be in store for him unless he secured a pardon; accordingly he resolved to go to Washington and see the President personally. Brother Tom knew the President well. They had served together in Congress and he thought a personal interview might achieve results which his letters had failed to do--doubtless the letters had gone to some department, and had never been seen by the President.

The result justified my brother's decision; on arriving at the White House and being admitted to the President's presence my brother began to state the purpose of his visit, but Johnson interrupted him before his first sentence was completed.

"How are you, Tom Avery?" he said cordially. "I am glad to see you. When did you reach Washington?"

"Only an hour ago, Mr. President. I came to Washington to see you. Unfortunately my property holdings are such as to exclude me from the general amnesty granted in your proclamation. I thought perhaps in my case a special pardon . . ."

"Oh bother, Tom!" interrupted the President. "Don't let's waste time talking about pardons. Of course you shall have one. You shall have anything I can give you. Mr. B.----," turning to his secretary "make out a pardon for Col. William T. Avery formerly of the Confederate army. Now, Tom, turning again to my brother, I want to hear about the boys in Tennessee. It is a long time since I have been in the dear old state but I love her just the same and when I get through my work in Washington I promise you I won't lose a day in going --

back to Greeneville and breathing the pure air of my old mountain home. Remember that tailor sign of mine in Greeneville, Tom?"

My brother smiled; yes, he remembered the sign--"A. Johnson Tailor." The President had shown it to my brother one time when they were together making campaign speeches in Greeneville. I myself saw that sign in the summer of 1879 when we fled from the yellow fever in Memphis and took refuge in Greeneville, East Tennessee. For all I know, the sign may still be there to indicate where a President of the United States once made cheap suits of clothes for country youths. My brother told me the President was not a bit inclined to cover up his humble past; he was not ashamed of having been a country tailor, and himself brought up the subject. "In those days when we were running for Congress," he added, "you didn't expect I'd land in the White House, did you?"

"I certainly did not," replied my brother.

"Well neither did I," laughed the President. Then he asked about some of their mutual friends and kept my brother chatting with him for nearly an hour, although a long line of people were waiting outside to see him.

My brother told me every detail of this interview soon after his return to Memphis; I made notes of it at the time, consequently what I have here written may be accepted as a pretty fair picture of Andrew Johnson just after he was sworn in as President of the United States Tom told me Johnson was greatly changed in his appearance, since the days they had "stumped" Tennessee together and served in Congress together. In those days some years before the war Johnson was a robust, carefree, smiling, happy-looking man; but the man Tom saw in the White House looked careworn, troubled and far from happy. And in truth Johnson had ample cause to be unhappy; the great men of his party, the men in power, such as Secretary of War Stanton, Thaddeus Stevens (called by his admirers "The Great Commoner"), Gen. Butler etc., hated the President almost as much as they hated Jeff Davis and were even then planning and plotting to drag him out of the White House and install in his place a man they could use.

My brother returned home with the hope that the pardon papers in his pocket would save his property from confiscation, and the cordial manner in which the President had received my brother made me hope that I, too, might have restored to me the property which Gen. Sherman had stolen from me, if I were to see the President and lay my case before him. Minor did not share my hope; he said Johnson was a renegade. Although born a Tennessean, he had sided with Tennessee's enemies. A man who deserted his people in their direst need and went over to their enemies was not a man from whom justice could be expected. So my husband argued. But I reminded him of what Andrew Johnson had just done for my brother.

"That was because he and Tom were old friends," was Minor's answer. "He doesn't know you and he won't do anything for you."

About that time the President of the railroad running from Memphis to Grenada, Miss., offered Minor the position of Treasurer of the Railroad, he accepted, and as the salary was three thousand dollars a year I thought Minor could afford to let me have money enough for a trip to Washington. "If I see the President personally and tell him how Gen. Sherman robbed me of all my property, maybe he will order it given back to me. But if he doesn't do that, at any rate I shall have a nice trip. I want to see how Washington looks after the war."

Such was my argument. Minor grumbled and said it was no time to be taking pleasure trips, that we should save every dollar we could and try to mend our fallen fortunes. I would have acceded to this view had I not secretly believed that the President would help me; as it was, I insisted on the trip and finally Minor let me go. Miss Mary Body, an educated, refined young lady, came to our home to care for our three little boys during my absence. My journey was quite without incident until just before we reached the Capital, then as I sat shivering in my seat--the weather was cold, a dreary, drizzling rain was falling and the cars of that train were not heated--an old gentleman who was sitting beside me said "Permit me." And forthwith he laid his shawl over my knees as he added: "I guess you are from the South and so feel the cold more than I do."

"I am not from the far South," I answered. "Tennessee is hardly further south than Washington."

"Oh, you are from Tennessee?" said the old gentleman. "How are your people getting on, now that the war is over?"

"We are all hard at work," I replied. "Our men are trying to get bread and meat for their families."

"That's good. That's much better than fighting."

Minor had cautioned me not to speak of the war, he had warned me that serious trouble--arrest and imprisonment--might result from even casual comment about the conduct of our conquerors. I promised him not to say a word that might offend any "truly loyal" citizen, but it is not always easy to hold your tongue when your feelings are wounded. When that old man said: "At work, eh? That's better than fighting," his tone as well as his words showed he meant it as a fling at my country and my countrymen. Northerners of that day had a habit of talking of Southern men as if they were lazy, as if they never worked, as if they depended on the labor of negroes. The old gentleman continued to talk about the South and presently he said:

"Old Jeff Davis is still in Fortress Monroe waiting to be hanged."

This brutal remark, following the other things he had said, put my prudence to flight; a flame of indignation swept over me; I pushed the woolen shawl off my knees as if it were contamination and dashed it on the floor. "I'd rather freeze!" I exclaimed, "I'd rather die than use the shawl of such a man as you!" Then I burst into a passion of tears. I cried partly because I was suddenly conscious of my imprudence in forgetting Minor's caution, partly because it hurt me to realize how venomously our conquerors hated our martyred Confederate President. I knew Mr. Davis well--God never made a more kindhearted, a more conscientious man; as a statesman he was true to his ideals, as a private citizen he was a courtly gentleman and a God fearing Christian. The old man who sat beside me *looked* kindhearted and good; if such a man could feel such hatred for our Confederate President, then chained to a stone wall in a Fortress dungeon, what must be the hatred of Northerners less kindly looking, less cultured than my traveling neighbor seemed to be? In a little while I regained my composure and begged the old gentleman's pardon.

"It is I who must ask your pardon," he said gravely. "I was thoughtless. We in the North think we have reason to treat Jeff Davis harshly, but that is no reason why I should hurt a woman's feelings. To tell you the truth, it did not occur to me that anybody could love Jeff Davis as we love Lincoln. I see how onesided I have allowed my thoughts to wander." After a pause he added: "My name is B. T. Davies. I am not a politician, nor an army man. I am a professor of mathematics in a boy's college. If I knew what takes you to Washington I might be of some help to you. Can you trust me?

I looked at him for a moment, then said impulsively:

"Yes, I can trust you. I would not have thought it possible for me to trust any man who talked of hanging Mr. Davis, but you look good. You *are* good and I will tell you why I am going to Washington."

Then I told him how Gen. Sherman had confiscated my property, how my brother was an old friend of President Johnson, how the President had recently received him, and how I hoped he would order my property to be restored to me. The old Mathematics professor looked at me kindly.

"I shall be glad to do anything I can for you," he said, "but I fear there is nothing I can do. And to be frank, I fear your mission will fail. Events have been moving rapidly the past few weeks; since your brother was in Washington the President has lost immensely in prestige and power. I do not believe he will dare give you your property back."

"Not dare?" I repeated. "Who could prevent him if he wishes to do it? I thought the President has the last word in such affairs."

"Ordinarily he has, but the times are not ordinary. I fear the Secretary of War now has the real power. However, don't be downhearted. It won't hurt to see the President, and I'll go with you, if you wish and if you think it will do any good."

I thanked Prof. Davies and told him I would be glad to have him accompany me to the White House; we parted at the depot after I had given him my address, which was a small, inexpensive hotel recommended to me by my brother. I have forgotten the name of that little hotel, but I have always called it the "Southern" hotel because in that day just after the war it was the headquarters of poor Confederates who went to the Capital for a pardon or on

172

other business. When I reached the Southern hotel a servant showed me into a little sitting room and told me to wait there while my room was being made ready. A fire was burning in an open grate and I put my feet on the fender to warm them, and then of a sudden I heard a voice behind me say: "What pretty ankles!"

Hastily drawing my feet under my skirt, I turned and saw a tipsy man standing behind my chair leering at me. I was furious. "Leave this room instantly!" I commanded. But the man only grinned and tried to take my hand.

"Don't get mad, sweetheart," he mumbled, "'taint a crime, is it, to admire a pair of pretty ankles?"

I pushed him from me and ran to the door and jerked the bell cord as hard as I could; a clerk came running in to see what was the matter. "I wish to go to my room at once," I said. "I do not wish to wait here. This man annoys me."

The clerk stared at me a moment, then at the tipsy man, then he said: "Our house is full. We have no vacant rooms."

I learned afterward that this was untrue; I had come to the hotel alone and that stupid clerk thought I knew the tipsy man and was in some way not altogether a proper person. I left the Southern hotel, wondering how my brother could have recommended me to such a place, and got a room in a more central, and I am sorry to say a more expensive, hotel. The next morning at breakfast a little lady who looked to be about forty years old made friendly advances toward me-- passed me things on the table, asked me where I was from and told me a lot of her family history. She told me she was from Vermont and had come to Washington to work in one of the Government departments. "The pay is good," she said. I get a hundred dollars a month and really I have very little to do. Would you like to get a position in one of the departments?"

I told her I was married and had three little children to look after.

"Oh, you are from the South?" she said. "Of course you couldn't get a place here even if you wanted one. I wonder why I didn't guess at first that you were a Southerner. Is your husband here?"

I answered No, but volunteered no further information. l remembered Minor's caution and resolved to be reserved with strangers. Professor Davies of course did not call for me, not knowing where I went from the Southern hotel; so at eleven o'clock I started alone for the White House and was told to wait in what I think they call the "East" room. While sitting in that room two gentlemen entered and asked if I was waiting to see the President? I told them I was. Then the two gentlemen took seats beside me and one of them said:

"The President is my father-in-law. I married his daughter. Maybe I can help you. You don't look a bit like a Yankee. Aren't you from the South?"

"Yes, I am from Tennessee."

"Ah, that is my state. My name is Patterson." He edged his chair closer to me and I smelt whiskey on his breath." I feel kin to people from my state, and I always kiss my kin."

He edged still closer to me, but I drew hastily away.

"If you talk that way," I said, "I shall not believe that you are from my state. Tennesseans do not annoy ladies."

The gentleman who had come into the room with him of the whiskey breath came to my rescue. "I say, Pat," he remonstrated, "you've been drinking a bit too much. Come away. You must not talk so to this lady."

"No offense meant, none at all," mumbled "Pat" as he permitted himself to be pulled away; and I don't suppose he did mean any offense. It was only an instance of what whiskey will make even gentlemen high up in the world say and do--but as the two men walked away I wondered what other adventures might be in store for me, seeing that such things as this could happen right in the White House. I was not left long to my thoughts; in a very few minutes a man came in and told me to follow him. I did so, and presently was facing the President. He nodded his head kindly; I bent mine politely. Never before had I seen a face so careworn, so joyless, as was the face of Andrew Johnson. Had he been chained to a wall in a prison, as President Davis was, the President of the United States could not have looked more woe-begone than he did look that morning I saw him in the White House.

As briefly as possible I stated my case and asked for justice; I specially called the President's attention to the fact that I had acquired my property long before the war, consequently that in confiscating it the Government had really taken a woman's property, not the property of a Confederate soldier. Alas, as Professor Davies had foreseen, the President no longer was a free agent!

"It is not my province to set aside military orders," he said. "You should see the Secretary of War." Then the President bent his head a little as if to say, "That is all. The interview is over." I thanked him and walked away. As I entered the East Room, there stood the old mathematics Professor who wanted to see Jeff Davis hanged. He seemed pleased to see me and told me he had called for me at the Southern hotel and that they had not been able to tell him where I had gone. I explained why I had not stopped at the Southern hotel. "The fools!" exclaimed the old Professor. "A blind man would know you were a lady. Have you seen the President?" I told him Yes. "What did he say to you?"

"Just what you foresaw he would tell me."

"You mean he told you to see Stanton?"

"Yes."

"Well, it will do you no good. Stanton is a hard, unfeeling man. However, let us go to him. You will at least have an interesting interview."

While the old mathematics Professor and I were in the East room holding this conversation we saw emerging from the President's office a lady whose dress and manner betokened a high station in life, but whose face was as sorrow stricken as if she were poor and starved. A gentleman advanced to greet her and we heard the talk between them. "What did Johnson say?" asked the gentleman in a low voice." I can see it was nothing favorable. Your face looks anguished."

"And I feel anguished," returned the handsomely gowned lady, tears coming into her eyes. "First the President asked me if I had met Stanton going out of the White House as I was entering; I did see him, but I looked through him and did not even acknowledge the bow he made me. I told Mr. Johnson this and he burst out angrily" 'The old scoundrel! Do you know what he has just been asking me to do, Mrs. Clay?" I said No, but I knew it was something devilish. "Well," said the President, "he came here to clamor again for the blood of Jefferson Davis and for that of your husband, too!" I said: "And you, Mr. President? What did you tell him? Will you let that man have their blood? You know they had nothing to do with Booth's crazy deed." "Yes, I know that, he answered," and then I pleaded with him to set Mr. Davis and my husband free. I told him how jailor Miles was torturing those two sick prisoners to death."

"What did Johnson say to that," asked the man, again speaking in a low voice; but I was so near that I heard him distinctly.

"He told me to have patience," answered the handsomely gowned lady with tears in her eyes. "He said my husband would be free soon but he could promise nothing for Mr. Davis. It is useless to see the President again. He is afraid of Stanton. That monster intends to murder our dear President."

When the handsomely gowned lady moved away, Prof. Davies told me she was Mrs. Clem Clay of Alabama. Gen. Clay, her husband was a prisoner with Jefferson Davis in Fortress Monroe. What we had heard of Stanton was not reassuring, still we persisted in my plan seeking an interview with him, and that same day the old mathematics professor and I found ourselves among a crowd of people in the anteroom of the Secretary of War waiting our turn to see him. Two men in that crowd specially attracted my attention. Both were very ugly but not of the same type of ugliness. One was thin, meager, garbed in citizen's dress which seemed to have been worn a long time--the coat and trousers were rusty and dirty and shiny; the face of this man gave one the idea that he suffered both bodily and mental pain. The other man I specially noted, who was talking with the man in the shiny, rusty clothes, looked as if he might be a big eater and a big drinker. His face was puffed, his eyes were blood shot, his head was bald, his nose big and red--and his head sloped from the end of his big nose to the top of his bald head! His body was misshapen and his eyes squinted as if they were looking both ways at once!! On the shoulders of this phenomenally ugly man were straps indicating high military rank; his uniform was blue. "A Union General, isn't he?" I asked Prof. Davies in a whisper.

"Yes," answered my friend the Professor. "That is Gen. Butler. The thin little man he is talking with is Thaddeus Stevens."

Of course I had heard of both Butler and Stevens; the former had made himself infamous in every Southern woman's eyes because of his order in New

Orleans permitting his soldiers to treat as "Women of the Town" Southern ladies who did not acknowledge the smiles and bows of Union soldiers; the man talking with Gen. Butler was noted as the radical leader who was trying to get Congress to divide up Southern lands into forty acre tracts and give them to the negroes. When I learned who the two men were I observed them more closely than ever, and I could now and then catch a sentence of what they were saying. I heard Gen. Butler say "Impeachment is the thing. I tell you, there is no other remedy." And I heard Stevens say, "Whatever plan is adopted there must be no let up until we down the traitor." Neither Gen. Butler nor Thaddeus Stevens paid the slightest attention to me or to the old mathematics Professor; if they thought we could overhear them they did not show it; they talked freely until a man came out from the adjoining room and told them Mr. Stanton was ready for them. They followed this man into the next room, the door closing behind them. When at last our turn came to be ushered into the Secretary's room we found Stanton at a table writing, he did not lift his head or even look up; he seemed not to know we had entered the room, so we took the liberty of seating ourselves and silently waited for him to speak to us. After about five minutes he ceased writing, deliberately wiped his pen, laid it down, then said:

"What do you wish?"

His face, his voice, his manner made me feel that I was in the presence of a foe. Nevertheless, I nerved myself to speak and act politely--it was no easy task, considering the feelings that surged within me I told him I had seen the President and at his suggestion had come to state my case to the Secretary of War.

"What is your case?" queried Stanton coldly.

I told him in as few words as possible.

"Where were you when Gen. Sherman took your property?" asked Stanton when at length I had finished my statement.

"In Memphis," I answered.

"And where was your husband?"

"In the army."

"The rebel army?"

"The Confederate army," I said; I should have answered merely, "Yes," but I couldn't do it. I knew our brave soldiers were patriots defending their homes against invasion; they were not rebels. The Secretary of War looked at me more coldly than ever.

"Confederate army or rebel army, it is all the same. What has become of your husband?"

"He is in Memphis."

"Do you live with him?"

"Yes."

"That is enough. What is a wife's is her husband's. Gen. Sherman did right. Rebels must suffer for their crimes. I shall not reward rebels."

176

Thereupon Mr. Stanton resumed his writing and I knew that further appeal was useless; without a word of comment or reply to his insulting speech about crimes and rebels I rose and left that cold-hearted man's presence. The kind old mathematics professor accompanied me also without a word until we reached the street; then he asked me what I intended to do.

"Go home as soon as I can," I answered. "The very air here chills me."

"Yes," he said softly. "It is too soon after the war for you to come here on such a mission. A little later things will work out all right, but not now. Men's minds are still too inflamed. When will you leave? "

"On the first train I can get that goes to Memphis."

"There is no train for the South until tonight," he answered. "Since you must wait till then, would you not like to see something of Washington? Have you been to the Capitol?" I told him No; I had never seen the Capitol. "Then," he added, "we shall go there first of all."

And we did--on a street car which started not far from where we stood in front of the Secretary of War's office but which did not take us very close to the Capitol building. We had to walk quite a distance and climb quite a hill before we reached the broad flight of stone steps. I sat on those steps a while to rest, then a few minutes later was seated in the Senate visitors' gallery looking down upon the noted Senators whom my good old mathematics professor pointed out to me. One Senator whom I well remember seeing that day was Charles Sumner of Massachusetts; I thought him a handsome man. He was tall, erect and though not exactly slender, was not at all inclined to obesity; his eyes flashed, showing keenness and intellect, but as I studied his symmetrical features the impression made on me was that he had little feeling, that he was cold, neither loving nor loveable, that although he was not cruel, not quite callous to humanity's woes, yet neither did he have much feeling, much sympathy for suffering, especially for suffering at a distance. When I saw Sumner he was not on the Senate floor; he was standing in an open door of a hall or lobby near the Senate, and talking to him was a round faced, kindly, honest looking man whom I took to be a farmer. But Prof. Davies told me it was Horace Greely.

"He is not a Senator," said Prof. Davies. "But he has more influence than half a dozen Senators. That is why Sumner is treating him with such deference. The man passing them on his way to the Senate floor is Gen. Schurtz. He is not a Senator either and will have to get out as soon as the session begins."

I looked and saw strutting into the Senate chamber a man in uniform with epaulets and gold braid and an air of importance; this man a few years later became a senator from Missouri, but he was not a member of the Senate the day I saw him and presently, in spite of his General's uniform and important air, he and a number of others who had no right to the floor, had to leave. I, too, took my departure soon after the session began, for the proceedings were uninteresting; and that night I took the train for Memphis.

CHAPTER XXIII

First decoration of graves of Confederate soliders. The Yankee Military Commander forbids the decoration. How my old sunday School teacher got the Federal Government to give me back my stores and houses.

I reached Memphis safely and at the depot was joyfully greeted by my loved ones. My three boys shouted with gladness and smothered me with kisses, while Minor smiled happily. I told him I would make no further effort to get my property. I said I would be satisfied if we could keep our children and live in a modest little home. With such a good husband, and with three such fine boys, I felt rich even though the great United States Government did steal from me the house and lands and rents that belonged to me.

When I told Minor of my interview with President Andrew Johnson and with Secretary of War Stanton there was every chance and every reason for the retort: "I told you so!" But my dear husband never once reminded me of the fact that he had warned me of the uselessness of appealing to the Yankee for justice; he merely shrugged his shoulders and said:

"Well, don't worry, Lizzie. At any rate you have had an interesting trip. Some of these days our boys will be instructed as well as entertained when you tell them of the public men you saw."

Wasn't that a good as well as a sensible way to take the situation? Some husbands would have quarrelled and made a fuss and grumbled mightily over the expense of a trip which only a little reflection would have shown from the outset was utterly useless. But, children, your dear grandfather was a wise man as well as a good man. He knew that it would *pay* to overlook my failings in unessential matters; and so, while sometimes my temper or my errors of judgment may have cost him some money and some unpleasant moments, in the long run was not his policy a wise one? In these days when so many married people rush into the divorce court the fact that Minor and I lived happily together for nearly sixty years ought to answer this question in no uncertain way.

The very afternoon of my return from Washington the Confederatates of Memphis observed for the first time the ceremony of decorating with flowers the graves of Southern soldiers. Minor hurried me home from the depot, so I could change my dress and go with him and our boys to Elmwood cemetery. Our old friend, Col. Matt Galloway, had announced in his paper some days before that the graves of Confederate soldiers would be covered with flowers; his editorial called on every true Southerner to go to Elmwood that day with an armful of flowers; and, after putting the flowers on the graves, then to listen to the address which would be made by Dr. Ford, a well known Memphis Christian minister. This announcement so greatly displeased the then military commander of Memphis that he sent an order to Mrs. Lowe, President of the Southern Society which had organized the plan to put flowers on the southern graves, commanding her and all other persons to desist from the "disloyal project." In the communication to Mrs. Lowe the Commander said:

"No loyal person will pay homage to rebels who had sought to overthrow the Nation. Peace has been declared, but the Government cannot permit rebels and traitors to eulogize rebellion and treason."

This, no doubt, was an alarming document; and had it been sent to a man perhaps its warning would have been heeded. But women sometimes do foolhardy things--perhaps they think their sex may make it harder to hold them responsible. Mrs. Lowe put that document in her pocket and cautioned her women friends not to say a word about it to any man. Thus it was that Dr. Ford delivered his address without being burdened by the knowledge that the Commander of Memphis considered what he was doing was an act of treason! Dr. Ford saw nothing wrong in paying tribute to dead soldiers, even though the Cause they so nobly fought for had been defeated; his address was beautifully phrased and feelingly delivered--it brought tears to the eyes of even the men who heard it--and in the end the military Commander did nothing about it. He fumed and fretted and wrote Mrs. Lowe again and sent his letter by an armed soldier, perhaps to make it more menacing, more impressive. But Mrs. Lowe answered sweetly that *she* had not delivered any address; *she* had not even strewn any flowers on Confederate soldiers' graves. As for Dr. Ford, he did not know that the great United States Government was afraid of dead Confederate soldiers and so he had spoken tenderly of them and Southern men and women had shed tears on their graves; and thus the military Commander found himself unable to do more than fume and grumble. Mrs. Lowe had not disobeyed his order, and Dr. Ford had not seen his order.

I am glad to say that by time another year rolled around the Union Commanders saw the "smallness," if not the meanness of such orders as that sent Mrs. Lowe, and they made no further effort to prevent flowers being strewn on the graves of Confederate soldiers. From that day to this the graves of our heroic dead have been visited once a year by the men and women of the South; flowers have been placed upon them; over them have been delivered eloquent addresses telling of their heroism, their lofty patriotism--and though at first there were mutterings in the North and although radical Congressmen denounced this "putting Treason on a pedestal," instead of making "Traitors odious," no attempt was made to stop the annual Decoration Day celebration. And now for many years past there has not been even a desire to forbid such tributes to the dead soldiers of the South, so completely have the passions and prejudices of the war faded away.

On the first "Decoration Day" in Elmwood a wooden obelisk was erected in the midst of the hundreds of graves and on the obelisk, in letters made of flowers, were the words:

"In Honor of our Gallant Dead"

A splendid marble shaft has long since replaced that modest wooden one, and similar marble monuments rise from every cemetery in the land where Confederate soldiers are buried. In November 1914 a fine monument, with appropriate statues and bas-reliefs, was erected in Forest Park, St. Louis, to commemorate the virtues and the patriotism of the men who gave their lives for the Southern Confederacy. And not even Grand Army men were found in the republican city of St. Louis to raise an objection! When I see such things as this done today in such a city as St. Louis, things so different from what was said and done a few years ago, I realize that at last the war really is over, and that we all are people of one common country. But that does not make me either forget or cease to love the brave men who fought and died for the southern Confederacy.

I have told you why Henry and Rose left Ridgeway and went to live in the city. For the same reasons we also left our country home to live in Memphis; Ridgeway was too near Fort Pickering; we saw too much of negro soldiers; they persisted in entering our yard and lolling about under our big oak trees, so Minor moved us into a small house at No. 95 Union Street in Memphis and there, soon after our arrival, came Isham G. Harris to see us. At the outbreak of the war Harris was Governor of Tennessee; when the Yankees captured Nashville, Gov. Harris escaped, taking with him a large sum of money belonging to the State School fund--just how much money he took I do not know, but it ran up into the hundreds of thousands of dollars. For four years Gov. Harris kept that money safely, carrying it from place to place as the Yankee invasion of the South progressed; and when the war ended, he brought every dollar back to Nashville and turned it over to the State Treasurer. He was as poor as a church mouse; not one cent of his own did he have; he could have kept some, or all, of that money for himself. But Isham G. Harris was not that sort of man. He gave every dollar of it to the State Treasurer, then came to Memphis so poor that he was glad to accept the use of Ridgeway rent free, until he began making an income from the practice of law. Gov. Harris had long been our friend; we were glad to help him; and soon after the South was restored to white rule the people of Tennessee sent Isham G. Harris to the United States Senate where he rendered conspicuous service to his state and to his country during the many years he remained in Washington. He was re-elected to a number of terms and was a Senator at the time of his death.

In Chapter XVII, I told you of the Kentuckian who owed Minor four thousand dollars and who was so eager to take up his notes and pay off his debt. As told in that chapter, payment was not accepted because the notes were not then due and there was no way then that I could use the greenbacks with which payment was offered. The notes were now past due, but the Kentuckian was now no longer eager to pay his debt; indeed he was not willing to pay at all, and when Minor pressed him and threatened to foreclose the mortgage the Kentuckian offered to pay in Confederate money, using the most absurd arguments in an effort to convince Minor that payment in Confederate money was permissible and would satisfy the debt. At that time, a year after Lee's surrender, Confederate money was worth about fifty cents a bushel and so Minor decided to go to Kentucky and enforce payment of the notes in lawful money, that is, in greenbacks. Greenbacks were not worth nearly as much as gold, but they were worth a thousand times as much as Confederate money and in the end Minor succeeded in making that dishonest debtor pay his debt in greenbacks.

I have spoken of a very evil Irish family, the Hickeys; let me now tell you of another type of Irishman. There was a certain Mr. Patrick Kenny, a contractor, who had done a good deal of work for my husband before the war. Mr. Kenny moved to Louisville during the war and there Minor saw him when he went to Kentucky to collect his four thousand dollars. Mr. Kenny, who had prospered exceedingly well in his contracting business, had Minor out to his home to dinner, and when Minor was leaving after dinner for his hotel his host shook hands with him and pressed upon him a tight little roll of paper.

"What is this, Pat?" asked Minor; examining the roll and finding it to be money he added: "What is this for? What do you want me to do with this?"

"I want you to keep it," answered Mr. Kenny. "It is yours I don't mean it as a loan, I mean it as a gift."

"But I cannot accept such a gift," returned Minor. "It is very good of you to wish to help me but I must not take money from you."

"I do not see why you cannot accept a little present from me," said Mr. Kenny. "You went into the army; you fought four years and came out of the war poor, while I kept my business going and made a lot of money. You were fighting for me. Why can't you let me do something for you?

Minor shook his host's hand heartily; he appreciated his big heart and generous intentions, but of course he could not accept such a present. Thereupon Mr. Kenny, who was genuinely disappointed at Minor's refusal to accept his gift, said he hoped Minor would at least let him make a present to our three little boys. Minor said Yes, provided it was not too big a present and then Mr. Kenny handed him three twenty dollar gold pieces, one for each of our boys. These gold pieces were the first money our boys ever had; at first Minor kept them for the boys, paying them ten percent interest which was used as spending money. As each boy reached the age of fourteen he was given his gold piece and told of the way in which the gift had come to be made. Didn't Mr. Kenny have a big, generous heart? And he was born on the same little green isle that gave birth to the dreadful Hickey woman!

When Minor returned from Kentucky he had his four thousand dollars and I felt so rich that I thought of buying a handsome gown which I had seen at

Lowenstein's store, but Minor told me I must wear calico for sometime yet; we still owed a good deal on our Union Street home, and when that was all paid, if any of the four thousand was left it would be better spent helping poor Confederate soldiers than in buying silk gowns. During the first year or two after Lee's surrender hardly a day passed but some poor Confederate soldier came to our door for help; they were ragged, shoeless, moneyless. Some wanted help to get on to their former homes in distant states, Texas, Louisiana and Alabama. Some wanted to get work in Memphis. Others were wounded and could not work. Every soldier who had come out of that dreadful war unhurt felt it his sacred duty to help those who were less fortunate, and so it was that a considerable part of that four thousand dollars which Minor brought back from Kentucky went for charity.

While we were living at No. 95 Union Street, Minor hard at work starting life all over again, neither of us with any further thought of trying to get back the property which Gen. Sherman had stolen from me, a miracle happened and my property was given back to me. When you hear *why* Gen. Sherman's order of confiscation was rescinded you will not say I am using too strong a word when I say it was a miracle. Surely nothing short of a miracle could have produced such a result. During all the years of war, and indeed for a long time prior to the war, I saw nothing of my old Sunday School teacher, Miss Ann Kesterson, whom I mentioned in Chapter IV, of these *Recollections*. Some two years after Lee's surrender Miss Ann came to see me--and then the miracle happened! It came about thus: During the four years of War Miss Ann had remained in Memphis doing Missionary work. She went about every day with a large basket on her arm; in this basket were food and clothing, which old Miss Ann distributed to the wives and widows and orphans of imprisoned or crippled soldiers After distributing the contents of the basket Miss Ann would take out of a capacious pocket in her dress a Bible, get down on her knees and fervently pray for God's blessing on the distressed women and children of the land. Although Southern born and at heart a Southern sympathizer Miss Ann was discreet and never by word or act did she permit her secret feelings to become known. When any alleged atrocity of the Confederates was spoken of in her presence she would piously say: "Lord forgive them. They know not what they do!"

In this way Miss Ann came to be well and favorably known to the Union officers quartered in Memphis, and her good work and "patriotic" sentiments were even reported to the "High-Up" authorities at Washington. Well, the day my old Sunday School teacher came to see me, among the many other things I told her was the way Gen. Sherman had stolen my property and the way President Johnson and Secretary of War Stanton had treated me in Washington.

"Betty Avery!" exclaimed my old teacher, forgetting that in the years that had passed since we had met my name had been changed to Betty Meriwether. "Do you mean to say the United States Government is taking your rents *now*, this long after Lee's surrender?"

"That is precisely what it is doing," I answered.

"And you a good anti-slavery woman?"

"I certainly have always opposed slavery," I said. "But what has that to do with the question?"

"It has a great deal to do with it," replied Miss Ann. "Seems to me you were once threatened with hanging because you were so bitter against slavery."

Several years before the war our old and good friend Col Matt Galloway, editor of the Memphis *Appeal,* had said to me laughingly: "Mrs. Meriwether, you preach mighty unsafe doctrines. If we didn't know you to be a good Southern woman we'd have a lynching Bee take charge of you."

This story had been repeated by our friends and was the only foundation for Miss Ann's remarks. I told her so, but she declared it was foundation enough.

"Get your bonnet," she said. "I want you to come with me. I think I can get them to give you back your property."

I had little faith in Miss Ann's ability to do this, nevertheless I put on my bonnet and accompanied her to the office of the Military Commander; the visit could do no harm and of course there was always the possibility of justice being accorded me. I knew from the way that the Commander received Miss Ann that she stood well with him, still I did not believe he would be willing to help me. He shook hands with Miss Ann in a most cordial manner and asked her how her good work was progressing.

"Splendidly," answered Miss Ann. "And I have come here to do some more good work. This lady is an old scholar of mine whom the military authorities have treated very unjustly. If Gen. Sherman hadn't been in such a hurry, if he had taken time to investigate a little he wouldn't have confiscated Betty Avery's property."

"Betty Avery?" repeated the Commander. "You introduced this lady as Mrs. Meriwether."

"So I did," said old Miss Ann complacently. "But before she was married her name was Avery, and I always call her Betty Avery. Her father was from the North; near Pittsfield, Massachusetts, and Betty was always an Abolitionist. As long ago as 1856 they came near hanging her here in Memphis for preaching freedom to the negroes."

The Commander opened his eyes and looked at me in amazement. "But are you not the wife of Col. Meriwether of the rebel army?"

Before I could answer Miss Ann said: "Of course she is, but she's also the daughter of Dr. Nathan Avery of Pittsfield, Mass. But, General, when it comes to a question of slavery, Betty Avery's husband was an abolitionist, too. He inherited a Kentucky plantation and a lot of slaves way back in the early 'Fifties, but do you think he would keep those slaves? No sir, not much. Col.

Meriwether was bitter against slavery. They came near mobbing him, too. But he was perfectly fearless when it came to a matter of convictions like freedom for the poor slaves. Mr. Meriwether set every one of his slaves free, set 'em free years before the war, and at his own expense sent some of them to Liberia in Africa and the rest of 'em to the free states in the North. "

"If all that is true how came it he fought in the rebel army?" demanded the Commander a little severely. I wondered how Miss Ann meant to answer that question, it would have been quite impossible for me to answer it in a way that would have satisfied that Union officer. But Miss Ann was equal to the occasion.

"General," she said, "a hundred people here in Memphis, as well as many documents and records made long before the war, will prove the truth of what I say regarding Mr. Meriwether's setting his slaves free. As to how he came to fight in the rebel army, if you ask my opinion I think he was made to do it. They threatened him in the one way that was possible to move a brave man."

"How was that?" asked the Commander.

"They threatened to persecute and mistreat his wife and two little children if he refused to join the rebel army!"

I sat almost stupefied with astonishment as Miss Ann made this reply; the story seemed to me too monstrous for any one to believe, yet that military Commander seemed to swallow it whole. He turned and surveyed me with a look as cordial as that he had bestowed upon Miss Ann.

"If what Miss Kesterson says is correct," he said kindly, "and I have no doubt it is--Miss Kesterson has endeared herself to us during the years of the war that our troops occupied Memphis--if you have really been made to suffer for your loyalty and your standing true to your convictions amidst a community of rebels and traitors, why then, Mrs. Meriwether, an injustice has indeed been done to you and we shall hasten to undo it."

I found it hard to listen to this; "A community of rebels and traitors!" I wanted to tell that Commander that the people he thus slandered were as much patriots as were Washington's soldiers at Valley Forge; they fought and froze to repel foreign invasion--and that is precisely what our brave Confederate soldiers had done. But I said nothing of this to that Commander. I was beginning to learn a little of Miss Ann's diplomacy. So all I said was that my husband and I had always opposed slavery, that we had sacrificed a fortune because of our convictions in that regard and that it was true, as Miss Kesterson said, that Southerners had talked of "hanging" me because I so openly advocated freedom for all the slaves. The Commander listened attentively, his whole attitude now gracious and cordial.

"An investigation will be made," he said when I finished speaking. "I have no doubt it will result favorably. My orderly will let you know."

Thereupon we went away, the whole episode seeming to me like a curious dream. But it was not a dream. The Military Commander did set inquiries on foot and of course when my friends learned what it was all about they not only told how I had been known as an opponent of slavery but magnified the story in such a way that in a few days they had me pictured as a perfect martyr in the cause of Negro freedom; I had suffered contumely and abuse because of my heroic stand in defense of the poor, helpless slaves. The jesting remark of Col. Galloway that a "Lynching Bee would take charge of me" if I didn't stop preaching freedom for negroes was magnified into a story that once the slave oligarchy was on the point of lynching me, and that I had saved my life only by flight and lying in hiding. The result of all this was wonderful. In exactly one week from the afternoon that Miss Ann Kesterson and I had that interview with the Military Commander of Memphis a Yankee soldier came to our home at No. 95 Union Street and handed me the following note:

"Dear Madam: I have ordered your tenants to discontinue paying rents to our army agent and hereafter to pay all rents to the owner of the property Mrs. Betty Avery Meriwether.

Respectfully.

Davies Tilson

Gen. Tilson was from New England; he was an ardent Abolitionist. My father's coming from near Pittsfield, Mass., and my record as an opponent of slavery had done what neither my appeals for justice to the President nor to the Secretary of War had succeeded in doing. It was a wonderful surprise to me; I had had so little faith in the whole matter that I had not even mentioned to Minor my visit with Miss Ann to the Military Commander. When he came home that night and I showed him Gen. Tilson's note Minor was dubious as to its genuineness but it proved to be quite as good as it seemed, and so of a sudden we found ourselves almost rich. For the rental value of my property had greatly increased since the Surrender. A corner grocery which rented for $125.00 in 1861 was now bringing $250.00; my dwelling houses were also renting for double the rents they had brought six or seven years before.

With this comfortable income assured, Minor decided to resume his profession as a Civil Engineer; he could now afford to wait for business to come to him. Accordingly he resigned his position as Treasurer of the Mississippi and Tennessee Railroad and got the Road to give that position to my sister's husband, Mr. Lamb; then Minor looked about for civil engineering work and because of his high reputation, was not long in securing positions of both prominence and profit.

CHAPTER XXIV

The Ku Klux Klan. My husband a Ku Klux. All that saved the South from utter destruction. First parade of ghostly Klan before my home in Memphis.

At the time of Lincoln's assassination in April 1865 there were 38,000 men and women "Suspects" in northern prisons and fortresses. "Suspects" were persons who were not known to have done anything unlawful, but who were suspected of being in sympathy with the South. During the last years of the war the man or woman in the North who was not openly, even violently, in favor of the Union and against the South was "Suspect" and thrown into prison. When Andrew Johnson became president he ordered these 38,000 suspects set free and set about re-establishing state governments in the South, but Congress, which consisted almost entirely of radical republicans, had no notion of letting democrats work themselves into places of power. Everybody knew, of course, that if re-admitted into the Union the Southern states would send only democrats to Congress and to the Senate. All the Southern states except Texas were reorganized and applying for admission into the Union by the early fall of 1865; Congress convened the following December and then began the great struggle between the executive and the legislative branches of the government. Mr. Johnson had always been a democrat; although he turned against his native state, North Carolina, and against his adopted state, Tennessee, and sided with the Yankees, that was because of his deep rooted love of the Union, not because he wanted to see the negroes freed, much less because he wanted to see them made the political masters of the white race.

The radicals in Congress resented Johnson's leniency toward the ex-Confederates; they resented his opposition to the plan of making the negroes the masters of the South and so before he had been in the White House a year Congress enacted a number of laws over the President's veto which showed the country what the South had to expect. One of these laws annulled the State governments then in peaceful Operation, divided the Southern states into Military Districts, placed them under martial law, disfranchised all white men who had not actively sided with the North (this meant practically that all White men were disfranchised) and enfranchised all black men! Thus began the period of "Reconstruction" which more properly should be called "Destruction"--for this law destroyed the homes and happiness of the South to an extent not caused even by the Federal armies in a hundred great battles.

The first result of Congress' "Reconstruction" policy was to cause a horde of carpet baggers to swarm down upon the South. Now-a-days when men go traveling they carry bags or suit cases made of leather, but in the late Sixties leather was not as cheap as it is now; traveling bags were made of ordinary carpets. Carpets, of course, were of all sorts of colors and figures, consequently when you saw a dozen men enter a railroad coach your eyes would be dazzled by a dozen different colored, gaudily patterned pieces of carpets made up into bags. The adventurers from the North who swooped down upon the South to make their fortunes all carried carpet bags, hence the name "Carpet Baggers" which was indeed, as a northern writer, Albion Tourgee, said in his book, *A Fool's Errand*, "A stroke of genius, it had all the essentials of a denunciatory epithet in a superlative degree. It had a sound without a defined significance, it was altogether unique." Under the malign influences of these self-seeking carpet baggers the poor, ignorant negroes made but a sorry use of the franchise thrust upon them. The white men of the South, the men of brains and property, the men with a long line of cultured, civilized ancestry were forbidden either to vote or to hold public office. For a while they stood silently looking upon the destruction which was going on all over the South under the ironic name of "Reconstruction"; for a while they felt powerless, in the face of overwhelming military forces, to prevent the carpet baggers from using the negroes as tools with which to exploit the South to the point of utter ruin and desolation. Negro legislatures would vote millions and millions of dollars of bonds for public works that were never executed; but the carpet baggers would get hold of the bonds and demand payment of the last dollar of both principal and interest. Then, too, under the evil counsel of the carpet baggers, the ignorant negroes became intolerably insolent and overbearing. It became dangerous for a white woman to leave her home and white men were elbowed off the sidewalks into the streets by their former slaves. If they resented such insolence they would be arrested brought before a carpet bagger Judge and fined, or imprisoned.

As you may imagine, My Children, under such circumstances life in the South became one long nightmare; then a miracle happened--for surely the way the South escaped from that frightful nightmare was little short of miraculous. Escape by force of arms was impossible; more than two million northern soldiers stood ready to crush an attempt to interfere with the negroes in their orgy of misrule and oppression. But not even two million northern bayonets could overnight remake the skull and brains of a being just emancipated from slavery or rid him of the credulity and superstition handed down to him by generations of savage ancestors. It was this fact which finally saved the South from such a devastation as no country has seen since the Duke of Alva laid waste the lowlands of Holland!

I do not know who first thought of the Ku Klux Klan, but I do know that General Nathan Bedford Forest, the great cavalry soldier who lived near us on Union Street, was the Supreme Grand Wizard; and Minor was one of his counsellors and lieutenants. I remember as if it were yesterday how Minor said to me one night:

"Put out all the lights in the house early tonight, but do not go to bed before midnight, if you wish to see a ghostly army."

Sometime before this remark Minor had gotten me to make him certain curious, long white garments--as if for a mask ball; he had absented himself from home at night a great deal and I knew that something out of the ordinary was "in the wind." But not until the night of which I now speak did I have any definite knowledge of that movement which was destined to extend in so marvelous a manner and ultimately work our beloved Southland's salvation. I did as he bade me, gave him the "mask ball" garments I had made him, then sat down to wait and watch for the "Ghostly Army." Baby Lee was still too young to take part in my vigil, but my two other boys, little Rivers and Avery, sat up with me and their eyes opened wide with amazement, and perhaps, too, with fear, when at midnight that ghostly procession began to file before our home. It seemed to be an army of horses but the horses' feet did not make the usual noise and clatter. Their hoofs were wrapped in cloth, their bodies were covered with flowing white cotton cloth, their riders wore white hoods and white gowns which trailed almost to the ground. Hardly a sound did either horses or riders make--truly, in the light of that midnight moon, it did seem like an army of ghosts! We watched it until it disappeared into Desoto Street, a street given over to negroes; and a few minutes later a lot of black men and women fled by our house running *away* from Desoto Street as if they thought the Devil himself were pursuing them.

Our negro cook, Sally Ann, was very religious; the Baptist preacher of her church often called on her and the day after that ghostly army passed No. 95 Union Street, old Parson Hodges came to our house to tell Sally Ann what had happened. I went back into the kitchen to hear him, and I shall give here the notes of his talk as I made them at the time--I thought then, and I think now, they are interesting as showing the impression made by the Ku Klux Klan in the beginning of their career upon a negro who, if not cultured, was at any rate enough above the average to be the preacher of a church.

"Hit wuz jes dis way," began old Parson Hodges, squaring himself back in his chair in my kitchen. "We had a pra'r meetin' las' night an' ebery ting wuz gwine on jes like hit alluz goes on, singin' an' prayin' and shoutin' so dat hit wuz nigh onto 'leben o'clock when de meetin' quit, an' when I got home hit wuz nigh onto midnight. I went out into de yard to draw a bucket ob water an' I had dun let de bucket down into de well an' drawed hit out agin when I heard dem ghosts comin' down Desoto Street an' when I turned my head an' saw 'em comin' I wuz purty nigh skeert to death. De bucket hit drop back into de well an' my legs shook so dat I could hardly stan' or say a word: well, Sally Ann, dem ghosts wuz ridin' ghost horses an' dey come right into my yard by de well an' one ob dem sez, sez he:

" 'You looks like a 'ligious nigger what's willin' ter help a po' spirit from hell! ' "

" 'Yas sah!' I sez, 'yas sah. What you wants me ter do?' I wuz dat skeert my legs began jes nacherly to gib way. But I didn't want dem ghosts ter git mad wid me, so I tole 'em plain I wuz willin' ter do jes what dey wanted me ter do."

"What did dey want you ter do?" asked our cook, who was listening to her preacher's story with dilated nostrils and wide open eyes.

"Dey wanted me ter gib 'em a drink ob water," resumed Parson Hodges. "You see, Sally Ann, dey uuz straight from hell an' hit's so monsus hot down dere dat dose po' ghosts wuz powerful thirsty. Dey kin drink mo' water dan a dozen mules. I drawed up a full bucket an' wuz gwine gib a gourdfull ter de fust ghost but he reached out an' took de bucket an' drank ebery drap out'n hit, den tol me ter gib him annuder bucketfull. Nacherlly I drawed hit fer him an' he drank ebery drap ob dat too. All de odder ghosts drank two buckets apiece an' one ob 'em sez, sez he:

" 'Dis is de bes drink I'se had since de Yankees shot me at de battle ob Shiloh an' sent me ter hell. Good bye, nigger. When you comes ter hell I'll git de debble ter be good ter you fur gibbin' me dis drink.'

"Den dey rode away an' I wuz too skeert to tell 'em I wuz a Babtis preacher in good standin' an' wuzn't no ways tinkin' ob goin' ter hell."

"How many ob dem ghosts wuz dey" asked Sally Ann in an awed whisper.

" 'Bout a million," answered Parson Hodges gravely. "I neber took no count ob dem, but dey wuz comin' down Desoto Street jes as far as I could see. Nacherlly I neber stayed out dar by de well no longer'n I had to. Jes as soon as dem ghosts what come into my yard got all de water dey wanted an' rode away I run into my house an' I nebber come out agin till broad day. Ghosts can't hurt you in de day, Sally Ann, but at midnight dey sho' is dangrus."

I wrote the above report of Parson Hodges' story to Sally Ann that same day and sent it to my friend Col. Galloway, the editor, but he thought it unwise to publish it at that time; the *Avalanche* was then pursuing the policy of making light of the story of Ku Kluxes, while the Memphis *Post* took the other cue and savagely denounced the white "rebels" of the city for masquerading in ghostly robes and "intimidating" the peaceful negroes. That word "Intimidate" during the next few years came to play quite a role in the political literature of the South. The "rebel" whites were accused of "intimidating" the loyal negroes from the polls, "intimidating" them from sitting by white women in street cars, "intimidating" them from elbowing white men off sidewalks into the street, etc. The negro who did any of these things, took seats by white women, went to the polls on election day to vote or shoved white men off the sidewalks into the streets, etc., were not "intimidated" at the time they committed the forbidden act; the million soldiers in blue prevented any day light "intimidation." But negroes soon noted that the Ku Klux ghosts paid visits only to such of their race as committed the forbidden acts; in extreme cases those ghostly visitors held ghostly trials at midnight in the depths of some dark forest and executed negroes by shooting or hanging before any of the million blue coated soldiers could interfere. Everybody soon came to know who and what the Ku Klux were, but nobody could *prove* what all knew, and so the carpet baggers became fairly apoplectic with futile hate and anger. Shortly after that first "ghostly" procession which my two little boys and I witnessed from our home at 95 Union Street, the *Avalanche* published this editorial paragraph:

"Our esteemed contemporary the POST is mistaken; that army on Desoto Street was not composed of wicked rebels, nor was it a band of Ku Kluxers. They were the daughters of Zion taking a moonlight ride, so don't be alarmed, Brother POST. The Daughters of Zion won't hurt you."

The "Daughters of Zion" were the negro women of a Church society; the POST, knowing the real meaning of that ghostly parade, became more bitter than ever at what it called the *Avalanche's* impudent mendacity; it declared the Government ought to send more soldiers down South and quiet this new rebellion before all the good work of Lincoln and Grant and the Union armies was undone. More soldiers were sent down South and Congress did take up the Ku Klux question in an effort to solve the problem; the carpet baggers strove with might and main to make the negroes see that the "ghosts" were nothing but whipped and conquered rebel soldiers dressed up in the cheapest kind of masquerade gowns--but all to no avail. The negroes persisted in believing the Ku Klux were ghosts fresh from hell and the soldiers in blue, despite their numbers, rarely if ever seemed able to appear on the scene in time to rescue anyone condemned to death by the ghostly council of Ku Kluxers. I remember the case of a negro who had been elected to a high office and who, spoiled by his worldly success, became obsessed with the desire to marry a white woman. Had he sought out the daughter of some "Truly loyal" Yankee who believed in miscegenation his fate might not have been so tragic; but this negro permitted himself to seek the hand of a Southern girl, the daughter of an ex-Confederate officer. When this officer, Major B., learned that his daughter had been annoyed on the street by the aspiring office holding negro he could not have been more indignant had a Black man fresh from Cannibal Land asked to marry his daughter. And when a letter from the Negro came, asking his daughter's hand in marriage, Major B.'s impulse was to shoot the fellow. In the days before the Ku Klux that is what he would have done, regardless of the fatal consequences to himself. But there was no necessity now for personal action. What Major B. did was this: he submitted the Negro's letter, together with an account of his conduct, to the "Council" of the Ku Klux. Not long afterward that negro office holder did not report at his office for duty; at his boarding house no one knew

190

what had become of him. Several days later his dead body was found swinging from the limb of a tree in a forest some miles from Memphis. Pinned to the body was a card on which were *printed* these words:

"DONE BY ORDER OF THE KU KLUX KLAN."

So outraged were the carpet baggers at this murder of a "Truly Loyal" negro, one of them wrote Major B. an insulting letter in the course of which he not only called him an assassin but a fool, in that he had not allowed his daughter to marry the "brave, loyal negro citizen." He, Major B., was a broken down, pauperized rebel; the negro suitor for his daughter's hand was a rising politician who, but for his foul murder, would doubtless have risen to be a man of wealth and power. Major B. turned this letter over to the "Council" and a few days later that carpet bagger was missing one morning at breakfast; his landlady went to his room and found there his clothes on a chair where he had placed them the previous night before retiring. But there was no clue to the question whether he had gone, or why he had gone. A search was begun and late that afternoon the carpet bagger was found tied to the trunk of the same tree from which the negro office holder had been hanged. There was no wound on his body, but from his neck to his waist he was naked, his shirt was torn to shreds; and his body was a mass of red stripes and bruises. The man had been lashed with a whip until he was insensible; it was some days before he recovered sufficiently to relate what had happened to him. Six masked men had entered his room in the night while he lay asleep and had threatened to kill him if he offered the slightest resistance or made the slightest sound. At the point of half a dozen pistols which the masked men held close to him he was forced to dress and get into a wagon and drive out into the country; there he was bound to a tree and whipped into unconsciousness!

Judged by present day standards those six masked men were wicked and cowardly; but they will not be condemned by the historian who knows what carpet bag and negro rule meant for the South. It was only by such stern measures that the carpet baggers and negroes were brought to treat the disfranchised and conquered Southerners with some small degree of justice and respect.

The Ku Klux Klan was organized in June 1866 in my home state of Tennessee and spread rapidly all over the South. People spoke of it as the "Invisible Empire," and well might they call it such, for it became more powerful than all the laws the carpet baggers and their negro legislatures were able to enact, supported though those laws were by the military power of the United States. Congress sent Committees to the South to investigate and hundreds of suspects were arrested, but no positive evidence could be obtained and all that the Congressional Committee learned was that more than a thousand men had been killed and many more than a thousand had been mutilated by the members of that "traitorous Klan." The Committees pointed out that all of the victims of the Klan were from three classes of persons, Negroes, Carpet Baggers and Scallawags (Southern men who turned against their state and sided with the Carpet Baggers). To the honor of our Southern manhood let me hasten to say that in all Memphis there were fewer than a score of Scallawags. Although profit and political promotion were the certain rewards for betraying the South, yet poor as were the conquered Confederate soldiers very, very few of them became Scallawags. And, although dire punishment awaited the man convicted of being a Ku Klux, Southern men joined the Klan by the tens of thousands! Judge Albion Tourgee, a Northern man, says in his book, *A Fools Errand*:

"Well did the Ku Klux call themselves 'The Invisible Empire.' In one state the Klan numbered ten thousand; in another state forty thousand--in all the Southern states the Klan could muster an army greater than the armies of the Rebellion-- an Invisible Empire with a trained and disciplined army of midnight marauders making war on the weakling powers that wise men had set up in the rebellious territory."

By "Wise Men" Judge Tourgee means the radicals in power at Washington who hated the South and who had disfranchised all ex-Confederate soldiers and set the recently freed slaves above them. Judge Tourgee continues:
"Yet after all it was magnificent--such an unfaltering determination, such an invincible defiance to all that had the seeming of tyranny!"
Seeming? If the carpet bagger--Negro rule of the South was only "seeming" tyranny, what would need to be done by the rulers of a land to constitute *real* tyranny? Judge Tourgee pays this further tribute to the Ku Kluxers:
"One can but regard with pride and sympathy the indomitable men who though conquered in war, yet resisted every effort of their conquerors to change their laws and their customs; and this, too, not only with unyielding stubbornness, but with success.
One can but admire the arrogant boldness with which they charged the Nation which had conquered them with perfidy, malice and a spirit of contemptible revenge....
How Rebels laughed to scorn the Reconstruction laws of which the Wise Men boasted! How boldly they declared the conflict was irrepressible! That the Negro could not, should not hold power over them!
It is wonderful and terrible! Yet in it we may recognize the elements which go to make up a grand and kingly people. They felt themselves insulted and oppressed. The Ku Klux must be counted as a desperate effort of a proud, brave and determined people to secure and to hold what they deemed to be their rights."

There is now being shown throughout the country a Photoplay called "The Birth of A Nation." My son Lee took me to see it a few months ago (January 1916) and I who lived through the agony attending the birth of our Nation in the Sixties wish to tell you, my children, that, thrilling as is that Photoplay, it is quite true to History. When I saw, the ghostly army moving across the screen I was taken back in memory to that midnight in 1866 when the real army of Ku Klux on cloth-shod horses rode silently by my Memphis home!

No doubt many abuses were committeed by the Ku Klux. In large bodies of men some unwise ones, some mean ones will inevitably be found. But, considered as a whole, the work of the Ku Klux was done in a patriotic spirit for patriotic purposes, and I rejoice to see from the Photoplay now having so wide a vogue that History is beginning to do justice to that wonderful secret movement. At the time it was misunderstood; in the North it was reviled. But in truth it accomplished a noble and a necessary work in the only way in which that work was then possible.

CHAPTER XXV

The impeachment trial of President Andrew Johnson. Minor's letters describe the scene. Pen pictures of General Butler, Thadeus Stevens, Senator Ben Wade and other managers of the Prosectuion. Speaker of the House Boutwell's "Hole in the Sky" speech. Jeff Davis becomes our neighbor in Memphis. His home life and family.

In a previous chapter I have told how the Yankees cut the Mississippi river levees, thus inundating a vast expanse of country every time the river was in flood. After the war the planters of the lower Mississippi valley tried to raise funds with which to rebuild the levees, but the cost proved so great, and the planters were so impoverished by the four years of war, that the work was abandoned. Then in 1868 it was determined to ask Federal assistance and the Mississippi valley planters employed Minor to go to Washington to present their case to Congress and urge an appropriation for the restoration of the levees which the Federal armies had destroyed.

Minor arrived in Washington in the spring of 1868 and learned within a few days that his mission was hopeless; for he found all Washington in fevered turmoil over the question of impeaching the President. Almost before he had hung up his hat in the White House the radicals in Congress manifested their dislike of Andrew Johnson; that dislike grew to violent hate and led to the enactment of the law known as the "Tenure of Office Act." That act practically deprived the President of all power, in fact made of him little more than a dummy, a figure head. The Act forbade the President from dismissing his own Secretary, or from removing his own confidential advisers, in case he should lose his confidence in them and wish to have other advisers. Johnson believed-- rightly as the event proved--that this Act was illegal, that it was an encroachment upon the constitutional rights of the Executive, and therefore he ignored it--in many instances, but most conspicuously in the case of Secretary of War Stanton. From the very day Johnson became President in April 1865 Stanton openly showed his dislike and his disrespect for the President and at length Johnson asked Stanton to resign. Stanton refused. Thereupon Johnson ordered him to get out and appointed Gen. Grant in his place. The Senate, however, refused to recognize even so popular a military hero as Grant, declaring that the President had exceeded his lawful powers and that Stanton was still the Secretary of War. Gen. Grant, who was himself unfriendly to Johnson, promptly accepted the Senate's view and withdrew from the Secretary of War's office. Then Johnson, perceiving that not even the appointment of a man like

Gen. Grant would placate his enemies, determined to appoint one of his own friends; his choice was General Lorenzo Thomas. Secretary Stanton lost no time in defying the President. No sooner was Gen. Thomas' commission announced than Stanton appealed to Gen. Grant for military protection. Gen. Grant at once put one of his generals, with a detachment of soldiers, in charge of the War Department building and at the same time Congress began the impeachment proceedings.

This was the situation that greeted my husband when he arrived in Washington. Naturally he was unable to get Congress even to consider the question of building levees so as to save the Mississippi valley from annual inundations. But Minor did not regret his trip; he regarded himself lucky in being able to witness a proceeding hardly less historic and interesting than the Impeachment trial of Warren Hastings. Every day during several weeks Minor sat in the gallery looking down on the drama in progress on the Senate floor, and every night he wrote me a hurried account of what he had seen and heard. I remember the description in one of his letters of Senator Bayard's indignation when Senator Ben Wade walked up to the Bar of the Senate to be sworn. Wade would have become president had Johnson been deposed, consequently the commonest sense of propriety should have told Wade not to sit as one of Johnson's judges. But in that day of passion and prejudice propriety was not much in evidence. Wade walked up to be sworn and then it was that Senator Bayard sought to shame him into decency.

"Stop!" cried the distinguished Senator from Delaware. "*You* have no right to sit in judgement here. You know if you vote against the accused it will be a vote for yourself for President of the United States. A Judge should be unbiased. How can you be unbiased, how can you be fair and impartial when the greatest political prize in the world will be yours in case the accused you are judging is convicted?"

Minor wrote me that Wade flinched when Senator Bayard cried out these words; his face flushed, but he made no reply and after a moment's hesitation, stood boldly up in front of the bar, lifted his hand and took the oath as one of the President's judges!

Seven men were appointed as managers of the Impeachment trial, James Wilson, George S. Boutwell (of Mass.), Gen. John A. Logan (of Ill.), Gen. B. F. Butler, Thadeus Stevens, Thomas Williams and John A. Bingham. The last named was the Judge Advocate who presided over Mrs Surratt's trial. On that tragic trial Bingham made the shameless and false assertion that Jefferson Davis *had hired* Booth to assassinate Lincoln; Bingham pretended to give even the very words Mr. Davis was alleged to have used when he hired Booth to commit the crime! And this shameless liar was to sit in judgement upon the President of the United States! Minor wrote me that all Washington regarded impeachment as certain; the jury was "fixed"; arguments and evidence would be heard as a matter of form, but the radicals were in a majority and they were determined to "get" Johnson, all law, Justice and the Constitution notwithstanding.

Gen. Butler opened the trial by reading a number of printed slips of paper He held the slips of paper in both hands and (as your grandfather wrote me) never was there a poorer reader; he mumbled his words, kept his head tucked down close to the slips of paper and spoke in a voice so muffled and indistinct that few people in the Senate chamber could hear him. Judge Curtis, who followed Gen. Butler, spoke in the President's defense; his delivery was so superior to Butler's, his analysis and refutation of the impeachment charges was so masterly, Johnson's friends were jubilant. They had not learned even yet how little a part justice and reason were to play in this remarkable trial. Following Judge Curtis came Gen. Logan with a stump speech rather than a legal argument. Minor wrote me that Gen. Logan seemed chiefly concerned over the fact that Johnson's deposition would put Wade in the White House and thus save the country from traitors and rebels! "If Andrew Johnson remains in the White House," said Gen. Logan, "we will lose the fruits of the victory won by Lincoln and the Union armies. We assert, and we shall prove, that Andrew Johnson has allied himself with rebels and traitors. Unless he is deposed the country will be under the control of democrat copperheads in the North and democrat rebels in the South! "

As wonderful as was Gen. Logan's "argument," it was tame indeed, compared with that of Speaker of the House Boutwell who followed him. Here is an extract from one of the many letters received from my dear husband during that interesting trial

"Boutwell began mildly, even modestly; but soon he dropped into a style of bombast of which I should think a school boy would be ashamed. Listen to this sample of his oratory and tell me if you don't think Baby Lee could beat it.

" 'Astronomers' Boutvell said, 'inform us that in the Southern Heavens is a vast space called the "Hole in the Sky." In that dark, dreary, cold "Hole in the Sky" the great author of the celestial mechanism has left a chaos. Were this earth capable of emotions of justice it would heave and throw with the energy of elemental force, and project this enemy (Andrew Johnson) of two races (the black and the white races) into that cold, dark, dreary region in the sky, there forever to exist in solitude and eternal tribulation!'

"Think of a man capable of making such a speech being chosen as Speaker of Congress! "

When Minor a few days after that speech saw President Johnson he asked him if he was not nervous, if he did not fear old mother earth might begin to heave and project him into that "dark and dreary hole in the sky?" Johnson made no reply but Minor wrote me that a grim smile parted his lips and a twinkle in his eye showed he appreciated Boutwell's wonderful speech at its true worth. From the day he delivered that speech Boutwell was called "Hole in the Sky Boutwell." Even the newspapers of his own political faith poked fun at him and asked him to locate the "Hole in the Sky" so that astronomers might take note of it; it had never been mentioned in any work on Astronomy and the world was curious to know how a busy Congressman had had time to make so wonderful a discovery.

William H. Evarts followed Boutwell in the President's defense and the wit and sarcasm with which he treated the "Hole in the Sky" speech delighted Minor more than anything else during the long trial. Altogether the Impeachment proceedings in Washington which began in February of 1868 and continued until late in the following May were as interesting and as remarkable as the Impeachment proceedings of Warren Hastings; some say it is to be hoped another Macaulay will immortalize the American trial as the great English essayist has immortalized the attempt to impeach the first governor general of British India.

Impeachment almost succeeded; it was defeated by one vote--that of Senator Henderson of Missouri. But the radicals were as stunned by the verdict as if it had been unanimous for acquittal. Stanton and Wade knew that their political power was gone forever. When the vote was announced, Stanton, who had been watching the call with breathless interest, turned ghastly pale; as he rose to leave the chamber he staggered so that Gen. Logan took his arm and helped him away. Senator Wade's face looked gloomy and sullen as he walked out behind Stanton, but he was able to walk without assistance. Poor old lame Thadeus Stevens rose up and shambled out, neither asking nor receiving support; he limped out on his crutch, his face plainly showing the venomous but now futile hatred of Johnson and of the South which scarred his soul. Minor wrote me that Boutwell bore the verdict well, considering the frightful things he had prophesied would befall the country if Andrew Johnson were allowed to remain on earth instead of being projected into that "cold, dreary hole in the sky!" By the vote just announced Johnson was to remain in the White House for another year and if Boutwell believed half he had said in his "Hole in the sky" speech, even another week of Johnson as President of the United States would work untold calamities upon the country and the people. Nevertheless Minor said that Boutwell, though appearing to be bitterly disappointed, did not seem crushed as did Stanton, Wade and Thadeus Stevens. Of course Johnson's friends were jubilant. They rushed up to the President, wrung his hands and showered him with congratulations. At last he was free to exercise the constiutional duties of his office without being constantly hampered and thwarted by even the members of his Cabinet. Stanton, of course, now no longer stood on the order of going, he went at once and was succeeded by a Secretary of War who was a true friend and adviser to the president. Stanton died the following year, as many people believed, of disappointment and a broken heart.

When my husband returned from Washington in May 1868 he seemed jubilant in spite of the complete failure of his mission with reference to the levees. He said he saw many signs on the political horizon which indicated the dawn of a better day for the South and events soon showed there was reason for this optimism. Our beloved Confederate president, after two years of martyrdom in a dungeon, much of the time chained to the stone walls like a wild beast, had been admitted to bail, and now the case against him was dismissed, thus in effect retracting the vile charges of treason and complicity in the assassination of Lincoln which had been brought against him. Large numbers of carpet baggers, finding they could no longer use the ignorant negroes as their tools to exploit the South, returned to the North, and those who remained in the South behaved themselves far better than they had done up to the time they hoped and believed Senator Ben Wade of Ohio would be installed in the White House in Andrew Johnson's place. The government of southern cities and states began to fall into the hands of the white race which had always lived and governed there. And so Minor's optimism was indeed warranted and we breathed happily once more as we saw the long night of "Reconstruction" giving way to a day of Freedom and Justice and common sense!

After a trip to Europe, following his release from the dungeon in Fortress Monroe, Jefferson Davis came to Memphis to live and I was astonished to see how well and how bravely he had withstood his misfortunes. He had endured that which might well bow any man's shoulders, but not even a dungeon and chains and manacles had been able to subdue that great man's lofty spirit. He still held himself as erect as an Indian, his head sat well and firmly on his shoulders, his eyes still held their native fire and force. Mr. Davis' features were finely chiseled; his face, his glance, his general aspect denoted benevolence and impulses that were pure and good. He was tall and slender, his step was firm and steady, and this vigor he maintained almost to the day of his death in 1889, although he was then a very old man. During the years we were neighbors in Memphis I saw much of him and of his family; he often was at our house and listened with much interest to my account of his brother in Tuscaloosa. Mr. Davis had courtly manners. His conversation was always grave and serious. Mrs. Davis was jolly and full of humor, but her distinguished husband never told a funny story, nor laughed at one. The most he did was to indulge in a grave smile. If anyone in his presence denounced his jailor, General Miles, Mr. Davis invariably remained silent and at the first opportunity changed the subject. He never complained of his treatment or of his fallen fortunes; when he came to Memphis he was practically penniless. Like Gen. Lee, he was offered big salaries by a number of concerns that sought to use his reputation as a commercial asset, but like Gen. Lee, Davis answered that his name was not for sale. In conjunction with other "Daughters of the Confederacy" I set about raising a fund with which to buy Mr. Davis a home. The very first man I approached, Mr. Jacob Thompson (who had represented the Confederate States abroad as their foreign agent), subscribed one thousand dollars. Mr. Robert Brinkley put his name down for five hundred dollars. My brother and my husband each subscribed for three hundred dollars--the balance would have been secured within a week. Then Mr. Davis heard of the project and immediately asked that it be discontinued; he said he rejoiced at such signal proof of the confidence and affection of his fellow citizens, but there were so many Confederate soldiers whose necessities were greater than his, they must be helped first and he begged us, if we had money to bestow, to bestow it upon moneyless and wounded Southern soldiers! This letter was written to me as Chairwoman of the Committee and was long treasured by me as a souvenir of the Confederate president and as a proof of his delicacy and patriotism; to my great regret it was lost, together with other valuable papers, when we moved from Memphis to St. Louis.

Mr. Davis' daughter Winnie, afterward known throughout the country as the "Daughter of the Confederacy" (she was born in the Confederate "White House" in Richmond during the war) was about the same age as my boy Lee and during their childhood they were great friends. One day when Lee was giving a birthday party little Winnie, about seven years old, was one of his guests; another guest was a little girl, the daughter of a neighbor, General Williams. This little girl, whose pet name was "Lady Bird," sat talking with little Winnie Davis.

"Have you a brother?" asked Lady Bird.

"Yes," answered Winnie. "I have two brothers."

"My brother," said Lady Bird, "is a big, tall man. He's 'most as tall as the top of the door."

The door was a very tall one, at least seven or eight feet. Winnie looked at Lady Bird curiously.

"Child," she said, "don't you know that boys don't grow that high?"

This remark, so gravely made as if she were talking to one infinitely her junior, interested me in little Winnie. I asked her how she liked the people in Europe-- this was shortly after the Davises came back from their trip abroad. "I liked them," replied the child. "They were kind to us."

"Did you see any of the distinguished people there?"

"We saw some Lords and Ladies," replied Winnie.

"I don't mean titled people," I said. "I mean did you see people who have done great things in the world?"

The child straightened herself up in her big chair and gravely replied: "I never saw anyone like my father. My father is a great man. He has done great things!"

Next day when I saw Mr. Davis I told him of this talk with his little girl and a smile parted his lips. "The dear child!" he said. "I never knew that she thought of such things." This little girl grew up into lovely womanhood; she was brilliant as well as lovely and the books she wrote gave promise of fame apart from that she had because of the distinguished name she bore. Alas!! cruel death cut her down in the very morning of her life and she was laid to rest by the side of her father. The loftiest and most beautiful monument in Richmond's beautiful Hollywood cemetery is that erected in honor of Jefferson Davis; the monument next in beauty and artistic design is that marking the resting place of the sweet little girl who used to play in my yard in Memphis, of Winnie, The Daughter of the Confederacy!

CHAPTER XXVI

My lack of orthodoxy distresses some of my friends. Letter from Jeff Davis on the subject. I publish a paper, The Tablet. Horace Greeley writes me to exchange with his New York Tribune. I refuse to pay taxes unless allowed a voice in the government. The Register of voters issues me a permit to vote "at any election in 1872." I speak in New England urging votes for women. Meet Henry George in Canada in 1881 and become a Single Taxer.

If you have read what I have written thus far, my dear grand children, you no doubt have perceived that although my parents were very orthodox and tried to rear me in their religious beliefs, doubts as to the truth of church dogmas came to me early in life; and of those doubts I have never been able to rid myself. Nor have I been always discreet enough to keep them to myself; as perhaps I should have done--at any rate when talking with orthodox friends. This lack of discretion on my part has sometimes caused a kind of wall to rise between me and very dear friends; indeed, it has in a degree prevented the relations between me and even my two sisters from being quite what they should be. Both my two old sisters are today, as they have always been, very religious and look upon me as one who has preferred error to truth. It is strange that I, reared by exceptionally orthodox parents, with the example of two good and loving sisters before me, should have so little religious faith, but so it is--not from any wish of mine, but simply because such is the nature of my brain and being.

Among the friends who, I thought, looked askant at me because of my lack of orthodoxy were our Confederate President and his wife. Mr. and Mrs. Davis were both devout church people and I should have known better than to discuss religious topics with them, but to me no topic under the sun has ever seemed too sacred to discuss. Truth can never be hurt by discussion, why then resent arguments supporting a doctrine contrary to the doctrine you entertain? This seems a very simple and a very sensible proposition, but I have lived long enough to learn that with some people religion is a thing concerning which no discussion is desired. In looking over my books of old letters I came across one from Jeff Davis to me written from Vicksburg in 1876. I had sent him and Mrs. Davis New Years congratulations and in acknowledging them Mr. Davis took advantage of the opportunity to refer to this subject of my rather "loose" religious convictions. As the letter throws a side light on Jefferson Davis' character I shall give it here in full.

My dear Mrs. Meriwether:

Your very kind and most welcome letter of the 1st. inst. has been this day received. I know not if many, as you suppose, did wish me a Happy New Year, but I do know there could be none whose greeting I would more value than yours. Be assured you sent me that without which I should be poor indeed, but with which I am yet equal to any fortune. The affection of the true, the conscientious, the self sacrificing is the treasure dearest and most enduring of all. Only one who has been broken by the storms of Fate and who finds himself a waif on the current of life and drifting near to the sea of eternity, can feel the full force of a friendship which follows him still. Cordially I thank you, and pray that God's blessing may be on you and yours.

I left your city under pressing business engagements, not--as you have been told--to go to a new home. Indeed, I do not know where my future residence may be. In one respect (it is to be feared in only one) I am like St. Peter. That is, when St. Peter was young he went whither he would; but when he was old he went where others carried him. My course must be as fortune drives.

Why do you think your "unpopular convictions" have put you at a disadvantage with me? You are quite mistaken, if for no better reason yet because I have so often felt the injustice of measuring my opinions by the numbers who concur in them. I could not depreciate one who boldly held to creed against the many headed monster thing. If I did not unmistakably manifest my regard and admiration it was not because they were not truly felt.

But there is another whose regard is better worth than mine, and concerning whom you make a like mistake. Mrs. Davis regrets your disbelief of things which she considers essential both to tremporal and eternal welfare? and the truths by which men should live, for which men should be willing to die. Did she not feel a personal attachment to you she would not regret your disbelief enough to have attracted your notice. Be sure you have mistaken a pained love for a "strange degree of disapproval."

Present me affectionately to your noble husband and accept for yourself the heart's best offering of your faithful friend.

JEFFERSON DAVIS.

Here is an earlier note I received from Mr. Davis:

Memphis, 17th Feb. 1872.

My dear Mrs. Meriwether:

Please find inclosed the price of one year's subscription for the copy sent to my wife, and believe me

Faithfully your friend
JEFFERSON DAVIS

The "copy" referred to was that of a weekly paper called *"The Tablet"* which I established and published and edited during the year 1872. Not being hampered by much sense of responsibility, as a man would have been, and having at that time a fairly vigorous pen, the *Tablet,* considering its brief life and limited circulation, attracted much notice. I remember a "tilt" I had with Horace Greeley which amused me greatly. Greeley was then editing the New York *Tribune;* I sent the *Tablet* to all the leading newspapers of the country, blue-marking a notice at the top of the first column of the editorial page asking publishers of other newspapers to put the *Tablet* on their exchange lists. The *Tribune* in response to this request sent me a printed circular letter calling attention to the fact that a metropolitan daily could not afford to place on its exchange list all the weekly papers which applied for that favor, but added that if the *Tablet* would run a six inch Ad. of the *Tribune* for the term of three months the *Daily Tribune* would be sent to the publisher of the *Tablet* for a term of one year! I published this *Tribune* letter on my editorial page with the comment that if the *Tribune* would run a six inch Ad. of the *Tablet* for three months I would send my paper to the *Tribune* for one year. Whether it was the sheer audacity of this proposal, or the manner in which I phrased it, that pleased Mr. Greeley, I cannot say, but I received a letter from him which, after great labor and calling into counsel my proof reader and printer, I found to be a cordial offer to exchange on even terms. Thereafter, and as long as Greeley remained with the *Tribune* (which was long after my poor little *Tablet* gave its last gasp and expired) the *Daily Tribune* came to me free of charge, a big "X" marked on the wrapper.

When the *Tablet* died in October 1872 several newspapers, among them the Panola, Miss., *Star,* seized the occasion as one to decry radical opinions and women's interference in "spheres" appropriate only to men. In my scrap book of 1872 I find a letter which I sent to the Memphis *Appeal,* and which was published by that paper in its issue of October 15th, 1872. Here is that letter:

Editor the *Appeal*:

While thanking you for your rebuke of the Panola *Star's* pert fling at woman, permit me to say a word regarding the life and death of my little paper. When I first mentioned my project of publishing a paper to the gentleman in whom I have the honor to be merged, and for whose financial judgment I have great respect, he looked at me in dismay and asked if I wished to head our family toward the poor house? Such a wish was far from my heart; I explained that I meant my paper to pay for itself from the start, and that when it ceased to pay for itself its publication would be promptly discontinued. Well, Mr. Editor, the Tablet did pay for itself as long as it was under my control! Subscriptions and advertisements poured in upon me in such generous quantities that at the end of the first quarter not only had all expenses been paid out of the paper's receipts, but a surplus remained with which I sent to St. Louis and bought a lot of type so that I could have the paper set up in my own office instead of having it done outside. In the course of time however, I found the work of being editor, contributor and publisher, all in one, too arduous for my health and strength; moreover, my family wished to go to Canada for the summer. Accordingly I sold the *Tablet* to Hutton & Shroyer, an old printing firm in Memphis; this firm met with financial troubles and some months after it bought the paper, and while I was in Canada, it decided to suspend publication. Your ill mannered Mississippi exchange, which jeers over that suspension as peculiarly a woman's failure, will probably abate his spitefulness when he learns that no woman had either ownership or management of the *Tablet* at the time of its demise. For four months it had been owned and published by two beings of the same sex to which the editor of the Panola *Star* belongs. The sale of the *Tablet* to Hutton & Shroyer was duly published in the paper at the time, had the juvenile editor of the *Star* kept up with the news of the day he might have spared himself the rebuke so properly administered to him by the Memphis *Appeal*.
Respectfully,

ELIZABETH A. MERIWETHER.

One of the things which arrayed against me such conservative newspapers as the Panola *Star* was my outspoken advocacy of votes for women and abolition of the liquor traffic. In these days when women vote in a dozen states, and when Prohibition has been adopted in more than a dozen states, advocates of those two measures are not vilified, even insulted and assaulted, as they were half a century ago. About that time Susan B. Anthony was arrested, imprisoned, tried and convicted for voting at an election; the law under which she was held guilty was enacted on May 31st 1870. The learned Judge held that Miss Anthony knew that she was a woman "and that the constitution of this state prohibits her from voting." I was convinced that Justice Hunt's ruling, if not illegal, was at any rate a denial of justice; I had been taught in my history that taxation without representation was tyranny and in order to bring the question home to our people in the South, as Miss Anthony's arrest and imprisonment had brought it home to the people of the North, I determined to vote in Memphis. In my case, however, there was no arrest and no imprisonment. I think the election officials in Memphis, knowing me and knowing my family, perhaps decided to consider me merely as a harmless "freak." At any rate, when I tested the matter I was allowed to cast my ballot; whether it was counted I cannot say. In my scrap book for 1871 is pasted the certificate which authorized me to vote. It reads as follows:

No. 355   Register's Office, 5th Ward.
                             Memphis, Tenn., Dec. 8, 1871

Mrs. Elizabeth A. Meriwether who resides at No. 95 Union St. is entitled to vote in the Fifth Ward of this city at any election during the year 1872.
                             A. R. DRAESHER,
                             Register of Voters for the 5th Ward.
(Property Holder of the Fifth Ward, A. R. DRAESHER.)

Some Southern papers thought the world was coming to an end, so horrified were they at the sight of a woman voting. Here is one of the many editorials on the subject which I find preserved in my 1872 scrap book:
"We enter our most earnest protest against the mothers, wives and daughters of Memphis being dragged into the corrupt cesspool of elections. We have been taught to look upon females as too pure to mingle in the strife and turmoil of the political arena and would feel greatly shocked to see some of our estimable female friends elbowed rudely at the polls in an effort to deposit their ballot. It will unsex woman to give her the ballot."
Here is an extract from the answer which I made to this editorial, and which was published in the Memphis *Appeal:*
"What nonsense to say the ballot would unsex woman! To believe such a thing is to disbelieve in Nature. All the political freedom on earth cannot change woman's destiny, which is to be the mother of the race. Maternal feeling is the strongest feeling in the human breast. Nothing but death can wipe it out. To say love of politics can wipe that feeling out of a woman's breast is bosh. If woman had to vote six times a day she would not love her baby one atom the less. Has Queen Victoria neglected her nine children because of politics? Yet she opens Parliament, signs State papers and confers with her Ministers. Did Maria Theresa neglect her big brood of babies? Yet Maria Theresa ruled an empire and was every inch a sovereign."
These activities of mine--publishing the *Tablet*, advocating votes for women, and actually, voting myself--made me known to many people in the North as

well as in my native South and I was urged to go to Washington and plead for justice to women before the comittees of Congress. In my "Letter" book for 1873 is this letter from Isabella Beecher Hooker (a sister of Henry Ward Beecher.):

Hartford, Conn., Jan'y 24, 1873.

Dear Friend:

I am very desirous you should go to Washington with your talk--I know how good and effective it would be . . . Our hearing before the Senate Judiciary committee last winter was the result of hours of talk with Senator Lyman Trumbull and other members of the committee, and of such threatening pertinacity as would have been impertinence itself in a matter of less national importance. I long ago came to the conclusion that the parable of the unjust judge must have been given for this age with direct reference to the encouragement of women, the traditional and neglected pleaders of the centuries. So every woman of us that has tongue and eloquence and power must besiege the heart of man while attempting to enlighten his sensual brain. The head is narcotized by the animalism of his nature and the readiness with which woman has consented to sit at his feet.

I inclose a letter to Senator Sumner that will secure you a kind private reception, if his health will permit, and I want you to read your MS. to him, or leave it with him for a day or two as he may prefer. He will read it faithfully and do it full justice. Also I shall urge Mr. Henry Wilson to invite a few congressmen to hear you in a Committee room. It is of great importance that a *Southern* woman be heard just at this time, and in case politicians desire to conciliate the South you will have the field before you. You must read your MS. aloud in your parlors at home and just as fast as possible acquire the arts of a public speaker. I know you will read well, and soon you can venture upon extempore speaking. Your first essay I read in Steinway Hall to an eagerly listening house, and I never enjoyed anything more--your argument is at once so logical, clear, profound, yet *spicy*--a remarkable combination--for an unpracticed writer it is wonderful.

Ever yours,
ISABELLA BEECHER HOOKER.

The letter to Senator Sumner, which I also find in my 1873 "Letter" book (I did not go to Washington and so kept the letter) reads as follows:

Hatford, Jan'y 24, 1873

Hon. Charles Sumner:

Permit me to introduce my friend Mrs. Meriwether of Memphis, Tenn., and to ask you to read her essay addressed to yourself and other leading abolinonists. I have asked Mrs. Meriwether to leave with you her essay on Blackstone which seems to me an uncommon effort for an unprofessional writer, and I feel confident you cannot fail to be impressed with the logical character of her mind and the trenchant style of her pen.

Permit me to express my deep sympathy in your recent sufferings and my earnest hope that relief will soon come to you and a permanent reestablishment of health.

My dear friend, I could not help praying our Heavenly Father that you might not be taken from earth till you had spoken at least one earnest word for the oppressed among women, even as you have for your own black brethren been ready to offer life itself. Must I hope in vain?

Sincerely yours,
ISABELLA B. HOOKER.

At that time I had not met Mrs. Hooker, nor did I come to know her personally until many years later. In 1881, long after I had followed her advice to read my "essays" in my home parlor and so acquire the arts of a public speaker, I joined Elizabeth Cady Stanton, Susan B. Anthony and other suffrage women in a speaking tour of New England and if I may judge from what many newspapers printed about me, I was not wholly lacking in the "arts of a public speaker." The Chicago *Tribune* correspondent wired his paper that "Mrs. Meriwether was very able and eloquent--she brought the house down with frequent applause." The St. Louis *Globe-Democrat* said:

"Mrs. Meriwether's keen sarcasm, wit and humor caused frequent bursts of laughter and applause."

The Boston *Herald* said: "One of the brightest, wittiest, most eloquent of the speakers." The *Morning News* of Portland. Me.. said:

"A most pleasing speaker. She held her audience from first to last." I could fill several chapters with laudatory notices of my speeches on Woman's Suffrage and on Temperance, but I fear I have already said enough on this subject. These things that were said of me when I was young and good looking are interesting to me, now that I am old and ugly, but of course they are of no interest to anyone else. I hope you will forgive me, my children, for saying what I have said on the subject.

To return to Mrs. Hooker: When our Suffrage meeting was held in Hartford I stopped at Mrs. Hooker's house as her guest and was greatly interested not only in her own personality but also in the intimate stories she told me of her famous preacher brother, Henry Ward Beecher, and of her still more famous sister, Harriet Beecher Stowe, author of *Uncle Tom's Cabin*. When I was leaving Hartford for Boston an amusing, although somewhat embarrassing, incident occurred at the railway station. I will quote from the newspaper account of the episode which I have in my scrap book for 1881:

"While the ladies who have taken part in the Women's Suffrage Convention in this city during the past two days were in the depot this morning waiting for their train Mrs. Elizabeth A. Meriwether of Memphis, Tenn., was accosted by two young men who said they were theological students and who acted in a most astonishing manner. One of them knelt down on the depot platform beside Mrs. Meriwether and began praying for the conversion of her soul. The lady, as soon as she recovered from her astonishment at being thus made the subject of attention of the crowd in the station, advised the young man to get up off his knees and desist from his prayers. 'Everybody will think you are making love to me,' she said.

"'I do love you!' he replied, 'just as Jesus loves you. And I want to save your soul.'

'I don't think it is love,' was Mrs. Meriwether's response. 'I think it is dyspepsia. You must not kneel to me here in public.'

"This rather cooled the young man's ardor and he got up. Officer Tom Kennedy says this is the first prayer he ever heard made in the new depot."

It was on that 1881 trip through New England and to Canada that I met a man who then was little known, but of whom the whole world was soon to hear--a man whose books have already caused a marked change in the world's conception of justice and of what constitutes just taxation. Some sort of a convention was going on in Montreal and to this convention came Henry George to expound and explain the theory of his *Progress and Poverty* which had been published a few months before. George was not an imposing man to look at; what little hair he had was red. His beard was of the same color, and he was short in stature, what I would call "stocky." But there was a fire in his eye and an eloquence in his speech which made me believe he was an uncommon man from the first moment I met him in the Windsor Hotel in Montreal. This belief was confirmed, of course, by reading his book, of which I wrote a review for a Southern paper; in that review which is preserved in my scrap book, I said:

"In the one year of its existence *Progress and Poverty* has already exerted an influence equaling that of John Stuart Mill's political economy. In fact this critical and suggestive work is destined to do much toward lessening the authority of the whole school of political economy heretofore known to the world--its effect upon peoples and govermnents will ultimately be even greater than the effect produced by Adam Smith's *Wealth of Nations.* "

My support by pen and speech of George's Single Tax theory caused my friends to become all the more confirmed in their view of me as a woman with "simply impossible" opinions. One of my friends said to me:

"Betty Meriwether, before the war you let your impractical theories cause you to sacrifice a fortune by letting your husband give away his slaves. And now you want Henry George to come along and take away your land. "

Of course I wished no such thing; but I did wish to see land values, which were created by the community, go to the community rather than to private individuals who did *not* create those values. I also believed it to be unwise to impose a penalty upon improvements created by labor, and to bestow a premium upon the holding of land unimproved, consequently I supported Henry George's plan--which after all was but an elaboration of, and an improvement upon, a theory advanced by Herbert Spencer in one of his early writings. Spencer subsequently "went back upon" his "unearned increment" argument, and upon the plea he made in his *Data of Ethics* concerning the fundamental right of *all* men to the earth being superior to the right of any individual man to any particular portion of the earth; but it never seemed to me that Spencer Old even half way refuted Spencer Young, and so I have counted myself a believer in Henry George's doctrine ever since I met George in the summer of 1881. When Mr. George returned in 1892 from his trip around the world I went to New York to attend the great reception which was given him; in 1892 he was not the almost unknown printer I had met in 1881 -- he was then known all over the world and admired for his great talents even by those who could not accept his economic teachings.

My next lecture tour after the New England trip was in 1883 through Arkansas and Texas. My talks on temperance were approved by the thoughtful people of the South, but on the question of political freedom for women an extreme and unreasoning prejudice existed which in some instances led to the doing of very wrong and very unjust things. I remember one misguided gentleman, the Rev. P. F. Bourland, a Methodist preacher in Sherman, Texas, who so strongly disapproved of Woman Suffrage that he attempted to prevent me from giving my lectures. He sent letters about the state to "expose" me as a "woman who is imposing herself upon the people as a temperance lecturer" whereas she "has no heart in temperance" but is using temperance as "a cloak to cover her infidel woman's right doctrines. " There was more, and worse, stuff in one of this preacher's letters which fell into my hands and when my husband saw the letter he immediately wrote the Rev. Bourland that he must promptly write an apology and retraction, or stand a suit for libel in the United States Courts. The Rev. Bourland did not permit his prejudice against "infidel woman's rights doctrines" to carry him so far as to become a defendant in a libel suit; he wrote the apology Minor demanded and thereafter my Texas lectures, if not approved, were at any rate not vilified. In truth, however, even at that early day Southern conservatism was beginning to become more rational, and a large per cent of my audiences seemed to be in sympathy with my views. As a rule the newspapers, although opposed to Woman's Suffrage, gave me fair treatment. One paper said: "Though we dissent from her doctrines we admire the courage, the vigor and the eloquence with which she maintains them. " Even the newspapers of the Rev. Bourland's city, Sherman, Texas, treated me nicely--as witness this from the Sherman *Courier* of February 28, 1883:

"The good audience seemed to animate the eloquent speaker with greater zeal and more fervent utterance. Mrs. Meriwether has the power to interest her hearers and holds them with a steady attention throughout her discourse. Her manner is that of a refined, cultivated Southern lady and as such we respect her enthusiastic advocacy of a cause, Eutopian* thought it be.

I have dwelt so much on my Texas and New England trips that I have neglected to mention the first public speech I ever made, which was on May 5th, 1876. I rented the leading theater of Memphis for that evening and owing both to the novelty of the subject and the fact that the lecture was free my first audience was large, if not enthusiastic. However, its lack of enthusiasm did not discourage me. I believed that in time the truth would prevail and I was content so long as the people would accord me a hearing.

---

* Eutopian? Only a third of a century has elapsed since the *Courier* published those lines, a short time in the life of either a Nation or a great cause. And yet in those thirty three years I have seen the triumph of that "Eutopian" cause. Only this month (June 1916) the democratic national convention here in my home city declared in favor of Woman Suffrage. All the other political parties have taken the same stand, so that from now on the political "crank," the party "heretic" will be, not he who supports, but he who opposes votes for women. In 1876 the democratic national convention met here in this same city to nominate Tilden for President. I was then still living in Memphis, but I came to St Louis to plead with the convention to give Woman justice. The Resolutions Committee treated me as a joke, and the newspapers said nothing of my arguments, they talked only of my millinery and described the dress I wore. In the same city where I was thus scoffed and scorned because of my advocacy of justice for my sex, forty years later the national convention of the same political party unanimously declares in favor of votes for women!

Is not this a triumph for which I may justly feel thankful? I think so, my children. And now that success has come to the two great causes which for sixty years have been so close to my heart I feel that my life's work is done and that I am ready to go whenever the call comes.

210

CHAPTER XXVII

My first novel, "The Master of Red Leaf," published in England. Praised by the London Saturday Review, the N. Y. Sun and other critical journals. Other books and novels. Amusing letters to me from my boys when they were children. I dance with the Grand Duke Alexis of Russia.

I wrote my first novel, *The Master of Red Leaf,*in 1872; its strong Southern tone prevented its finding a Northern publisher, but when it was published in England in three volumes the press of New York, Boston, and other Eastern cities gave it lengthy notice. I have many of these notices in my scrap books where you may read them if you have curiosity to know what was said forty years ago about your grand mother's first novel; in these *Recollections* I shall quote from only two of my critics, the London *Saturday Review* and the New York *Sun*. Both of these journals stand high for critical acumen, consequently I was no little pleased at what they said.

The *Saturday Review* said:

"The Master of Red Leaf is distinctly an original novel. From the first words .. . . to the last scene in the tomb of a nameless race there is no pause in the excitement. The first essential of a novel of this kind is that it should carry the reader on and powerfully move his curiosity. This *The Master of Red Leaf* undoubtedly does--the reader feels that it is all true. Hester's description of life on a Southern plantation is exceedingly interesting . . . The rapidity and energy of this curious tale are remarkable. "

The New York *Sun* said:

"The Master of Red Leaf is a book that merits more than ordinary attention . . . There is some reason to apprehend that the future historian may concur with the author in pronouncing the preservation of the Union rather a pretext than a generative cause of the uprising in the North. We can call to mind no history nor elaborate disquisition on the causes of the late war in which the essential antithesis in the attitude of the Northern and the Southern people is more distinctly recognized than is Mrs. Meriwether's novel. We would direct notice especially to certain passages which demonstrate the author's comprehension of the political problem solved by slaughter and devastation and which at the same

time indicate the keenness of her observation and the range of her experience. Her analysis of the African character is incisive and striking. "

In the last paragraph of the *Sun* review, which was several columns long, the writer said:

"We have left ourselves no space to speak of the book's technical worth but we can assure the reader that, aside from its value as a transcript of Southern life and thought at a most critical juncture, he will find *The Master of Red Leaf* a well constructed, spirited and very interesting novel. "

Unfortunately I neglected to write the date on this clipping from the *Sun*; it assigned "M. W. H. " whom old newspaper readers will remember as a Reviewer who attained considerable literary fame in the early days of the *Sun* when Charles A. Dana was at the paper's helm.

Following the publication in England of *The Master of Red Leaf* I wrote *Black and White* and several other novels, also *Facts and Falsehoods about the War of the Sixties,* an historical review of Fact VS. Fiction, concerning the causes of the war and the men who fought that war; but I shall not devote space to any of my other books excepting the novel of my old age, *Sowing of Swords*, which was written when I was nearing ninety and the publication of which was attended by such circumstances as to make some reference thereto worth while. Thinking a woman nearly ninety could be imposed upon, the publisher of my last novel acted in such a way that I had to send him to jail. But I will tell of that in a later chapter.

My children, once the war ended and the stirring days of "Reconstruction" gave way to self government by the white men of the South, Memphis settled down to the quiet, uneventful life of the average small city, consequently there will not be much more for me to tell you that you will care to hear. In looking through my letter and my scrap books I find little that would interest you, unless it be a few specimens of the letters your father wrote to me when he was a child. Here, Lee Jr., is a letter which your father wrote me when he was eleven and a half years old; I cannot recall what occasioned the letter, but evidently - your father had done some mischief and as a punishment I had taken from him his "paper"--what "paper" I have not now the slightest idea. I give you the letter verbatim, and even "Punctuatim," just as your father wrote it:

Memphis Tenn 6 July 187

Fair Godess

did you but know what miseries I have sufered since I have felt the efects of your wrath, you would surely give me my paper and much more quickly when you here me promise with my left hand on the Bible and my right raised to God to try to be an obedient boy and to try to check my selfishnes I am also very sorry for my past offence

your affectionate yet sad boy
LEE MERWETHER.

P. S.
I rest in peace relying on your many virtues and above all on your better judgement.

Adieu and Au revoir.

Accompanying this appeal was an essay on "Selfishness," from which I judge Lee had been guilty of that particular sin; here is the essay, the title, as you see, spelt in a novel way:

Shelfishness

Selfishness is one of the worst of evils and is at the bottom of almost every crime. There are many reasons why one should avoid selfishness (correctly spelled here). It makes every one despise a person who is selfish.

A mother despises a selfish child.

I am compelled to confess that I am shelfish but I hope I have not gone too far to reform. I have a mother who is not shelfish. She is fairer and more spotless than the sun and far more generous I hope I will fall in her ways with these assurances together with asking your pardon I beg to remain your humble and loving son

LEE MERIWETHER

You will note how the little diplomat worked in a lot of compliments about me-- "Fairer than the sun and far more generous!" I have no recollection of the episode at all, but no doubt that compliment gained the offender a pardon in full. A year and a half later, on his thirteenth birthday, Lee handed me this letter:

Christmas 1875

Dear Mother:--

This is my thirteenth birthday. For thirteen long years you have watched over me with the care and solicitude which only a mother can evince for her offspring. I have ever been loved by you; Though when I was bad you have at times been quite cold in your outward bearing, still there was a spark of love left in the deepest recesses of your heart. This spark I most devoutly hope will never be extinguished.

213

It was you, mother, who brought me into life and O what can I do to repay that debt of existence? I know of but one way and that is by love and filial affection which I shall give with all its strength. Through all my failings, Mother, your hand has guided me from doing harm. For this I and the community in which I shall live will thank you and most richly will you deserve it. In my sickness you have proven to be more than a match for death, that grim monster who is finally the conqueror of all.

For these reasons I, Lee Meriwether, have on my 13th birthday taken my pen in hand (by the way, a gold pen) to tender my thanks and undying affection.

This letter is entirely in Lee's hand writing and the diction is his; the back of the letter is marked:

"A birth day present to my mother."

My son Lee, the "Baby Lee" of Tuscaloosa day, always tried to "write" himself out of the consequences of his misdoings. Here is an amusing specimen, written when he was fifteen years old. Although he was living with me, he did not hand the letter to me; he sent it through the post office marked "Important."

5th March 1878

Dear Mother:

Please do not throw this down before reading it all. I think it best to write an account of what I feel sure you think was most base of me, viz. my conduct last night. I beg of you to believe what I say and then, if posilble, give me your pardon which I so earnestly crave.

Yesterday I gave you my promise to bring Julia home after the pyrotechnical display on the bluff. The intention of keeping that promise never deserted me. You may ask why then did I break it? Believe me when I say I did my best to avoid breaking it. You know how dense the crowd was. Just as we were cutting across the grounds a hack or some other kind of vehicle drove up. I was not aware it was so near until I heard Julia shriek "The horses are right behind us!" Then I jumped to one side while Julia jumped to the other side. When the vehicle had passed by, you, dear Mother, were no longer in my view. I strove hard to find you. I stood where I had last seen you and peered around with what keenness of vision the darkness of the hour permitted, often crying out "Mother!! Father!" But alas! amidst so great a crowd I was not heard. I went about in all directions, hoping to find you, but all in vain. At last, after the pyrotechnic display, I hurriedly went towards the Opera House thinking to find you there, but again was I doomed to disappointment. Then, and only then, did I give up all hope of finding you.

Dearest Mother, the above is a true report. I know you think my "jumping aside" was intentional but I will take my oath such was not the case.

Mother, may I hope for your forgiveness--may I dare say your love?

214

Trusting that you may once again look kindly on me, I am your loving son

LEE MERIWETHER

P.S.

If there is anything for me to hope let me know, if there is no hope, say nothing, for your very presence will tell me all. It was only this morning--when you so coldly said "That is sufficient"--that I understood the sad words "Thou art so near, yet so far."

In the summer of 1876 Minor took me and our three boys to see the Centennial Exhibition in Philadelphia; after visiting the Exhibition we spent a month at Dr. Trall's "Water Cure" on the Delaware river at Florence Heights, N. J., and there I became a believer in what was then called a "Hygienic" diet. From this diet all condiments are excluded; no salt or pepper or meat ever appeared on Dr. Trall's table. His bread was made of whole wheat flour and contained nothing but the flour and water, no salt, butter, lard or other "shortening." To a palate inflamed by condiments this regime was not agreeable, but to a natural, normal palate it was good enough to cause one to eat all one really needed to eat; I always opposed foods so rich and so palatable as to tempt one to eat merely for the sake of eating. I became really fond of Dr. Trall's rolls made of unbolted flour without any seasoning, but none of my family cared for them; they were so hard, almost flinty, that my boys called them "Trojans," meaning that they were as hard as the curios which Dr. Schliemann was about that time excavating from the ruins of Troy. At length, however, my youngest boy, Lee was won over to the Hygienic theory and in looking over my book of old letters I came across the following sent to me by Lee when he was sixteen years old:

4 March 1879, 1 p.m.

Darling Mother:

It is with great pleasure I announce to you the change I am undergoing and through which I hope triumphantly to pass. I trust you will not think me vain when I say I shall deserve your warmest embraces when next we meet. I am now thoroughly hygienic--no salt, no butter, no forbidden food of any kind now passes my lips! This morning I had a delicious breakfast of Trojans (Oh most sweet Trojans!) apples, raisins (of course in moderate and *hygienic* quantities) and one egg! Think of this, dear Mother, and then marvel at the great change. I can hardly realize that once I, like a cannibal, would eat salt and butter and meat. This morning when I saw father eating bacon with his eggs I really felt sorry for him--to think that his taste should be so perverted! Before me now are four Trojans, two bananas and one apple which I shall eat with a relish as soon

215

as I finish this epistle. And this evening at six I shall eat another hygienic meal, with the addition perhaps of a little weak tea, which I trust you will forgive because I have to go out for my German lesson.

This, mother, I send you as a truthful report upon my diet; if you were here with me I could live on your love, but as you are two hundred miles away I must have the more substantial Trojans.

Your loving son,
LEE

I regret to say that this reform in Lee was a transient one; his enthusiasm died out as quickly as it had come and by the time I returned to Memphis from my first visit to St. Louis (in 1879) he seemed quite as fond of meat and butter and salt as his father. As I have said, however, my boy Lee always had a way of "writing" himself into my good graces, and sometimes he attempted to use this talent to help him get out of trouble with his teacher. Years after Lee had finished school Mr. Carey Anderson, a son of Lee's Latin Professor, sent me a letter written by Lee to Professor Anderson in July 1875 and which Mr. Carey Anderson found among his father's papers after his death. It seems that in rebuking Lee for not knowing his lessons Professor Anderson told him if he would spend less time on dress and more time on study it would be better for his brains. And so Lee wrote the following letter and handed it to his teacher next morning:

31st JULY, 1875

Captain Anderson:

Dear Sir: I beg to inform you I do not think my dress is to blame, and in proof I remind you that to put on a clean pair of pants takes no longer than to put on a dirty pair. The same with a shirt and coat.

To put on a clean shirt takes two minutes; to adjust my cravat two minutes; to put on my socks and shoes two minutes; to put on coat and pants two minutes.

As for my ring, I do not take it off. And I don't think I look at myself in the glass more than six minutes, thus making fourteen minutes to complete my toilet. Accordingly I do not think it can be my watch chain, or any part of my dress, that causes my bad lessons. I think it is because I am too fond of play and reading novels. But I intend to reform and give you no occasion to complain of my lessons.

With your consent I shall continue to come to school with a clean face, clean pants, shirt and coat, and watch chain and ring.

Yours respectfully,
LEE MERIWETHER.

This, of course, was a very pert letter for a boy of twelve and a half years to send his teacher, but Captain Anderson must have thought it amusing or he would not have preserved it so many years among his papers.

Here is another letter Lee wrote that same year after I had punished him for disobeying my orders to attend to certain household duties:

253 Beale St., Memphis, Tenn.
A. D. 9 Jan. 1875

This day, A. D. 1875, I do solemnly swear by the beard of Mahomet that what I am about to state is true:

On said day, Jan. 9, 1875, Mrs. Meriwether sent me to lock the doors of the coal shed and stables on lot No. 253 Beale St. in M. Tenn. I also state in the nonperformance of said duties assigned to me I was stood up against the wall from a quarter to seven sharp until 20 minutes to eight P.M.

I also do of my own free will state that in nonperforming said duties I committed a gross error and think my punishment well merited and I now beg pardon of my most noble and deserving mother who brought me into the world.

Your most humble son and servant,

LEE MERIWETHER.

P. S

Written at eight o'clock sharp on the 9th day of Jan. A. D. 1875, just after finishing my time standing up against the wall.

P. P. S.

I will think of the cow hereafter. Au revoir.

LEE

(Pen sketch of cow here)

My second son, Rivers, who was three and a half years older than Lee, must have been implicated in that cow difficulty, for in my scrap book is the following apology written by him:

9 January 1875.

The reason I did not put up the cow is this: Lee told me Maggie had to come out there again and so naturally I inferred the cow had not been milked. And Lee further told me that my honorable mother, the commander, ruler, boss, queen and empress of the Meriwether family, had commanded him to lock up the door and so I did it.

RIVERS B. MERIWETHER.

Did what? Forty one years have rolled by since my dear boy wrote that note; I cannot remember what it was all about, and Rivers' note hardly throws much light on the question. Because I commanded Lee to lock up the cow my Boy Rivers says he "did it." Clear as mud, isn't it? I have heard you, my grandson Lee Jr., use that expression, and I think it exactly fits this occasion. The above two little letters throw a pretty fair light on the different trend of thought of my two boys. Lee, twelve and a half, is grandiloquent; Rivers, aged sixteen, is sober, matter of fact. I will give one more sample of Rivers' writings, this one when he was aged ten:

Memphis, Oct. 10, 1869.

Dear Dady:

I love you very much. I am going to school Monday. When are you coming home? Alice sends her love to you in the most affectionate manner. We are not going to the commercial writing school, but we are going to a man named Mr. Brown and nearly every boddy says he is the best teacher a going. Miss Boddy brought him around to see us.

RIVERS BLYTHE MERIWETHER.

To even matters up between my boys I must also give two specimens of the letters written by my first born son, Avery; the first letter was written at the age of ten:

Memphis Tenn., 16 Feb'y 1868.

Dear Father:

I can't tell how much I miss you. Lee says his lesson every day. He has no black spot on him yet. As Lee was hunting his breeches this morning he said: "Oh, how I wish I had dear Dady's old, rough beard to rub my cheek on!" Lee then said: "Oh, Mama, will you cry if I love dear Dady the most?" Mother answered, "You may love Dady the most while he is gone but when he comes back you must love me the most." Lee says tell Dady that I love him a million universes full. So do I. At night Rivers brought the ax up stairs and told Lucy to split open the heads of any robbers who should come. No robbers came that night. Rivers, Lee and I went to dancing school yesterday. Madame Liese said she would not charge for Lee. Good bye dear father.

Your affectionate boy,
AVERY MERIWETHER

P. S. Mother, Rivers, Lee and I send you a great deal of love.

The second letter of Avery's which I shall give was written, when he was eighteen years old, to me on my fifty second birthday; Avery was then at college in Kentucky (the Kentucky Military Institute) and I was at home in Memphis:

K. M. I. Jan'y 19th 1876.

218

Dear Mother:

This is your birthday and I never thought of it till this moment. On the birthdays of the emperors of Rome the Senate decreed a thanksgiving; the shops were closed and the day was spent as a hallowed one.

To you, dear mother, I decree a thanksgiving--and only wish I could tender it in person. I love you more than the Senate honored emperors.

It is customary to give presents on such a day as this, I am able to give only a boy's love to his mother--mine is unbounded! From time immemorial gifts have been used as marks of friendship--often as a pretense, not always for love are they given, but sometimes as reminders of self. The Grecian horse given to the Trojans was a gift of treachery, so were the golden vessels from Nero to his mother. The magnificent presents from one potentate to another are given for a purpose, rarely from disinterested friendship.

But, dear mother, I value your love more than all princely presents. Will you accept my love in return? Hereafter I shall try so to bear myself as to make you proud of me. If I am as faithful to my duty as you are to yours I shall surely succeed.

You, with a true mother's solicitude, have always watched over us; I confess at times I have chafed at the restraints imposed upon me but this was boyish folly. I now see the good of your past advice and only wish I could live my life over again to profit by it. By a foolish freak of Nature children seem unable to understand until too late that the restraints imposed by their parents are wise and beneficial, when we are old we understand it, but then it is too late to be of benefit to us.

Mother, sometimes I dream I am at home talking to you--then the roll of the drum drives dreams away and out of bed must I hop, as Byron says, "ere the morning star." It seems odd to eat breakfast before the sun is up. As I leave the breakfast hall every morning I see a beam of the lazy sun shining over the Kentucky hills--a slothful example indeed, for K. M. I. beats the sun!

Your loving son,
AVERY MERIWETHER.

My dear grand children, do you not think I have a right to be proud of this letter, and proud of the boy who wrote it?

Before finishing this chapter, which is based upon the results of my rummaging through my old letter books and scrap books, I shall mention an invitation card which was tucked away in one of the books, and which brought back to my mind the one occasion when I not only saw Royalty, or at least

"Near" Royalty, but actually danced with it--or should I say with him? The card reads thus:

RECEPTION BALL

Overton Hotel,   9 o'clock p.m., Memphis, Feb. 2d 1872.

In honor of His Imperial Highness The

GRAND DUKE ALEXIS

Committee:

Mr. F. S. Davis, Chairman.

Following the name of the chairman are the names of twenty other prominent Memphians who constituted the Committee and underneath these twenty names, in my hand writing, is this notation:

"Nov. 30, 1894: thirteen of these Committeemen are no longer living."

Alas! As I write these lines in May 1916 not one of that Committee remains; it is probable that of all the hundreds of gay men and women who greeted the Russian Grand Duke that February night in 1872 I alone am still among the living! Such cards as this impress upon me more forcibly than anything else that I have indeed outlived my day and generation.

The Grand Duke was of course bored by the ball; how was it possible for him to take any interest in the people of a small Southern city on the Mississippi river? But he tried not to show his *ennui;* he dutifully submitted to be introduced to all the prominent men and graciously offered himself as a partner in the dances to the ladies. While dancing the Duke kept his hat in his hand, whether because he feared some one might take it as a souvenir, if he left it out of his sight, or because it is the custom of Dukes to hold their hats in their hands while dancing, I do not know; but I remember that petty detail distinctly, and I am as much puzzled over it now as I was then. There were so many women who wanted to dance with the Grand Duke that each dance was made very short--for which no doubt the Duke and his partners were thankful. I know I was very glad when my turn with His Highness ended, for I wasn't accustomed to Grand Dukes and really was at a loss what to say or do. I know not if the Grand Duke Alexis still lives; the last I heard of him was in 1905 when, unless press reports were mistaken, he took some part in Russia's war with Japan.

CHAPTER XXVIII

Two old letters. Beginning of the end. My Brother Tom's death. Death of my sons. The novel of my old age and the lawsuit it caused. I prosecute my Publisher. My last trip to New York. The end.

In the last chapter I gave specimens of letters written by my sons when they were little boys forty years ago; before putting up my "Book of Old Letters" I will give two more specimens, the first written by my husband's mother just after she married in Virginia and was about to go forth into the west to make her home in what was then almost the "Wilderness" of Kentucky. My husband's maternal grandparents were named Minor; this old letter, yellowed by almost a hundred years, was left by the young bride in her mother's desk where it was not found until three days after the bride had left her Virginia home to settle in Kentucky. On the back of the faded, yellowed sheet is endorsed:

"Found in my darling's desk 3 days after she was gone--Sept. 15th, 1822. Lucy Minor."

I can imagine that mother's feelings on rummaging through her daughter's desk, after she was gone never to be seen by her again, and finding this letter:

Mother:

I can not trust my voice to utter the feelings and emotions of my heart at parting from friends so dear to me--parting perhaps forever! For I can not disguise from myself the uncertainty of our ever meeting again, though it is our firm resolve to return as soon as possible--but how many events may occur to alter the firmest resolves!

I have from various circumstances always felt a deeper interest in my family than is usually felt by children and I am persuaded that I shall continue through life to feel it. I earnestly hope that you will remember me as a child as long as your memory lasts. The memory of my dear father I shall always cherish and endeavour to impress on the minds of my children some portion of the admiration and veneration for his character that I feel myself. I can not believe that so bright an example can be wholly lost to posterity.

Farewell, dearest mother. May every blessing that a virtuous woman deserves attend you! May the consciousness of performing your duty be your support through the arduous task of rearing a large family to virtue! I shall never forget that I owe all my happiness in life to the care of my revered parents in my youth. I hope you may be as successful in inspiring all your children with love and gratitude as you have been with me. Once more, Farewell!

M.A. MERIWETHER

Below the signature, written by the mother of the young bride after finding this letter in her daughter's desk, are these lines:

Yes, my darling, you have been a dutiful and affectionate child to me, and may Almighty God bless and reward you in this world and the next. If my other children could resemble you it would be all I could ask of Heaven.

LUCY MINOR

In those days it was a "Far Cry" from Orange County, Virginia, to the Kentucky home whither Garret Meriwether took his bride, and so it was that the mother and daughter never met again. The next letter, which will be the last, children, that I shall copy from my old letter book, was written by Dr. Charles Meriwether a great uncle of my husband, to his grand father "Parson" Will Douglas; note, children, the formal manner in which parents and grand parents were addressed in those days; also note the reference to the "*rising* young poet Robert Burns."

Glasgow, Scotland, Jan. 12, 1790.

Honored sir:

I take this opportunity to inform you of our safe arrival in Scotland after a short voyage and fine weather; but both these could not render it agreeable to me for I was excessively sick the whole way over. We called at Norfolk to lay in our sea stores and there met with your nephew Mr. Jeames Douglass who kindly entertained us while we staid; he keeps a wholesale store and appears to be making a fortune.

After our arrival here we called on your friend Mr. McCaul who has undertaken to transact our bussiness for us . . . My friend and I are recovered from the small pox but it has detained us so long from the classes that I fear we shall get little good of them this season.

I will send you by the first post the poems of a Mr. Burns, a rising young poet here who is quite famous. They are wrote in the Scotch dialect and are much esteemed in this country. My compliments to you, grand mother and all my other friends, and that happiness may attend you all is the earnest prayer of

Your affectionate grand son

CHARLES MERIWETHER.

In spite of the small pox young Charles Meriwether finished his medical studies in Scotland with honor and subsequently became one of Virginia's most esteemed surgeons.

But now, children, I must put away these ancient letters and hasten to the end of my story which, I promise you, is not far away. My parents died, the one in 1846, the other in 1847, then for thirty three years Death passed by me and mine. I began to think we were immune, or rather I gave the subject no thought at all, so happy was I during that third of a century with my children, my husband, my brother and sisters all enjoying health and moderate prosperity. But though long in coming, Death does come at last to every family and so at last he came to mine. Thirty six years ago this month, on a day in May 1880, on Main street in Memphis I met an old friend, General A. R Taylor, (who still lives in Memphis) and stopped to speak to him. At that moment a man who knew General Taylor but who was a stranger to me paused in passing and said:

"Taylor, that's sad news about Tom Avery--he was drowned yesterday."

For an instant I did not realize the import of the words my ears heard; but I knew my brother had gone to Arkansas on a fishing trip and in a moment I felt my legs giving way beneath me. I would have sunk to the pavement had not Gen. Taylor put his arm about me and supported me. My dear brother whom I loved so much, who had become so distinguished in his state and Nation, was lost to me forever! The newspapers not only of Tennessee but of the whole country paid tribute to Tom's talents as well as to his loving heart and domestic virtues, but sweet as were such tributes they did not soften the blow which his untimely death gave me. Thirty three years intervened between the death of my mother and that of my brother; only three years elapsed after Tom's death until I lost my first born, my darling son Avery. How great this second blow was to me may be judged by the following extract from a letter which I wrote at the time of his death and which was published in the "Memorial" number of "Meriwether's Weekly," the literary journal which my dear boy was editing and publishing during the last three years of his life. My boy died while away from home and after only a day's illness, on July 22d, 1883, just a week after his twenty sixth birth day, and here is what I wrote the day after he was put away from me forever:

For twenty six years he was the light of our home and our hearts! Our first born, our darling, our darling! We loved him, we love him yet, his father and I, more than life. His death has forever darkened our skies and hung our world in black. He was a boy no human could know without loving; tender, true, strong in moral purpose, always sunny, always joyous! He never entered our presence without a beaming face and never left us without a kiss . . . He hated tyranny and sympathised with the oppressed. His Ovum Vovo published in pamphlet form is a satire on a certain phase of American politics of no ordinary merit, had so fine a satire on English politics been published in London it would have won celebrity for its author. His pamphlet *English Tyranny and Irish Suffering* exhibits a grasp of the Irish Question which few older men possess ...I call to my darling but he answers not. I stretch out my arms to embrace him, but I clasp only the empty air. Never again shall I hear his voice, never again feel the tender touch of his caresses! Oh how cruel, how cruel is death!

A third of a century has passed since Avery's death; during those thirty three years other dear ones have been snatched from me, but the loss of the others was not such a blow to me as was the loss of my first born boy. In a glass jar on my desk before me as I write these lines is the little dress which I made for Avery when he was born; I have kept it all these years and wish it put beside me in my coffin when I die--the little garment which I made fifty nine years ago for my first born, for my darling boy, for my tender and true and brilliant son! A few months after Avery's death, in November 1883, we moved to St. Louis and Death let us alone for thirteen years, then in February 1896 I lost my second son, Rivers--but not until he had been married ten years, and left two lovely daughters who are some consolation to me now, although both are married and seldom visit me. In January 1899 I lost my grand daughter Marie Rivers Meriwether (my son Lee's little girl), and finally on June 6th 1910 the time came to say farewell to the partner of my joys and sorrows for so many years, to my dear husband who had been so good and true and loving to me for more than fifty four years. He died in our St. Louis home, 3716 Delmar Avenue, in his eighty fourth year and now lies buried in beautiful Bellefontaine cemetery where I shall soon lie beside him.

Minor's death came after an illness of several months and during those sad months I tried to lift some of the grief from my heart by writing a novel. This book, which I entitled *The Sowing of Swords* was not finished until a short time before my husband's death and, in an unhappy moment for me, about the time I finished the MS. I received a letter from the Neale Publishing Company of New York asking if I had any books to publish and stating that it made a specialty of publishing works concerning the South and appealing to Southern readers. I sent the Neale Company my MS. and soon came a reply praising my story highly and urging me to have it published "in time for the lamp light season." Among other things Mr. Walter Neale, president of the Publishing Company, wrote:

I am confident your book will create a decided sensation both North and South; we think it should be widely saleable, not only for its inherent worth, but for the reason that it makes a strong appeal to Southern patriotic societies.

Mr. Neale offered to publish the MS. if I would defray "part" of the cost, which--owing to the expensive style of publication he had in view--would be large; my "part" he estimated at $600.00. Very foolishly I said nothing of all this to my son; I believed Neale when he wrote that he had a mail list of customers numbering thirty thousand, of whom he estimated so many would buy my book as to make its publication highly profitable, and I sent him six hundred dollars. Then a curious change came over Neale; my book which before he got my money, seemed to him a work of genius, a work that should be published at once so as to be in time for, as he expressed it, "the lamp light season," now seemed to possess for him no merit at all. When at length I took my son Lee in my confidence and got him to inquire of Neale why my book was not published, Neale wrote my son the fault was mine, not his; my book was the "crude stuff of a ten year old child," his editors had worked on the MS. for weeks, they had practically to rewrite it etc. My son Lee is a lawyer and a man of sense; he wrote Neale that my book was neither better nor worse than when it had been first submitted for his examination; Neale had then declared it to be a work of great merit and contracted to publish it, and published it must be or the law would be invoked in my behalf.

Following this correspondence the Neale Publishing Company published *The Sowing of Swords*, or rather *printed it*. No publication, in the real sense of the word, was made or attempted and at length, in the fall of 1912, I went to New York to prosecute the suit which I had instituted against the Neale Company. I presume it is unusual for a woman nearing ninety to travel a thousand miles alone (no one accompanied me on the journey from St. Louis to New York) in order to prosecute a law suit; at any rate the New York newspapers published lengthy reports of the case and some of them, the *Herald*, the *World* and others, published my picture--not a good picture, I thought, though it was perhaps the best the artist could make under the circumstances--sketching me as I sat on the witness stand in the court room in Brooklyn. On account of some legal technicality my civil suit was dismissed but even as he dismissed it Justice Kelly of the Supreme Court in Brooklyn declared from the Bench that the treatment accorded me had been outrageous and advised that I prosecute Neale on a criminal charge. This I did; I went direct from the Supreme Court in Brooklyn to the office of District Attorney Whitman (now Governor of New York State) and swore to my complaint, and Neale was arrested, tried in the Jefferson Market Court on Sixth Avenue and found guilty of violating section 551 of the penal laws of New York. Neale gave bond and appealed to a higher court and ultimately escaped going to jail, for an old woman nearly ninety can't stay indefinitely in New York, a thousand miles from her home, to testify in a criminal prosecution. I rather fancy he was surprised at my appearing in New York at all. He knew my home was distant from the metropolis; he knew it would cost much money for me to buy railroad tickets and pay New York hotel bills; he knew, too, that I was old. And so no doubt this worthy "publisher" thought himself quite safe from me. I have reason to believe, however, that in the end he was sorry he acted as he did, even though he did get my six hundred dollars. As for me, I enjoyed my visit to New York; it was the first time I had been there in many years; I knew nothing of the Subway and when my son Lee, who met me at the Pennsylvania Station on 34th Street in New York, took me in the subway to Brooklyn I did not realize that I was in a tunnel; I supposed I was on an "El." train and after peering out of the window without being able to see a thing I turned to my son and asked why it was so dark? "Since when," I queried, "has New York become so smoky and foggy?" Lee laughed at this question but I saw nothing to laugh at. How was I to know that people voluntarily travel down in a hole in the ground when there are surface and elevated cars they might use?

I remained in New York from October 1912 until late in January 1913, then perceiving that the law's delays are as great now as when Shakespeare made Hamlet denounce them, I told the District Attorney I could wait no longer, that I had to go back to my home in St. Louis and so the case of the State of New York vs. Waiter Neale had to be dismissed. Before dismissing this episode, lest you imagine Neale's criticism of my book after he got my money is more warranted than the good things he said of it *before* I sent him my six hundred dollars I want you to read one or two things that newspapers said about my *Sowing of Swords*. The San Francisco Examiner of Dec. 10, 1910, said:

"Mrs. Meriwether is a brilliant writer . . . A truly remarkable book."

The St. Louis *Globe Democrat* of August 20, 1910, said:

"Not the least claim to consideration of this book is that the author has reached an age when literary work usually ceases . . . The cleverly alliterative title should not go uncommended . . . '*The Sowing of Swords or the Soul of the Sixties*' must be rated as a fascinating volume."

The *Oregonian*, Portland, Ore., of March 4, 1911, said:

"It is an intense, passionate story . . . As 'Uncle Tom's Cabin' gave the story of the South from a Northern standpoint, the writer of this book has given us an insight into Dixie homes from a Southern standpoint."

And here is a letter which I received only recently from a gentleman in Memphis--a stranger to me who had come across my book by chance:

Memphis, Tenn.. March 15th, 1916

Dear Mrs. Meriwether:

For some time I have intended writing you how much I admire your *'Sowing of Swords'*. In my opinion you alone have written the South's answer and in the strongest appeal possible. Your rhetoric and your work are powerful; the manner in which you have woven thoughts and facts together shows positive genius. General A. R. Taylor of this city told me of this work--told me to read it, and I did. When I finished it I mailed it to Col. Chas. E. Hyatt, President of the Pennsylvania Military College Chester, Pa.; his comment was highly appreciative. The late Judge Walter Malone roomed near me; one evening he read the first chapter of your book, 'Remorse.' Judge Malone said 'Wonderful!'

Please pardon this letter from a stranger--I felt in my blood that I just had to tell you how your book impressed me.

Very respectfully,

F. FRAYSER HINTON.

173 Union Ave.

This praise is, I admit a little extravagant--prompted no doubt by the feeling that for a nonagenarian to write a novel at all is deserving of praise; at the same time if my *Sowing of the Swords* was the "crude stuff of a ten year old child," which is what Mr. Neale said it was, *after* his company got my six hundred dollars, I do not believe that Mr. Hinton would have written the above letter, nor would the newspapers have published such criticisms as I have here quoted.

* * * * * * * * * * * * * * *

And now, my dear children, I must lay down my pen; when one is on the wrong side of ninety the story necessarily comes to an end. Were I younger the passing of the years might see me engaged in doing things worth at least a moment's mention; as it is, I must content myself with merely watching the passing show and in living over the past in my imagination. It will not be long before I shall not be able even to play the role of a passive spectator. My son tells me I shall live to be a hundred, but I hope he is mistaken. The zest of life departs when health and strength give way to disease and weakness. And how can I, at my age, expect to escape these ills many more years, or even many more months? Above all, I do not want to "die at the top" first; should that misfortune be my fate, should my mind give way before my body, I want you to promise me, my dear, dear children, that in the years to come you will think of me as I was when my mind and my body had some of their strength, and not as they were when destroyed by the burdens of nearly an hundred years.

My work now is done; I have lived a full life; I am content now, surrounded by my son and my grand children, to turn my eyes toward the setting sun and calmly, serenely await the end.

INDEX